New International

A MAGAZINE OF MARXIST POLITICS AND THEORY

NUMBER 6 1987

Contents

EDITORS: Michel Prairie and Mary-Alice Waters

MANAGING EDITOR: Steve Clark

BUSINESS MANAGER: Jim White

Many of the articles that appear in *New International* are also available in French in *Nouvelle Internationale,* in Spanish in *Nueva Internacional,* and in Swedish in *Ny International.* All four publications are available at www.pathfinderpress.com.

ISSN 0737-3724
ISBN 978-0-87348-641-5
Manufactured in Canada

First printing, 1987
Tenth printing, 2014

IN THIS ISSUE

FIDEL CASTRO, IN A 1980 SPEECH, called the revolutionary governments in Cuba, Nicaragua, and Grenada "three giants" in the Caribbean "on the very doorstep of imperialism." A substantial portion of this issue is devoted to political lessons drawn from the experience of these three giants.

One product of the Cuban, Grenadian, and Nicaraguan revolutions has been progress toward greater solidarity and collaboration among anti-imperialist, democratic, and communist organizations throughout the Caribbean. The counterrevolutionary coup and subsequent U.S. invasion of Grenada in October 1983 was a bitter defeat with repercussions throughout the region. But the accomplishments of revolutionary Grenada and Nicaragua, together with the example of socialist Cuba, were strong enough to make possible the founding of the Anti-Imperialist Organizations of the Caribbean and Central America.

This organization was launched in June 1984 at a conference in Havana. Today it encompasses some thirty-seven political parties and movements—of diverse political origins and programs—from twenty-two countries in the English-, French-, Spanish-, Dutch-, and Creole-speaking Caribbean and Central America. The new organization came out of a discussion among Caribbean political groups following the overthrow of the Grenada revolution. Debate focused not only on the causes of that defeat, but also on the need for a response to the stepped-up aggression by U.S. imperialism in the region.

The founding statement of the Anti-Imperialist Organizations explained:

"Central America and the Caribbean have been linked since before the discovery of the New World. With the conquest, however, they were chained to different metropolises. Thus, we have long been separated by colonialism, and this separation was reinforced by U.S. imperialism in the last few decades; by the permanent plundering of each people in the region; and by the lack of communication, the political repression and the disinformation imposed throughout the Caribbean and Central America, which only the peoples' struggle has managed to overcome, little by little—the struggle in which we recognize one another and affirm our nationalities, in the defense of our wealth and in the search for a political regime that guarantees our countries' freedom and socioeconomic development.

"Above all, we recognize that we are brothers because we are confronting the same enemy, which oppresses and exploits us. Now, faced with U.S. imperialism's aggressive policy, the peoples of the Caribbean and Central America need close unity, diverse means of rapid communication, mutual support, encouragement, and shared criticism in order to survive, struggle, and win.

"We need ongoing exchanges in order to effectively coordinate our own resistance—coordination based on all that unites us and which enables us, as brothers and comrades, to tackle the differences and matters that separate us."

The organization's ten-party coordinating committee is broadly representative of the geographical and political mix of Central American and Caribbean groups that belong to it. The coordinating committee currently includes the Socialist People's Party of Curaçao, the Left Front of the Dominican Republic, the Maurice Bishop Patriotic Movement of Grenada, the People's Progressive Party of Guyana, the Communist Party of Guadeloupe, the Workers Party of Jamaica, the Puerto Rican Socialist Party, the Farabundo Martí National Liberation Front of El Salvador, the Progressive Labour Party of St. Lucia, and the February 18 Movement of Trinidad and Tobago.

THE HAVANA DECLARATION of the Anti-Imperialist Organizations denounced the U.S. invasion of Grenada and "reaffirmed the need to defend the human rights of all the Grenadian people, including the right to work, to freedom of expression and to freedom of association, and the right of all persons who are accused of crimes to select their legal representatives and to have a free and just trial—all of which have been violated by the illegal, servile puppet regime and its U.S. masters."

Stating that the defeat of the Grenadian Revolution constituted a serious setback for the Caribbean and international revolutions, the declaration continued, "the participants in the meeting denounced the execution of Maurice Bishop and other revolutionaries and expressed their conviction that, sooner rather than later, the people of Grenada would once more take up the torch of national and social freedom given them by their beloved leader and martyr, Maurice Bishop."

"The Second Assassination of Maurice Bishop" is a contribution to the discussion among all those revolutionaries who are looking for a way to take up Bishop's torch. In October 1983 the door to a U.S. invasion of Grenada was thrown open by the murderous counterrevolutionary actions of Bernard Coard and his political backers on the island. The U.S.-imposed regime that governs Grenada today has surrendered even the most minimal display of independence from its colonial masters. It was the only government to vote with Washington in the Organization of American States to approve U.S. economic sanctions against Nicaragua. It has twice been the only delegation from a colonial or semicolonial country to join Washington in opposing United Nations resolutions calling for sanctions against the apartheid South African regime.

IN GRENADA ITSELF, the neocolonial government has slashed education, health care, and other social services. The drug trade and prostitution are once again flourishing. Unemployment has skyrocketed and continues to mount.

The U.S.-organized occupation forces were withdrawn from Grenada within a year after the December 1984 elections staged to legitimize the regime they had placed in power. On several occasions since then, however, Grenada's prime minister Herbert Blaize has called in troops from the so-called Regional Security System set up under Washington's tutelage following the 1983 invasion. In addition to the country's regular police, U.S. occupation authorities have trained a paramilitary cop force called the Special Services Unit that has victimized trade unionists, political activists, and young people. This goes hand-in-hand with steps to establish a repressive court and prison system, marked by total disregard for the fundamental rights of defendants and prisoners.

An example was the trial last year in which Bernard Coard and thirteen other Grenadians were found guilty of murder and sentenced to death on charges stemming from the events of October 19, 1983. The U.S. and Grenadian governments hope to take advantage of the unpopularity of these defendants among Grenada's working people to make more palatable the violations of national sovereignty and democratic rights that mark this new "justice" system. But the prison abuse, denial of basic courtroom rights, and barbaric death sentences imposed on the defendants were aimed at intimidating anyone in Grenada or elsewhere in the Caribbean who opposes imperialist domination. The outcome of the trial confirmed Fidel Castro's statement that those who sat in judgment on Coard and the others have no "right to keep that extremist group in prison or to try them, because no invading force has the right to run the courts and enforce the laws."

Another goal of the current Grenadian government and its masters in Washington is to prevent the rebuilding of any political organization that speaks and acts on behalf of the island's working people. Over the past several years, however, the Maurice Bishop Patriotic Movement and Maurice Bishop Youth Organization have spoken out against U.S. domination and the reactionary policies of the Blaize regime at home and abroad. The MBPM and MBYO distribute a newspaper, *Indies Times,* and organize public activities to protest government policies and maintain popular consciousness of the revolution and its accomplishments.

The U.S.-dominated government that has been established in Grenada is the enemy of workers and farmers there and throughout the Caribbean. It will have to be replaced by a workers' and farmers' government, just as the dictatorship of Eric Gairy was toppled on March 13,

1979, by a revolutionary people under the leadership of the New Jewel Movement led by Maurice Bishop. That task will require the forging of a strong revolutionary workers' party through the struggles by the working people of Grenada in the years ahead.

Understanding both the achievements of the 1979–83 Grenada revolution and the political lessons of its destruction is an indispensable part of rebuilding a revolutionary party there. The disastrous consequences of the counterrevolutionary political course charted by Bernard Coard and the faction he organized need to be explained, and their efforts to malign Maurice Bishop and distort his revolutionary political legacy have to be combated. The aim of "The Second Assassination of Maurice Bishop" is to contribute to this effort.

"In today's world and tomorrow's world, to be a revolutionary is to be a communist," Fidel Castro told the delegates to the congress of the Union of Young Communists in April of this year. The tasks posed for communists in Cuba today is the topic of the two speeches by Castro published in this issue. The speeches are from the February and December 1986 sessions of the Cuban Communist Party's Third Congress.

The Cuban revolution is at a historic turning point, and the questions dealt with by Castro, as he explains, are important not just for Cuba but for "the whole of international revolutionary thought." The new course being charted in Cuba, and the Cuban communists' analysis of the reasons for it, are a major contribution to assessing the experiences of constructing socialism over the seven decades since the Bolshevik-led revolution in Russia. These speeches by Castro can be productively studied alongside works on these matters by other outstanding communist leaders of this century: Lenin's writings from the final months of his active political life (see the forthcoming Pathfinder book, *Lenin's Unfinished Fight: Articles by V.I. Lenin*); Leon Trotsky's *The Revolution Betrayed* (Pathfinder); and Che Guevara's "Notes on Man and Socialism in Cuba" (in Pathfinder's *Che Guevara Speaks*).

The participation of the Cuban Communist Party brings an irreplaceable element into the developing process of political collaboration and discussion within the Anti-Imperialist Organizations of the Caribbean and Central America. Another unique contribution is made by the participation of the Sandinista National Liberation Front of Nicaragua. Following the Anti-Imperialist Organizations' founding congress in Havana, a subsequent plenary meeting and special conference—both in 1986—have been held in Managua. In this issue we are publishing translations of works by two leaders of the FSLN. "Nicaragua Is a Caribbean Country" is the welcoming speech by Sandinista leader Lumberto Campbell to the February 1986 meeting in Managua of the Anti-Imperialist Organizations of the Caribbean and Central America. "Revolution Is the Birth of Light" is a 1985 interview with FSLN Commander Tomás Borge from the Cuban literary magazine, *El Caimán Barbudo.*

Two other articles in this issue focus on the class struggle in the two imperialist countries in the Americas.

"Land, Labor, and the Canadian Socialist Revolution" by Michel Dugré is translated from our French-language sister publication, *Nouvelle Internationale* (Fall 1986). Based on an analysis of the evolution of the economy, class struggle, and capitalist state in English Canada and Quebec, Dugré deals with questions of communist strategy that have been discussed in previous issues of *New International* (see in particular the articles by Jack Barnes and Doug Jenness on "The Workers' and Farmers' Alliance in the United States" in the spring 1985 issue).

Dugré sheds light on how two imperialist powers, not just one, came to exist on the North American continent. He describes the crisis facing exploited farmers in Canada, and presents some proposals for the kind of program needed by workers and farmers to forge a fighting alliance against their common exploiters, the Canadian capitalist class and its state. Dugré's explanation of questions such as how the demand for nationalization of the land was taken up by militant farmers' organizations and sections of the labor movement in western Canada in the 1920s and 1930s will be of great interest to working people not only in Canada but also in the United States, where that demand has rarely been championed beyond a small organized communist vanguard.

Larry Seigle's article on "Washington's Fifty-Year Domestic Contra Operation" addresses a question vital to the interests of workers and farmers throughout the world—the fight against attacks on democratic rights and political freedoms by the FBI, CIA, and other U.S. government police agencies. The occasion for Seigle's article is the campaign launched by the Political Rights Defense Fund (PRDF) to mobilize international support for the fight by the U.S. Socialist Workers Party and Young Socialist Alliance against FBI spying and disruption. In August 1986 Federal District Judge Thomas Griesa handed down a decision in the lawsuit against federal political police operations filed by the SWP and YSA fifteen years ago. In a historic victory for political liberties, Griesa ruled that the FBI's decades-long campaign against the two communist organizations was in violation of the U.S.

Constitution and Bill of Rights.

The victory has raised the stakes in this fight. Judge Griesa is currently considering the scope of the injunction outlined in his ruling against government use of illegally obtained files on the SWP and YSA. Once that question has been resolved, the fight to prevent the government from getting all or part of Griesa's ruling overturned in the appellate courts will begin.

Growing recognition that blows struck for democratic rights and against government secrecy in the United States benefit working people everywhere is adding a new international dimension to the campaign around the SWP and YSA lawsuit. Endorsements of the Political Rights Defense Fund, which has organized public support and financial backing for the case since its inception, have begun to come in from figures in the labor movement and other organizations around the world.

A RELATED VICTORY for political rights was won in May of this year, when the U.S. Immigration and Naturalization Service granted a temporary work permit to Héctor Marroquín, a Mexican-born socialist who has been waging a ten-year fight against deportation because of his membership in the SWP. Marroquín, who has been living in the United States since 1974, now has legal status for the first time and has gained a much stronger position from which to win his right to permanent residency. The Political Rights Defense Fund is organizing the campaign in defense of Marroquín's rights, as well, and PRDF will be stepping up efforts to win new sponsors for Marroquín's case as part of its international campaign.

Héctor Marroquín's case is an important front in the battle in the United States for full citizenship rights and equality by millions of foreign-born workers from the Americas, Asia, Africa, the Middle East, and elsewhere. These immigrants are a growing part of the U.S. working class and many of them are in the forefront of its battles against the capitalist rulers for better living standards, working conditions, and expanded political rights. The victories in both the SWP lawsuit and the Marroquín case, especially if they can be secured and built on, narrow the latitude of the capitalist government and employers to victimize immigrants on the basis of their union or political activities. They are victories for the entire U.S. labor movement and for workers and farmers around the world.

Since the SWP and YSA lawsuit was launched in the early 1970s, the Political Rights Defense Fund has gained the endorsement of trade union bodies, Black and women's rights groups, immigrants' rights organizations, and hundreds of individuals in the labor movement, farm activists' groups, civil liberties associations, and organizations of the oppressed. With the new stage in the fight opened by the August 1986 court decision, PRDF has launched a major effort to win thousands of additional endorsers and to raise financial contributions.

We urge our readers throughout the world to lend support to this fight by signing up to be a sponsor of the Political Rights Defense Fund and sending in a financial contribution.

A number of people worked on the translations from Spanish and French for this issue. They are: Mike Baumann, Robert Dees, Cindy Jaquith, Harvey McArthur, Fred Murphy, Ruth Nebbia, Selva Nebbia, and John Riddell.

THE SECOND ASSASSINATION OF MAURICE BISHOP

by Steve Clark

IN MID-OCTOBER 1983 a faction led by Deputy Prime Minister Bernard Coard in Grenada's army, government, and New Jewel Movement (NJM) overthrew the workers' and farmers' government brought to power by the March 13, 1979, revolution.

Prime Minister Maurice Bishop, backed by other NJM leaders and the overwhelming majority of the island's workers and farmers, resisted this counterrevolution and attempted to reverse it. On October 19 the Grenadian people launched an uprising to restore their government to power. They shut down workplaces, poured into the streets of the capital, St. George's, and freed Bishop, who had been placed under house arrest by the Coard faction. Estimates of the crowd range from 15,000 to 30,000—equivalent for that island of 110,000 people to an outpouring of 35 to 65 million in the United States.

Troops loyal to Coard's faction turned their guns on the mass demonstration, killing many participants and wounding others. They assassinated Maurice Bishop and five other revolutionary leaders—Fitzroy Bain, Norris Bain, Jacqueline Creft, Vincent Noel, and Unison Whiteman. The working people of Grenada were stunned and demoralized.

One week later, on October 25, United States armed forces stormed the island and occupied it. The Coard faction had handed free Grenada to imperialism on a silver platter. The country once again was shackled with a government subservient to Washington.

Discredited worldwide by these crimes and their disastrous consequences, Bernard Coard and his followers have tried ever since to cover their tracks by conducting a second assassination of Maurice Bishop. Their political targets include all those revolutionaries—in the Caribbean, North America, and elsewhere—who champion and seek to learn from Bishop's political legacy.[1]

The first assassination succeeded in eliminating Maurice Bishop himself. But Bishop's accomplishments and example as a revolutionary internationalist leader proved more enduring than Coard had reckoned. As the truth came out about what actually happened in October 1983—through the efforts of surviving Grenadian revolutionaries, Cuban president Fidel Castro, and others—the original explanations presented by Coard and his followers were increasingly repudiated by communists, anti-imperialist fighters, and progressive-minded people throughout the world.

HOW DID COARD'S ACCOMPLICES at the time seek to explain the October 1983 bloodbath?

Their first cover-up story was presented on the night of October 19, in a Radio Free Grenada broadcast by Gen. Hudson Austin. Austin presented the slanderous lie

ENDNOTES BEGIN ON PAGE 128

that Bishop "had declared his intention to wipe out the entire leadership of the party and the army" and "had linked up—openly—with counterrevolutionaries in order to do so."[2]

In a public statement that same day, Coard's colleagues condemned the "right opportunist and reactionary forces" led by Maurice Bishop. The declaration claimed that Bishop, shortly before his death, had said "that he did not want to see socialism built in this country" and "openly stated that he was going to build a new Party and a new Army—to defend the interest of the bourgeois."[3]

Another statement the following day declared that "Maurice Bishop and his other petty bourgeois and upper bourgeois friends had deserted the working class and working people of Grenada. He instead pushed them in front to cause trouble and bloodshed in the country. No man who has love for the working class and working people would push them into causing bloodshed."[4]

As each of these charges was exposed as a lie, the Coardites dropped them from their public pronouncements—without a word of explanation. Today, Coard hypocritically speaks of "the tragic death of Cde. Maurice Bishop and others." He laments that, "Those who slandered the name of the Grenada Revolution including Cde. Maurice Bishop, and tried tricks to assassinate Cde. Maurice Bishop, are now crying crocodile tears—while the people who feel this loss the most are those on trial."[5] (In December 1986, Coard and thirteen of his followers were convicted of murder and sentenced to death by a Grenadian court in connection with the October 1983 events. The violation of national sovereignty and democratic rights posed by the proceedings in this U.S. imposed, colonial-style court are dealt with in the "In This Issue" column of *New International.*)

Coard and his supporters have not dropped their efforts to exterminate the political legacy of Maurice Bishop, however. Instead, with Coard himself as the master chef, they have cooked up some new concoctions that, while no less poisonous, they hope will be a bit more palatable.

BERNARD COARD PRESENTED this new story in his August 1986 statement from the dock during the trial in Grenada. The 107-page transcript of Coard's account forms the basis for various shorter versions peddled by his apologists.[6] In his trial statement, Coard bombards the truth with a drumfire of outright lies, personal slanders, and vile innuendos. Not content with a volley of smears against Bishop and his close political supporters, Coard turns his fire once more against the workers and farmers who sought to salvage their revolution on October 19. Coard states:

> It's very important to understand crowd psychology if we are really to understand October 19, 1983.
>
> We have to understand the dynamics of a crowd, especially a huge crowd, especially one being whipped up and agitated by certain elements.
>
> Think about it. Consider this example. Suppose there is a fire at a store. Citizens will gather and they will stare at the store. Suppose then one or two persons break a showcase window. This will trigger a few other elements to do likewise. And if a couple people then, seeing some nice goods in the showcase window, start to take one or two things home—otherwise known as looting—you would be surprised how many other law-abiding citizens, who have never

> in their lives stolen anything, will do likewise!
>
> People one to one can be reasoned with. It's different with a large crowd. There is a "herd psychology."[7]

Coard's observation does indeed shed light on the events of October 19, 1983. But not for the reason Coard intends. To the contrary, the contempt for working people displayed by this statement illuminates the opposing *political* roads marked out by Coard and Bishop during the March 1979–October 1983 revolution and the years leading up to it.

Coard did not proceed along the historic line of march of Grenada's workers and exploited farmers, seeking to advance their class interests in the context of the particular historical and social conditions inherited by the revolution. Instead, he and his backers favored the use of bureaucratic mechanisms to impose their preconceived doctrines on the Grenadian working people. For Coard, the exploited producers in city and countryside were not the *subjects* of revolutionary social change, not its *makers,* but instead the *objects* of policy by an administrative apparatus.

Coard sought to build the New Jewel Movement as a tightly controlled staff to operate that apparatus, not as a growing political vanguard of the producing classes helping to expand working people's involvement in the administration of the Grenadian state and economy. Coard organized to keep the party small and narrow. Decisions that affected the state, the government, the unions, the mass organizations, the producing classes were more and more concentrated in the hands of a small, self-selected, and self-perpetuating group inside the New Jewel Movement.

Coard organized a secret faction loyal to himself inside

the party, the army officer corps, and government agencies. In order to entrench their control, he and his backers resorted to cronyism, administrative fiat, ultraleft demagogy, and finally bloody repression. Fidel Castro has accurately recognized the Coard faction as a "Pol Pot-type group."[8]

MAURICE BISHOP'S political starting point was the opposite of Coard's. Bishop relied on the organization, mobilization, and political education of Grenada's workers and farmers to advance their class interests and those of their oppressed and exploited allies throughout the Caribbean, the Americas, and the world.

"As we worked together to safeguard and consolidate our victory, our people's genius was set free and began to sparkle with brilliance," Bishop said on the third anniversary of the revolution. "For as we began, as a people, to confirm concretely that organization was our greatest weapon, our conviction became doubly reinforced that it was only mass participation and revolutionary democracy that could genuinely move us forward."[9]

Maurice Bishop knew the Grenadian people and they knew him. He was knowledgeable about the concrete history, socioeconomic conditions, and class relations of Grenada and the Caribbean, and of their place in the worldwide struggle for national liberation and socialism. On that basis, he sought to chart a revolutionary course, making use of the rich experiences and lessons of the international workers' movement.

Bishop was a true internationalist—one for whom internationalism was not a matter of ritual bows in the direction of other nations and struggles, but instead a life-or-death question for the Grenada revolution itself. "The success of our revolution cannot be an isolated event,"

Bishop told a mass rally in Nicaragua in February 1980. "The very worldwide nature of imperialism attests to the need for revolutionary solidarity among oppressed peoples everywhere."[10]

There was no better gauge of Bishop's internationalism than his tireless efforts to promote active solidarity with socialist Cuba. He was attracted to the Cuban revolution because it showed a way forward for Grenada and for other oppressed and exploited peoples. In his speech to the September 1979 summit meeting of the Non-Aligned Nations in Havana, Bishop said that the Cuban revolution "is now the best example of what socialism can do in a small country for health, education, employment, for ending poverty, prostitution, and disease."[11]

In a speech to the Grenadian people on the second anniversary of their revolution, Bishop pointed to Cuba's selfless assistance to nations and peoples throughout Africa, Asia, and the Americas. The Cuban people understand "from their own history the meaning of true internationalism," Bishop said. He emphasized that "the solidarity, the friendship, the depth of feelings, the unity, the cooperation, the anti-imperialist militancy that keeps us together can never, ever be broken. . . ."[12]

Given the strong internationalist bonds that united the Bishop leadership and the leaders of the Cuban revolution, Coard bitterly turned on Cuba when his faction launched its all-out assault against Bishop in September and October 1983. The political attitude toward socialist Cuba was a gauge with which to measure Coard's revolutionary internationalism, too.

Coard attracted to his banner those in the NJM who not only had the least confidence in the capacities of Grenadian working people to defend and advance the revolution, but who also had the least conviction that Grenada's fate was inextricably tied to those of the oppressed and exploited throughout the Caribbean, Central America, and the world.

Maurice Bishop summed up his approach to the Grenada revolution in his speech on its third anniversary in March 1982:

> The great strength of the revolution, first and foremost, lies in the unbreakable link between the masses and the party; between the masses and the government; between the masses and the state. This is what gives our revolution an invincible force, because the masses see the party, see the state and the government as theirs; not something foreign and strange, or apart or isolated from them, but living, throbbing entities that embody their aspirations, their interests and their hopes.[13]

This wasn't just oratory. Maurice Bishop *acted* on this understanding of the relationship between the party, government, state, and the masses of workers and farmers.

BERNARD COARD and his supporters destroyed the Grenada revolution in October 1983 when they placed Maurice Bishop under house arrest, overthrew the government that the workers and farmers had established in March 1979, and then unleashed a bloody reign of terror. It was those counterrevolutionary acts, Fidel Castro has explained, "that made it possible for the Reagan administration" to carry out a successful invasion and occupation of Grenada. "If Bishop had been alive leading the people," Castro said, "it would have been very difficult for the United States to orchestrate the political aspects of its intervention. . . ."

Following the events of October 19, however, the U.S. invading troops "were not going to be met with the people's resistance, for the simple reason that the people were outraged, traumatized by the attitude of this group that had fired upon the people and assassinated Bishop."[14]

Contrary to the claims by many commentators—conservative, liberal, and radical alike—the U.S. invasion of Grenada was not a political and military victory for the so-called Reagan Doctrine. The Grenada revolution was not defeated in a war with U.S. imperialism. The Coard faction had already destroyed the revolution and with it the Grenadian people's organized capacity to preserve the country's national sovereignty.

Today, Coard and his apologists deny that any fundamental political questions divided them from Bishop. Coard supporter Richard Hart, for example, asserts that "there were, in fact, no substantial differences of opinion within the NJM as to the policies to be pursued by the PRG." He dismisses "suggestions in the media to the effect that there was within the party an ultra-left group favouring some kind of instant socialism."[15]

In his August 1986 trial statement, Coard himself insisted that he had no political differences with Bishop. "One of the lines pushed heavily in all this [U.S. government] propaganda," Coard said, "has been . . . that 'Bernard Coard is a hardline Marxist and Communist' and 'Maurice Bishop is a wishy-washy Socialist.' That Bernard Coard wants Communism right away, and Maurice didn't want that, or wanted it slower."[16]

Coard fails to mention where the U.S. government procured grist for its propaganda mill—conveniently so, since Coard himself was the biggest supplier. Take, for example, his remarks at a meeting of the NJM Central

Committee on September 17, 1983. "There are two trends on the C[entral] C[ommittee]—[a] petit bourgeois revolutionary democratic trend and [a] M[arxist] L[eninist] trend," Coard said. Over the past several years, Bishop "found himself vacillating between the M.L. trend and the petit bourgeois trend in the party."[17]

There is a reason Coard and his supporters focus on the way the issue of political differences inside the NJM has been posed by the U.S. government, the big business media, and other opponents of the revolution. It makes it easier for them to dismiss the question. Yes, both Maurice Bishop and Bernard Coard considered themselves Marxists and communists. Yes, both publicly declared their aim to advance toward building a socialist Grenada. No, neither Coard nor Bishop ever said that "instant socialism" was possible.

But these broad generalities are empty of any real political content. The actual record demonstrates that Coard and Bishop differed sharply over the character, pace, and tasks of the Grenada revolution. Coard's secret faction *in practice* advocated bureaucratic and ultraleftist policies that Maurice Bishop, with diminishing success, sought to resist. Their political trajectories were bound to collide, although the outcome was not preordained.

What is the evidence for this conclusion? That is what the remainder of this article will present.

I. THE GRENADA REVOLUTION AND ITS TASKS

IN ORDER TO EVALUATE the opposing political courses of Maurice Bishop and Bernard Coard, it is necessary to look at the economic and social structure of Grenada and the resulting tasks posed for a revolutionary workers' party leading a workers' and farmers' government.

Grenada is a small, predominantly agricultural island. It became independent of direct colonial rule by Britain only five years prior to the March 1979 revolution but remained under the heel of British and, increasingly, U.S. imperialist domination.

When the New Jewel Movement took power, more than one third of the population was dependent on incomes from farming or farm labor as their source of livelihood. Among Grenadians fortunate enough to have a job—unemployment stood at 50 percent just prior to the revolution—many made their living in the marketplace, on the docks, or in other ways closely linked to farming.

The bulk of the island's farm output, however, went neither to feed the Grenadian people nor to advance their living standards. Most of the food consumed on the island was imported; in 1979 this accounted for almost one-third of Grenada's imports. At the same time, the country's major agricultural products—cocoa, bananas, and the spices nutmeg and mace—were almost entirely for export (primarily to Britain). These commodities made up more than 90 percent of Grenada's export earnings.

As a result, the working conditions and income of the Grenadian people were extremely vulnerable to price fluctuations on the world capitalist market. Even when these prices were relatively high, Grenada was denied most of the revenues from the crops cultivated and transported by its farmers and workers. Instead, the owners of the imperialist-operated businesses that controlled the bulk of the processing and marketing firms were enriched.

Two-thirds of Grenada's farmers held title to the land they tilled, but the big majority of these farmers had plots too small to sustain themselves and their families. Nearly

90 percent of farms were less than five acres; two-thirds were under two acres. On the other hand, half the total acreage was owned by a handful of Grenadian capitalists accounting for fewer than 2 percent of the farms. Very little land was foreign-owned.

As a result of these conditions, many farmers also had to work as wage laborers, either on one of the big plantations or in town. Neither the exploited majority nor exploiting minority of farmers had much incentive to modernize production methods under this setup; the former could not do so given their tiny landholdings and paucity of resources, while the latter reaped handsome profits from the extensive hiring and intensive toil of plentiful cheap labor.

Tourism came second to agriculture in employment of Grenadians. Profits from tourist services, however, contributed little to the development of productive economic activity in Grenada. Moreover, under the colonial and neocolonial regimes prior to March 1979, tourism reinforced the island's subordination to imperialist domination. It promoted degrading and parasitic practices such as prostitution, the drug trade, and every variety of hustling aimed at the tastes of well-to-do tourists.

The majority of wage workers in Grenada were employed as agricultural laborers, in tourism-related jobs, or as retail clerks or government employees. Less than 10 percent of the working population was employed in manufacturing at the time of the revolution, and the largest factory—a brewery—hired on only some 75 workers. Several thousand workers had jobs in construction or on the docks.

The tasks of the revolution in Grenada were conditioned by the country's subordination to imperialism, its economic structure, and its class relations. British and

Canadian capital dominated banking and the import/export trade on the island. The local Grenadian capitalist class was composed largely of big landholders, hotel and restaurant operators, wholesale traders, wealthy storekeepers, some import/export dealers, and a handful of factory owners.

Although Grenada was an agricultural country with very little industry, precapitalist systems of land ownership and labor exploitation had been largely supplanted over the past century by the capitalist system of money rents and mortgages burdening small farmers and the exploitation of wage labor on the plantations and in the towns. Grenada had gone from capitalist chattel slavery in the first half of the nineteenth century to capitalist debt slavery and wage slavery in the latter half of the twentieth.

THE VICTORIOUS UPRISING in March 1979 opened an anticapitalist revolution—one whose most pressing immediate tasks were democratic goals such as land reform, labor rights, and elementary political freedoms, as well as liberation from imperialist domination in order to develop productive economic activity.[18]

The revolution brought to power for the first time in Grenada a government not subservient to U.S. and British imperialism and the local landlords and capitalists. The new workers' and farmers' government began to carry out a revolutionary democratic program. From the outset it also began promoting the organization of working people in town and country to advance their class interests against the power and prerogatives of the large landowners and capitalists.

Given the tiny industrial base, small urban working class, and the concrete character of the economic backwardness of Grenada, however, the transition to a planned economy based on state property in industry, banking, and big trade was necessarily a process that could unfold only over a number of years. Most important, it could advance only in tandem with the expanding organization, mobilization, and political consciousness of the workers and exploited farmers, whose class alliance formed the social base of the revolutionary government, state, and vanguard working-class party.

GRENADA'S PRODUCTIVE FORCES, both in agriculture and industry, had to grow and be modernized. An adequate system of roads, electrification, water and sewage pipelines, communications, and international sea and air transport had to be built up. Local industries to process and package the island's agricultural commodities for export, and to reduce reliance on imported consumer goods, had to be developed. Revenues from tourism would need to be redirected from the enrichment of a few local and overseas capitalists to the advancement of agriculture and industry.

Meanwhile, Grenada's economy remained capitalist. The working people through their government and the New Jewel Movement needed to make use of the technical and managerial skills of middle class and professional layers who were willing to cooperate in expanding production and cooperate with capitalists willing to continue investing in productive enterprises. The revolutionary government guaranteed the ownership rights of capitalists so long as they did not sabotage the economy or participate in illegal acts.

This course was necessary until the development of Grenada's productive forces, the growth of the state sector in industry, banking, and trade, and—above all—the political and administrative experience of the working people would make possible the transition to socialist property relations. Even then, the revolutionary government had no intention of expropriating owners of small shops, inns, and other modest enterprises.

The tempo of a revolutionary transformation of property relations in Grenada could not be predetermined. That would depend on the concrete evolution of the class struggle and the economy in Grenada and internationally. During this transition period, the workers' and farmers' government, together with the unions and other mass organizations, decisively altered the relationship of class forces to the advantage of working people in their struggles for better living and working conditions. This included the adoption and enforcement of labor laws guaranteeing union rights and regulating the wages and job conditions of rural and urban workers.

Moreover, the new People's Revolutionary Army and People's Militia gave the workers and farmers a way to defend their political power against counterrevolution instigated by U.S. imperialism and by local landowners and businessmen. Without this armed power, the transition to a new, nonexploiting society would be a utopia. Some 3,500 Grenadians received army or militia training between March 1979 and October 1983.

Everyone in the leadership of the New Jewel Movement professed agreement with the proposition that the socialist task of expropriating the Grenadian bourgeoisie was not on the short-term agenda of the revolution opened by the March 1979 victory. "With the working people we made our popular, anti-imperialist, and democratic revolution," Maurice Bishop said in March 1983. "With them we will build and advance to socialism and final victory."[19]

"At this time, we see our task not as one of building socialism," Bernard Coard explained in a 1979 interview. "It is one of re-structuring and re-building the economy, of getting production going and trying to develop genuine grassroots democracy, trying to involve the people in every village and every workplace in the process of the reconstruction of the country. In that sense we are in a national democratic revolution. . . ."[20]

But how did this work out in real life? How did Maurice Bishop and Bernard Coard seek to chart a course for the New Jewel Movement and the People's Revolutionary Government (PRG) during the four-and-a-half years of the Grenada revolution? What did they do in practice to politicize, increase the confidence, and expand the involvement of Grenada's workers and farmers in economic, state, and party affairs?

Origins of New Jewel Movement

Bernard Coard's efforts to misrepresent himself and his supporters as the "real" communist leadership of the Grenadian working class date back to the early years of the New Jewel Movement and its precursors in the first half of the 1970s.

The New Jewel Movement, like many other revolutionary organizations in the Caribbean, was a product of the Black Power movement in the islands in the late 1960s, and early 1970s. This was a movement of young people, largely based in the islands under current or former British colonial rule (Jamaica and Trinidad were the first islands to gain formal independence in 1962).

Black Power activists wanted to fight for genuine national independence and self-determination and against racist oppression and economic superexploitation of all peoples of African slave origins in the Caribbean and the Americas. They had been inspired by the post–World War II anticolonial battles and victories in Africa; by social struggles such as the anti–Vietnam War movement in many countries; and—as the name of their movement indicated—by the Black Power currents among young fighters against segregation and racist discrimination in the United States, as well as by Malcolm X.

As a student in Britain in the 1960s, Maurice Bishop had been chairperson of the West Indian Students Society at London University and was active in the Campaign Against Racial Discrimination in that country. He returned to Grenada in early 1970, just as students in nearby Trinidad were linking up with workers and small farmers in an uprising that shook the foundations of the capitalist government of Prime Minister Eric Williams. This uprising—put down in blood under a state of emergency in April—marked the high point of the Black Power movement in the Caribbean.

Inspired by the uprising in Trinidad, Bishop organized a solidarity demonstration in Grenada in May 1970. "In those days, demonstrations were something new to Grenada," he later recalled, "and many people thought we were crazy parading up and down with placards."[21] But things were beginning to change.

Over the next few years Bishop led a support committee for striking nurses, participated in a mass protest against a wealthy British landowner blocking access to a public beach, and took part in other social and political struggles in Grenada.

In 1972 Bishop and Kendrick Radix launched an organization based in St. George's called the Movement for Assemblies of the People. That same year Unison Whiteman, another young fighter influenced by the Black Power movement, formed an organization called JEWEL (Joint

Endeavour for Welfare, Education and Liberation), which based its political activity among small farmers and plantation laborers in the southern part of the island.

In 1973 these two organizations fused to form the New Jewel Movement. Among its early leaders and cadres were Bishop, Whiteman, Radix, Hudson Austin, George Louison, Selwyn Strachan, and Jacqueline Creft.[22]

THE NJM RAPIDLY demonstrated its capacity to mobilize mass opposition to the corrupt and oppressive regime of Eric Gairy, who presided over the transition to independence from direct British rule in 1974. In May of that year, it sponsored a rally of 10,000 to demand the people's involvement in drafting the new constitution. Over the next half decade the NJM helped initiate and lead struggles for democratic rights and better conditions for workers and farmers. NJM members organized unionization drives and participated in the 1976 elections, winning three seats in Grenada's parliament.[23]

Through his leadership of these battles, Maurice Bishop won the recognition of tens of thousands of working people as a committed spokesperson for their interests and an effective political organizer.

The NJM also began to advance politically beyond its militant nationalism and anti-imperialism toward proletarian internationalism.

In a 1977 interview, Maurice Bishop told the Cuban weekly *Bohemia* that the movement in Grenada had initially been deeply influenced by "the ideas of 'Black Power' that developed in the United States and the freedom struggle of the African peoples in such places as Angola, Mozambique, and Guinea-Bissau." It was above all "through the Cuban experience," Bishop said, that "we got to see scientific socialism close up. . . . Our party began to develop along Marxist lines in 1974, when we began to study the theory of scientific socialism."[24]

When the NJM was formed, Bernard Coard was not living in Grenada and was not among its founding members. At the time, he was teaching at the University of the West Indies in Jamaica, where he worked closely with Trevor Munroe of the Workers Liberation League (forerunner of today's Workers Party of Jamaica). Coard declared himself an NJM supporter from the outset, however, and collaborated with Bishop in drafting its founding manifesto.[25]

In 1976 Coard returned to Grenada and joined the NJM, becoming a member of its Political Bureau. For several years Coard had been linked with a group of secondary school students and other young people in Grenada, who in 1975 formed the Organization for Research, Education and Liberation (OREL). OREL briefly published a newspaper called *The Spark*. "In those early years," Kendrick Radix said in a 1984 interview, "they attacked the New Jewel Movement, which was already rooted in the people, as a petit-bourgeois party. Yet at the same time, they approached the NJM leadership proposing an amalgamation into the New Jewel Movement. . . ."[26] In 1976 the OREL members joined the NJM.

Once back on the island, Coard quickly became OREL's leading figure. The OREL included Liam James, Leon Cornwall, Ewart Layne, John Ventour, Chris Stroude, Basil Gahagan, and Nazim Burke.[27] The OREL cadres considered themselves to be the "Marxist-Leninist" component of the New Jewel Movement and regularly held meetings separate from the rest of the party, normally in Coard's home.[28] (Seeking to justify Coard's claim to "ideological guidance" of the NJM from its origins, a September 1983 report prepared by his faction stated that he had "formed the first M[arxist-] L[eninist] study group in 1974. . . ."[29])

Under Coard's leadership, OREL began functioning as a secret faction of the NJM behind the backs of the party's leadership bodies, with its own discussions, goals, and discipline. "Certain unprincipled meetings started to develop," Kendrick Radix explained in a 1985 interview. "Coard introduced methods of internal canvassing, preparing opinions in advance" among the membership, Radix explained, "rather than dealing with matters on their merits in leadership bodies."[30]

Radix and some other NJM members at the time proposed Coard's expulsion from the Political Bureau and from the party in 1977 because of OREL's factional functioning.[31] Bishop intervened to resolve the dispute, however. Coard agreed to disband OREL, and an Organising Committee of the NJM was set up in 1978 under Coard's chairmanship. Subsequent events, however, demonstrate that the OREL grouping continued to operate as a permanent secret faction inside the NJM.[32]

II. OPENING YEARS OF THE REVOLUTION

On March 13, 1979, the New Jewel Movement organized an armed uprising against the U.S.-backed dictatorship of Eric Gairy. Thousands of Grenadians responded to a radio appeal by Maurice Bishop to come into the streets, ensuring victory.[33]

The new People's Revolutionary Government (PRG) wiped Gairy's repressive legislation off the books, expanded trade union rights, advanced women's equality in the workplace, instituted free medical care, built new schools and health clinics, established free public education and adult literacy programs for the first time, lowered the prices of food and other necessities, improved housing, took measures to benefit small farmers and farm workers, and carried out many other projects to aid Grenada's working people.

Asserting that Grenada was in "nobody's backyard," the PRG exercised its right to a foreign policy free from subjugation to Washington and London. It established economic and political relations with Cuba, Nicaragua, and the Soviet Union, and joined the Movement of Non-Aligned Nations.

In addition, the new government began taking steps to deepen the participation of workers and farmers in the revolution. Unions and mass organizations of women and youth were established, as well as a people's militia. By 1981 councils were launched in villages, neighborhoods, and workplaces to provide a forum for working people to question government officials and raise their own grievances and proposals.

An important political dispute within the New Jewel Movement broke out between Bishop and Coard during the first months following the revolutionary triumph. The conflict arose over how to combat the escalating counterrevolutionary provocations by the owners of the *Torchlight* newspaper.[34] The vast majority of shares in this weekly publication were held by D.M.B. Cromwell, a Grenadian capitalist, and by the owners of the reactionary Trinidadian newspaper, the *Express.*

The *Torchlight* rapidly went beyond editorial opposition to the policies of the People's Revolutionary Government, repeatedly featuring false and provocative articles aimed at creating panic inside Grenada and isolating the new government in the Caribbean. The *Torchlight,* for example, ran a front-page article alleging that PRG official and

NJM leader Kendrick Radix was plotting to overthrow the government of Antigua, a nearby island. Under the headline, "Click, Click, Got Ya'," the newspaper featured photographs of Bishop's personal security guards. It reprinted a completely groundless article from a West German scandal sheet claiming that the PRG was permitting the Soviet and Cuban governments to build a submarine base on the island. And it publicized the location of an army training camp.

The *Torchlight*'s publishers consistently refused to publish coverage of the policies and views of government and NJM leaders, including responses by them to the paper's scurrilous gossip. When Bishop requested to discuss these matters before a meeting of the newspaper's shareholders, "they rejected it outright," recalls former PRG cabinet member Lyden Ramdhanny. "They said that they would have nothing to do with Prime Minister Maurice Bishop, that it was an internal matter and we would handle it in our own way."[35]

BISHOP ENERGETICALLY exposed the *Torchlight*'s provocations and falsifications. In combating this reactionary voice of the exploiters, however, Bishop was convinced that the revolution would emerge stronger if the PRG could avoid closing the paper down, or do so only as a last resort. Among the PRG's first measures had been repeal of Gairy's antidemocratic newspaper law—aimed at the *Torchlight* as well as the NJM's *New Jewel*—requiring the payment of $20,000 in order to publish. Grenadian workers and farmers treasured this and other political freedoms that they had conquered in overthrowing the Gairy dictatorship. While shutting the *Torchlight* might have been unavoidable at some point if its publishers aligned themselves with forces engaged in counterrevolutionary acts, the big majority of Grenadian working people, given the evidence, would have understood the need for such defensive measures to preserve their revolution and its gains.

In line with this approach, Bishop made the following public response to the *Torchlight* editor's rejection of the PRG's request not to publish photographs of the prime minister's security guards:

> Because of the People's Revolutionary Government's well known desire to encourage a free press, we did not prevent [the reporter] from taking photographs. We had hoped that he would have put patriotism and concern for the safety of the leadership of the country above cheap journalism. We have certainly noted the irresponsibility of the Acting Editor and his newspaper in publishing these pictures.[36]

To help raise the political consciousness of Grenada's working people, Bishop unmasked the reactionary aims, class exploitation, and social inequalities that lay behind the *Torchlight*'s hypocritical championing of "freedom of the press." He pointed out that the political conduct of the newspaper's owners had nothing to do with freedom of the press, but instead with their determination to resist revolutionary change that threatened their minority class interests. He explained that the *Torchlight*'s publishers were facilitating efforts by U.S. imperialism and Grenadian and other Caribbean reactionaries to destabilize the PRG. To these ends, these exploiters were abusing the vastly disproportionate control over means of communications and information made possible by their wealth.[37]

Bishop's opinion on how to deal with the *Torchlight,* however, was not shared by Bernard Coard, who was anxious to shut it down, the sooner the better. He viewed Bishop's approach as reluctance "to take firm decisions on key issues."[38] In October 1979 Bishop traveled to New York City to address the United Nations General Assembly. In his absence, Coard used his position as acting head of state to scuttle Bishop's policy.

A FEW DAYS AFTER Bishop's departure, the *Torchlight* appeared with the front-page headline: "Rastas to Protest." The article reported plans for an antigovernment protest announced by Ras Nang Nang, a follower of the Rastafarian religion. In the wake of the Black Power upsurge of the late 1960s and early 1970s, the Rastas had substantially expanded their following among young people in Grenada and other English-speaking Caribbean islands. Support for the Rastas (whose members braid their hair in "dreadlocks" and smoke marijuana as part of their rites) was one form taken by the widespread youth rebellion against the repressive, neocolonial regimes on these islands.

In the 1970s Gairy and other Caribbean regimes carried out brutal campaigns against the Rastas. In Grenada, Gairy's hated Mongoose gang victimized Rastas, sometimes by assaulting them and cutting off their dreadlocks. The *Torchlight* supported Gairy's repression of the Rastas. Maurice Bishop acted as the attorney for many victimized Rastas during these years, further establishing his political reputation as a champion of the oppressed throughout Grenada and the Caribbean. Following the overthrow of Gairy, many Rastas rallied to the PRG and joined the People's Revolutionary Army. A few Rasta leaders, however, subsequently came to oppose the PRG's policies, especially as the government cracked down on the drug trade, including large-scale cultivation and sale of marijuana.

The article in the October 10 *Torchlight* falsely claimed that the PRG was barring Rastas from school and tracking them down at gunpoint around the island. The article said that "massive numbers" of Rastas were planning to demonstrate against the government to protest these policies.

This article fit into the *Torchlight*'s pattern of counterrevolutionary provocations aimed at destabilizing the PRG. Nothing about the circumstances surrounding this one particular article, however, posed such an emergency that action could not have been postponed until Bishop's return a week later. Nonetheless, Coard took advantage of his powers as acting prime minister to order the closing of the *Torchlight* on October 13. When Bishop arrived back in Grenada on October 18, he was confronted with the fait accompli.

Bishop then sought to make the best of the bad situation created by Coard's preemptive action. The front-page article on the shutdown that appeared in the *Free West Indian,* Grenada's prorevolution weekly, two days after Bishop's return stated:

> Government sources say the *Torchlight* newspaper, banned last weekend by the PRG, will return to the streets in a few weeks but with a different management and ownership structure. Government does not plan to take over the newspaper but will insist that its ownership structure be broadened. . . . The plan is to 'democratise' the paper with limits placed on the number of shares individuals or organizations can

> hold and to outline guidelines that would ensure that *Torchlight* publishes the views of all sections of the Grenadian society. It is also expected that there will be a change in the management structure.[39]

On October 26, the PRG issued a new law restricting newspaper ownership to citizens of Grenada and barring any shareholder from owning more than 4 percent of the total. A reorganized *Torchlight* was never reopened, however.

Coard and the 'Grenadian Voice'

With popular support growing for the social and economic programs of the PRG, U.S.-backed counterrevolutionaries in Grenada stepped up their efforts to destabilize the government. In October and November 1979, the PRG discovered an arms cache and documents outlining a plot to assassinate government leaders; more than thirty people were arrested in connection with this plot.[40] In the spring of 1980 a small group of former NJM members sought to undermine support for the PRG among Grenadian youth by stirring up opposition to the government's moves against marijuana growers and traders. In June 1980 counterrevolutionaries set off a bomb under the speakers' platform at a mass rally, killing three young women and injuring almost 100 other people.[41] Later in 1980 a soldier and a militia member were shot and seriously wounded, a militia camp was fired on, and there were arson and bombing incidents.

Washington was stepping up its economic sabotage and military pressure against the PRG, as well. U.S. officials sought to block loans and aid to Grenada by Washington's European imperialist allies and international lending institutions. As part of its Ocean Venture '81 war games in the Caribbean, the U.S. Navy staged a thinly veiled mock invasion of Grenada.

At the same time, opponents of the revolution inside and outside Grenada were stepping up propaganda efforts to discredit the PRG. "In 1981 counterrevolution, fueled by the CIA, was moving in certain areas in terms of the Rastafarians . . . business sectors . . . the dockworkers and in the trade unions, and the church," Kendrick Radix explained in a 1985 interview. "They were probing to destabilize the country and to overthrow the revolution internally. The question was how we were to deal with it."

In this political context, Radix continued, "Coard again proposed some very draconian measures, which led to a great debate inside the party on how to deal with the situation." In the opinion of Bishop, himself, and others in the NJM leadership, Radix said, Coard's proposals "would have fueled the counterrevolution and caused the revolution to collapse in 1981. The more mature elements within the party managed to hold sway."[42]

The first clash between Bishop and Coard took place following the appearance in mid-June of a mimeographed newspaper calling itself the *Grenadian Voice.* Its owners—listed in the paper as the "Committee of 26"—were wealthy Grenadian landowners, businessmen, and professionals. These included former shareholders of the *Torchlight.* Lyden Ramdhanny was present at the cabinet meeting in June 1981 when Bernard Coard proposed, in response to the appearance of the *Voice,* "to confiscate all of the large holdings in St. George's . . . to nationalize everything as a lesson to the bourgeoisie and that strata."[43]

Given the tremendous weight of St. George's in Grenada's overall commerce and industry, Coard's proposal would have meant the expropriation of virtually the entire

Grenadian capitalist class. This would have reversed over night the course carried out by the PRG and NJM since the March 1979 victory, without any political preparation or involvement of the nation's workers and farmers.

Coard's proposal confirms the later assessment of George Louison that

> the Coard clique . . . had the idea that the party could do anything, declare anything, and that the rest of the society had to fall in line on 24-hours' notice. In other words, they lacked an appreciation of the genuine need of the masses of the people to be in tandem with the activities of the party. They must understand those actions so they can carry them out also.[44]

Coard's proposed expropriation measures could have been implemented only administratively, largely by government authorities. While some Grenadian workers and farmers would have backed such a measure if PRG leaders convinced them it was necessary to preserve the revolution, most would have soon concluded from experience that this had been a disastrous mistake. Conditions did not yet exist in Grenada for a nationalized and planned economy.

Moreover, other layers of workers and farmers would have been disoriented and made more vulnerable to counterrevolutionary appeals, while middle class and professional layers supportive of the PRG would have turned against the revolution in unnecessarily large numbers. The flames of anticommunism would have been fanned.

At the conclusion of the June 1981 PRG cabinet meeting, Ramdhanny was convinced that Coard's proposal was going to be implemented. Following that meeting, however, Ramdhanny never heard anything more about Coard's plan. Only after the overthrow of the revolution did Ramdhanny learn that Bishop had successfully defeated the proposal in the NJM's leadership bodies.

The NJM leadership, however, did decide to bar further issues of the *Voice* or of any other new publications for one year. This decision was announced in a June 19, 1981, speech by Bishop.[45]

The New Jewel Movement justified the shutdown of the *Voice* by explaining that the paper's shareholders had previously issued pamphlets calling for counterrevolutionary violence; that one shareholder was involved in a plot to kill militia members and soldiers; and that the group was linked to the CIA. A few weeks after the banning of the *Grenadian Voice,* four of its sponsors—attorneys Lloyd Noel and Tillman Thomas, businessman Leslie Pierre, and union bureaucrat Stanley Roberts—were arrested for involvement in CIA efforts to topple the PRG. No formal charges were ever brought in connection with any of these matters, however.

Coard's Rasta roundup

On June 24, 1981, three top PRG defense officials—Majors Ewart Layne and Einstein Louison, and Deputy Minister of Defence and Interior Liam James—came before the Political Bureau. They were there "to discuss the present threat being posed by the rasta elements—particularly since it was learnt that they are planning to attack one of the PRA camps on Friday—and possible measures to deal with that situation." Their proposal was that the government round up 300 Rastas and cut off their dreadlocks.

According to the minutes of the meeting, Bishop "stated that he was totally against taking up 300 of them and cutting their hair as was proposed." Coard, on the other hand, "reminded the meeting that the Party . . . had always been reluctant to take firm decisions on key issues." Coard cited the examples of the *Torchlight* and Ras Nang Nang from late 1979.

The minutes indicate a wide-ranging discussion. Even Liam James, one of Coard's leading supporters from OREL days, expressed reservations about the proposal. He said that he had raised the matter with the Cuban ambassador, who "showed concern about the issue and felt that we would be isolated regionally and internationally." James also "questioned what would be the attitude/mood after the operation, the implications for the youth work, how will the rastas be influenced to work, the reaction of the population."

As an alternative, James proposed "that in order to 'legitimise' our grabbing any rastas, we should allow them to carry out their attack as planned and then take them." Bishop, clearly horrified by this suggestion, rejected it. He pointed out that "it could very well end up in people being killed on both sides."[46]

THE MATTER WAS DISCUSSED further at a Central Committee meeting later that day.

Neither Maurice Bishop nor Bernard Coard were present. Unison Whiteman initiated the discussion, explaining that "there is evidence that the rastas are planning to go on an offensive in the Northern part of the country within days and that we must consider preventative measures." Whiteman acknowledged, however, that "one of our greatest weaknesses is the lack of precise information."

Phyllis Coard, a prominent leader of the Coard faction, repeated the proposal "that the key rasta leaders should be picked up." She proposed "about 50 rastas," instead of the 300 raised earlier that day at the Political Bureau meeting. According to the minutes of the meeting, Phyllis Coard stated her opinion that

> we have to handle the situation with "manners" [firmness]; should look at not only the reaction of the rastas, but also at the rest of the masses; the rasta movement has weakened our support base; should not play up the line that this is a move against the rasta movement generally; we don't have the capacity to hold all the rastas in the country. . . .[47]

After some discussion, there was agreement to move ahead with the arrests. There is no reference in the Central Committee minutes to Bishop's opposition to the proposal that had been raised in the Political Bureau that morning. Recognizing the adverse political ramifications of this measure, Vincent Noel urged the establishment of "a propaganda team for the dissemination of the news regionally," and said that the NJM "must consider the possibility of a national address" by Bishop to explain any detentions.

The arrests began the following day. A list of these detainees dated July 22, 1981, indicates that seventy-six people in all were picked up. Fifteen were held for only a few days; of the remaining sixty-one, thirty-three had "declared themselves avowed Rastafarians" and another six had dreadlocks "but disclaim any connections with Rastafarians." The list said that nine of those with dreadlocks "have elected to cut their hair since detention and have done so"; of these, five had been released and four were still being held.

No charges were ever brought against the Rastas who were arrested, and the detentions and reasons for them were never publicized or explained to the Grenadian people. Nevertheless, a subsequent list of detainees, dated January 1, 1982, indicates that most of those picked up remained in jail at that time.[48]

Even if on a more limited scale than originally planned, the Rasta roundup had been carried out. And the revolution was the weaker for it.

Stepped-up effort to isolate Bishop

In mid-1981, Coard's secret faction stepped up their maneuvers to undermine Bishop's position in the leadership bodies of the NJM.

In late July Coard and his backers engineered the removal of longtime NJM leader Vincent Noel from the Central Committee and Political Bureau. This proposal originated in the NJM's Organising Committee, which had been chaired by Bernard Coard since its establishment in 1977. The Organising Committee brought in a report to the July 22, 1981, Central Committee meeting on inadequacies in the work of the NJM's Workers Committee, chaired by Noel.[49] The report stated that Noel "had failed to push the work forward" and that he himself acknowledged that his work had been indisciplined.[50]

Commenting on the Organising Committee report, Bishop said that the functioning of the Workers Committee had come up "time and time before" in the party, but that no serious attention had been given to this work. He said that "the Central Committee and the Political Bureau should shoulder some of the blame in this respect."

Coard, striking the theme that he and his backers would raise with increasing frequency over the next two years (and would level ever more directly at Bishop in particular), condemned the leadership's "timidity, unprincipled[ness] and softness in dealing with such a situation."[51]

At the conclusion of the meeting, Noel was not only removed as chairman of the Workers Committee, but from the Central Committee and Political Bureau, as well.

Coard also maneuvered to advance the position of his supporters within the top officer corps of the People's Revolutionary Army. The minutes of the September 23, 1981, meeting of the Political Bureau recount Coard's strong objections to a proposal on the makeup of the army command structure. At the time, the two highest-ranking army officers beneath Gen. Hudson Austin were Maj. Einstein Louison and Maj. Ewart Layne. Under the proposed reorganization, Layne—a longtime Coard supporter and OREL cadre—was to become army chief of staff, while Louison was given the higher position of deputy secretary of defense.

According to the minutes of the September 23 meeting, Coard "called this a compromise, since it is his strong feeling that the leadership of the Army should be changed." The Political Bureau agreed that these would be "temporary changes for a period of six months."[52]

While Coard had to accept this "compromise" in September 1981, he got his way the following year. Ewart Layne, by then promoted from major to lieutenant colonel, became deputy secretary of defense. Einstein Louison, still a major, was assigned the subordinate position of chief of staff. What's more, Liam James, another OREL cadre and leader of the Coard faction, became the PRA's only other lieutenant colonel; in mid-1981 James had not even been an officer. Thus, by the end of 1982, both of the highest-ranking army officers below Gen. Hudson Austin were solid leaders of the Coard faction.[53]

Coard's supporters also organized the ouster of Don Rojas as editor of the *Free West Indian* in December 1981. Without prior notice, Rojas was called before a meeting of the assembled staff of the newspaper, subjected to a "criticism" session, and informed that he was being replaced as editor. Although Bishop was head of the Ministry of Information, which was responsible for the *Free West Indian,* he was not informed of the decision to remove Rojas. This decision was organized behind Bishop's back by Coard supporter Kamau McBarnette and cadres from Trevor Munroe's Workers Party of Jamaica who were functioning in Grenada.

Rojas, who had edited the newspaper for two years since being appointed by Bishop, was replaced by McBarnette and then, several months later, by a WPJ cadre. Rojas was put on probation in the NJM for a few weeks, but was reinstated after Bishop took the initiative to ask Rojas to serve as his press secretary.[54]

Coard discovers a 'petty bourgeois trend'

At an April 21, 1982, meeting of the Central Committee, supporters of Coard's secret faction began to call attention to a "petty bourgeois" trend in the NJM leadership. Under the discussion of a report on the "State of the Party," Phyllis Coard listed as the number one problem "the petty bourgeois attitude still existing in a number of comrades, including the leadership."[55] No specific names were cited at this point.

At this Central Committee meeting, Bernard Coard also called attention to "a crisis in party organisation" affecting the NJM. Although this would emerge as a major axis of the campaign against Bishop over the next eighteen months, all that Coard is recorded as saying in the April 1982 minutes was that, "Our main problem is that we are trying to do too much."[56]

An August 27, 1982, Central Committee meeting discussed a major report by Bishop on the NJM's political perspectives and decided that it should be presented to several general meetings in September of all the party's full, candidate, and applicant members. That report was subsequently printed for discussion and education in the membership under the title, "Line of March for the Party." It was never distributed publicly.[57]

There is no indication of opposition to Bishop's report in the minutes of the August 1982 Central Committee meeting (prior to September 1983 the NJM's minutes never recorded votes). Nonetheless, Bishop's report itself refers to "some confusion" inside the NJM on the character and tasks of the revolution. "It is extremely important for us to get a better understanding of where we are, of what we are trying to build and of how we will be able to build it," Bishop stressed.[58]

The Grenada revolution, Bishop said, "is a national-democratic, anti-imperialist Revolution." He continued:

> I did not say a socialist revolution as some comrades like to keep pretending that we have. Obviously we do not have a socialist revolution. . . . We cannot proceed straight away to the building of socialism but must first pass through a stage where we lay the basis, where we create the conditions, including the socio-economic and political conditions, for the building of socialism and the creation of the socialist revolution, that is, for the full coming to power of the working class.[59]

The Grenada revolution, Bishop said, necessitates class alliances—"an alliance in the first place between the working class and the petty bourgeoisie, in particular the rural peasantry, and in the second place an alliance with those elements of the upper petty bourgeoisie and the national bourgeoisie who, for different reasons, are willing to be involved in building the economy and the country at this time."[60]

The NJM's task during the national-democratic stage of the revolution, Bishop said, is to

> ensure the leading role of the working class through its Marxist/Leninist Party backed by some form of the dictatorship of the proletariat. But please note that I said *some form* of the dictatorship of the proletariat, because obviously at this stage we cannot have the dictatorship of the proletariat or the working class, but the form we should have at this first stage is the dictatorship of the working people.[61]

Despite the unanimous adoption of the "Line of March" report, however, this document actually masked deep differences over the character and tasks of the Grenada revolution inside the Central Committee.

The New Jewel Movement

The "Line of March" report tenuously patched together two conflicting views of the kind of party that the NJM should be striving to build through its leadership of the workers' and farmers' government in Grenada.

On the one hand, the report advocated "strengthening the Leninist character of the party by bringing in the best elements of the *working people and in particular the working class*" into the NJM.[62] This reflected Bishop's conviction that the party had to base itself more solidly among the most self-sacrificing, hard-working, and politically conscious sections of the oppressed and exploited masses.

On the other hand, the membership requirements codified in the report reinforced efforts by Coard to preserve the NJM as a small and narrow apparatus *to administer* working people, instead of a growing vanguard political instrument *of* working people. "We believe it must become more and more difficult for comrades to become full members and candidate members," the report stated in its concluding paragraphs, "and it must become more difficult for new comrades to remain as members and candidate members. . . ."[63]

At the time the "Line of March" report was presented in fall 1982, the NJM had only about 350 full, candidate, and applicant members. A year later the party as a whole had not grown at all, and the number of full members had actually dropped from 80 to just over 70.[64]

The New Jewel Movement's exclusionary membership policy was presented in the name of "Leninist standards of discipline, consistency and seriousness."[65] To the contrary, however, Bishop's inability to break through the Coard faction's lockout of working people from the NJM blocked its development toward a mass revolutionary proletarian vanguard.

Following the March 1979 victory, the New Jewel Movement did not move decisively to transform itself into a party of a qualitatively different type, as was both possible and necessary. In the new political situation created by the establishment of a workers' and farmers' government, the NJM had to take steps toward incorporating into its ranks and leading bodies those working people who in practice were showing leadership capacities. It had to move toward becoming a party of the self-sacrificing cadres looked to as leaders by their fellow working people in the factories, fields, and other workplaces; in the unions and the women's and youth organizations; in the army and the militia.

The party could have become a school of communist

politics to these vanguard workers and farmers, helping them generalize their experiences and place them in the framework of past and present lessons from the international class struggle. The party, the state, and the working people and their organizations would have intermeshed more and more as the revolutionary government consolidated and advanced.

Instead, however, the NJM after March 1979 actually grew more distant from the working people with each passing year. While Bishop was ever turning outward to politicize the population and draw broader and broader layers into the work of the revolution, Coard's faction narrowed in on tightening its control over the Organising Committee, the Political Bureau, and the Central Committee.

Through Bishop's political work, larger and larger numbers of Grenadian workers and farmers were politicized and won to the revolution and its programs. Bishop's speeches were party-building speeches. But the policies instituted by Coard and his supporters blocked this political progress from being registered in the membership and leadership of the NJM itself.

The party "was very small and had lost touch with the people," George Louison has explained. "Very serious people who were committed to the struggle had not been allowed to join the party."[66]

This question has also been commented on by Don Rojas, Bishop's former press secretary and NJM member, in a 1985 article on the sixth anniversary of the Grenada revolution. The capacity of the Coard faction to capture the NJM's leadership bodies, Rojas wrote, "was facilitated by the very small size and the class composition of the party. . . . It had all too few workers and farmers who had proven their leadership capacities in the unions, organizations of rural producers, and in the National Women's Organization and National Youth Organization."[67]

Land reform without land to the tillers

One of the most debilitating aspects of the NJM's membership policy was its bar against small farmers joining, on the grounds that they were property owners and the NJM was a workers' party. This policy excluded the big majority of exploited working people from even being eligible for membership in the New Jewel Movement.

In a 1985 interview, George Louison cited the example of one individual who was among those who helped prepare the insurrection against the Gairy regime on March 13, 1979. Following the victory, Louison said, "there is nothing that we could have asked him to do for the revolution that he did not do. Now, what does such a comrade do to become a member of a revolutionary party? . . . The only problem he had is that he is a small farmer, and the position was taken that people with that kind of property could not be in the party."[68]

Every Marxist party strives to build itself as the mass political vanguard of the working class of its country. But that goal is not advanced by barring members from other social classes, least of all other exploited producers. The criteria for membership in a proletarian party begins with an individual's agreement with the organization's *working-class political perspectives* and his or her proven willingness—in deed as well as word—to carry out systematic political activity under its direction.

A revolutionary party's success or lack of success in consolidating a working-class majority in its membership depends on the existing political situation and how well that party provides leadership to the struggles of working people. There can be no more favorable conditions for the construction of a mass proletarian party than being in the leadership of a triumphant revolution and of a workers' and farmers' government.

The NJM's membership bar against working farmers displayed an ultraleft prejudice, pure and simple. Whatever the rationalizations for this policy, there was nothing Marxist or Leninist about it. No political party led by Marx or Lenin ever barred exploited farmers from its ranks.[69] Neither has the Communist Party of Cuba. Nor was the NJM's policy a "proletarian" one. In fact, it went hand in hand with the NJM's failure to bring the most politically active and class-conscious workers and union cadres into the party.[70]

In a 1985 interview with George Louison, I asked whether this membership policy had its inspiration with the Coard faction. "That was partly so," Louison answered. "The proposals, the initiatives came from them. . . . But we all allowed ourselves to be pushed in that direction."[71]

The NJM's membership bar on small farmers reinforced another leftist policy that undermined the worker-farmer alliance and weakened the revolution. During its four-and-a-half years in power, the PRG did not carry out a program to provide land to the tillers. It did not carry out a real land reform. This was in a country in which one-third of the work force were farmers and in which 90 percent of these farmers tilled plots smaller than five acres, and two-thirds smaller than two acres.

The revolution, of course, brought many benefits to farm laborers and small farmers in Grenada. From its origins, the New Jewel Movement had championed their struggles against the big capitalist landlords, imperialist-owned processing and marketing companies, and the

Gairy dictatorship. Following the March 1979 victory, the PRG guaranteed working farmers that it would never take away their land. It strengthened the union rights of farm workers and promoted the formation of an organization of small farmers. It instituted profit-sharing, and equal pay for women laborers, on the big state-owned and private farms. It provided farmers cheap credit. It lowered the price and increased the availability of seed, fertilizer, implements, and other items farmers needed to produce. It reorganized the marketing board and began to establish Grenada's own agroindustries to loosen the dependence of farmers on the big processors. It upgraded rural roads, irrigation, and training and extension services. It established a state-run tractor and machinery pool. Farmers and farm workers benefited from the many programs that met the needs of all Grenadian working people—the literacy program, free public education and health care, pipe-borne water, the island's first public transit service.

But the PRG never provided the main thing that small farmers want and need in order to make a substantial gain in their productivity and living conditions—*guaranteed use of sufficient land.* It is difficult for farmers to make a go of it when they have only two to five acres of land to till—no matter how easy their credit, how plentiful the seed, how efficient their marketing, how big the state tractor pool, or how good the roads. Once farmers have more land, and can begin to take advantage of some economies of scale, then all these measures become an enormous aid to them in working it productively.

With only some 55,000 acres of cultivable soil on the island, such a land reform would necessarily face physical limitations. But some one-third of this land was unutilized or underutilized. The PRG consciously rejected any redistribution of this idle land among the island's exploited farmers. Nor did it distribute any of the lands expropriated from Gairy or any state-owned lands taken over in 1979.

The New Jewel Movement's justification for this policy was that Grenada's agricultural productivity would be impaired by breaking up large private or state-owned landholdings. Such a course would simply be a repeat of Gairy's "land for the landless" policy, it was argued. Instead, the government should concentrate on promoting state farms and cooperatives on large plots conducive to modern machinery and agricultural techniques. This policy, it was claimed, was the only way to expand social labor and cooperation in farming and foster the eventual socialist transformation of agriculture.

But this approach elevated technical and administrative mechanisms supposedly leading to "economic efficiency" (often fallacious, as we will see) above the political necessity for a durable worker-farmer alliance to defend and advance the revolution and its social goals. This fundamental of revolutionary working-class strategy was taken up in the "Theses on the Agrarian Question," drafted by Lenin and adopted by the Second Congress of the Communist International in 1920.[72] Land must be distributed by the revolutionaries, Lenin said in support of this resolution, "otherwise, the small peasant will see no difference" between the old social order and the new. "If the proletarian state power does not act in this way," Lenin said, "it will be unable to retain power."[73]

At that 1920 communist gathering, Lenin's support for distributing land to the peasants was challenged by minorities on both the right and the ultraleft wings of the delegates. Lenin answered the charge of a German centrist, according to whom "to do anything for the small peasant at the expense of the big landowner is alleged to be petty-bourgeois action." Lenin explained that this delegate "says the landed proprietors should be dispossessed and their land handed over to co-operative associations."

"This is a pedantic viewpoint," Lenin replied. Even in an advanced capitalist country such as Germany, he said, much of the land on big estates is still either idle or tilled with methods that are far below those necessary for modern agricultural methods. "Large-scale farming can be preserved," Lenin said, "and yet the small peasants can be provided with something of considerable importance to them."[74]

WHILE THERE IS NO EVIDENCE that Maurice Bishop opposed the PRG's land policy, there are indications that Bernard Coard was its primary architect. Let's briefly review the evolution of this policy.

In mid-1980 the government announced the formation of the National Cooperative Development Agency (NACDA). A government commission toured the island identifying land that was being underutilized, which the PRG could then negotiate to lease from the owner. Land obtained in this way, however, was not turned over for use by small farmers or landless farm laborers. Instead, it was made available to NACDA to encourage the formation of cooperatives by groups of unemployed young people, many of whom had never farmed. As summed up in the slogan "idle lands for idle hands," the idea was that jobless youth would be allotted some land to work cooperatively and provided with the training, credit, implements, and marketing outlets to establish productive units. This was supposed to alleviate unemployment and at the same time promote agricultural development along socialist lines.

NACDA was never very successful. In November 1981 there were only twelve such cooperatives involving 160 young people and a total of 146 acres. (As a standard of comparison, there were more than 8,000 small and medium farm families in Grenada. Together with some 120 big landowners, these farmers held the great majority of the cultivable land on the island. There were also twenty-five state farms at that time, employing 1,000 workers and cultivating 4,000 acres.)

RESISTANCE TO NACDA'S cooperative project came from two directions. First, not many unemployed young people had been convinced to join the farm co-ops. And not many large landholders had been willing to lease land to the government. By mid-1981, the NJM was discussing ways to solve these problems.

In April 1981 the Central Committee decided to begin organizing voluntary production cooperatives among small farmers, as well. But the emphasis of government policy remained on cooperatives for unemployed youth and development of the state farms.

To deal with landlord resistance, a Land Development Utilization Law was adopted in September 1981 empowering the PRG to take out a compulsory lease on any idle landholdings of more than 100 acres. A draft of the law was presented by George Louison, the minister of agriculture, for consideration at a July 22, 1981, meeting of the NJM Central Committee. The minutes of that meeting record the main remarks on the law as those by Bernard Coard. According to the minutes, Coard said

> that the youths are the main factor of the Land Reform Programme. He stressed that it must be of

> number one priority to bring unemployed youths from the different parishes [districts] to make such a project fruitful. . . . He also emphasised the programme needs two thousand five hundred youths. . . . He concluded by saying that the youths are the existing reserve army of labour.[75]

Thus, according to Bernard Coard, the "main factor" in Grenada's land reform were not the farmers and farm laborers. It was the jobless youth. The main political goal was not to strengthen the worker-farmer alliance, which formed the bedrock of the revolutionary government.

In fact, Coard actually presented the new Land Reform Act as a measure that might arouse opposition to the revolution among small farmers rather than broaden their support. At an August 19, 1981, Central Committee meeting called to discuss how to combat stepped-up counterrevolutionary activity, Coard "questioned where is the peasantry at and where will they be when the Land Reform Act is passed." The minutes record that other CC members also were worried that, "The Land Reform Act will cause some general concern."[76]

By January 1983, the NJM Central Committee had been forced to acknowledge the failure of its initial land policy. A Central Committee resolution adopted that month proposed to "change the focus of NACDA to developing cooperatives among existing farmers only. New co-ops among unemployed must be ceased."

Nonetheless, the resolution stuck tough to the commitment not to distribute a single acre of land to individual working farmers. The NJM's goal, the document said, must be to "begin the process of collectivisation and transformation of the countryside." At the same time, the party had to figure out "what strategy and tactics must be applied toward the large owners. How to lay the basis for their nationalisation, prevent any land fragmentation while at the same time utilizing their managerial skills in production."

The document then listed several priorities. The first was to make the state farms "the leading vehicle for beginning to lay the basis for the socialist transformation of agriculture." This included the decision to place all confiscated idle lands "under the control of the restructured" Grenada Farm Corporation, which managed the state farms. Funds originally allocated for the land reform project were to be turned over to the GFC.

The second priority was "to win the peasantry gradually to socialism by building the alliance of the working class and the peasantry through a programme of concessions. . . ." These "concessions" included such things as cheap credit, tax breaks, road improvement, seed and fertilizer banks, and machinery pools.

The Central Committee resolution ended by stating that, "The CC concluded that the development and modernization of Agriculture holds the key to winning the peasantry to Socialism and the transformation of the countryside along socialist lines."[77]

THE RESOLUTION'S GUIDING ASSUMPTION that large-scale co-ops or state farms lead, *in and of themselves,* to more efficient agricultural production is a myth. That depends on many factors: the type of crop or animal product, soil quality, the existing level of mechanization and irrigation, and—above all—the degree to which the rural producers see the revolution and its programs as being in their interests. Land-hungry working farmers will be encouraged to increase their output if they are provided with a decent plot to till, and if the revolutionary government *on that basis* backs them up with a wide variety of support services.

The distribution of land to working farmers, moreover, need not result in an uncontrolled proliferation of new exploiters in the countryside. That can be checked by legislation barring the rental, mortgaging, and sale of land or its use as collateral; by the organization of farm workers and enforcement of laws protecting their conditions; and by rationing, price policies, and other measures to regulate marketing.

A policy of land to the tillers is not an obstacle to the development of state farms. Some large, formerly capitalist-run farms can and will be converted into state-run farms that play an important role in agriculture, especially in the production of particular commodities.

Nor does the distribution of land to small farmers pose a barrier to encouraging the formation of cooperatives—either credit and marketing cooperatives among independent landholding farmers or production cooperatives based on land cultivated in common. To the contrary, this is the only effective road toward cooperatives. By increasing the revolutionary commitment of working farmers, such a course will encourage more of them over time to voluntarily join with other producers to help advance farm production along the most efficient lines. As forms of cooperative marketing and production expand on a voluntary basis, together with improved mechanization and scientific methods, workers and farmers will make progress toward social labor in agriculture. That has been the course along which the cooperative movement in Cuba has made big strides.

No schema, no economic mechanism can ensure expanding political support for a revolution among the rural producers and increase production of food and fiber. The starting point has to be a concrete, political one. The revolutionary government and party must recognize farmers who exploit no labor—the vast majority—as *fellow toilers* of the working class, with a direct stake in combating a common exploitation by the capitalists.

The NJM too often approached exploited farmers not as fellow working people but as a petty-bourgeois layer who, as property holders, were inherently unreliable as allies of the working class. But the vast majority of Grenada's farmers owned no capital. Their tiny landholdings did not enable them to exploit labor, lease acreage, extract profits and rents, and accumulate more capital.[78]

These working farmers were not petty bourgeois—not small-time capitalists. They were working people who were directly exploited by the same U.S., British, and Grenadian capitalists that exploited urban and rural wage workers on the island.

Coard demands 'stringent Leninist measures'

Coard's secret faction openly went on the offensive against Bishop at a Central Committee meeting in October 1982.

The minutes record that the October 12–15 meeting had been called by Bishop as "an extraordinary plenary to discuss a letter of resignation [from the CC and Political Bureau] from Cde. Bernard Coard . . . and to examine the issues raised in the letter related to the state of the Party and the crisis in the work of the higher organs."[79]

Coard did not attend the meeting. Instead, say the minutes, NJM leader Selwyn Strachan "was asked to summarize his discussions with Cde. Coard in relation to the matter of his resignation." According to Strachan, "Cde. Coard had indicated that his decision to resign from PB and CC was taken 6 months previously."

Key to Coard's decision to resign, Strachan said, was the "strain" caused, among other things, by "the undermining of his authority" as chairman of the party's Organising Committee. Coard "made reference to the slackness of the CC and its unwillingness to speak up on issues, the lack of preparation for meetings by CC comrades, and the unwillingness of the CC to study."

"In order to take corrective action," according to Strachan's summary of Coard's views, "it would result in personality clashes" with Bishop. So Coard instead proposed his own resignation, which he presented as "not negotiable." Nonetheless, according to Strachan, Coard said that, "In the final analysis stringent Leninist measures are required" to resolve this crisis in the party.

At the very top of Coard's list of such "Leninist measures" was to "change Chairmanship of CC"—*that is, to remove Bishop from that position.* Coard also proposed to "chop dead weight from CC" and "expand the Political Bureau." Coard's backers took steps to implement these latter two measures at the close of this October 1982 Central Committee meeting; they would wait another year before moving on the first.

Following Strachan's report, "The meeting agreed to address itself to the issues raised by Cde. Coard in his conversation with several CC members." The Central Committee "concluded that the Party stood at the crossroads," the minutes record. One direction "would be the petty bourgeois route which would seek to make [Bernard Coard's] resignation the issue"—a not-too-subtle reference to Bishop, who had convoked the meeting to discuss that resignation and its political ramifications. "This would only lead to temporary relief," the minutes continued, "but would surely lead to the deterioration of the Party into a social-democratic Party and hence the degeneration of the Revolution."

"The second route," according to the minutes, "is the Communist route—the road of Leninist standards and functioning, the road of democratic centralism, of selectivity, of criticism and self-criticism and of collective leadership." In other words, the "Communist route" corresponded to the "stringent Leninist measures" proposed by Coard.

This outcome to the October 1982 meeting shows how far the Coard faction had already gone toward its goal of capturing control of the NJM's Central Committee. Its majority remained narrow, however, and Coard's supporters had still not established control over the Political Bureau. Bishop's political authority among class-conscious working people continued to grow.

At the October 1982 meeting, therefore, the Coard faction took steps to firm up its majority in the NJM Central Committee and to tip the balance in its favor in the Political Bureau. Kendrick Radix was removed from the Central Committee and Political Bureau, while Coard's "resignation" was more than offset by the addition of Liam James, Ewart Layne, and John Ventour—all cadres of Coard's faction since the mid-1970s. Moreover, the minutes record that "Phyllis Coard will be assessed in March on the question of membership of the Political Bureau," while "Whiteman will be severely warned for his weak performance."

To justify these measures, the Coard faction pointed to the "low level of ideological development" of those they were trying to push out of leadership bodies. Radix was berated for his "bad attitude to study," and Whiteman was among five Central Committee members singled out for a "crash course in Marxism-Leninism." Coard, although no longer a Central Committee member, was assigned to teach the course. Two of the three readings were to be pamphlets by Joseph Stalin—*Foundations of Leninism* and *Dialectics* (probably a reference to *Dialectical and Historical Materialism*).[80]

III. THE REVOLUTION'S FINAL YEAR

IN EARLY 1983 Washington intensified its political and military pressure against Grenada. In March the U.S. government carried out a provocative, large-scale military maneuver in the Caribbean. Over a period of a few months, U.S. President Ronald Reagan, Vice President George Bush, Secretary of State George Shultz, and Secretary of Defense Caspar Weinberger all leveled widely publicized attacks against Grenada. In particular, they beat the drums against the international airport being built, with Cuban help, to facilitate tourism and trade, raising the charge that this project was in fact a military installation for Cuban and Soviet armed forces.

The Grenadian government responded to these threats by increasing the political mobilization and military readiness of the population. At the same time, it sought opportunities to answer and expose the imperialist lies about Grenada. Upon the invitation of the liberal U.S. lobbying organization TransAfrica, Bishop visited the United States in June 1983. Reagan and Shultz snubbed the Grenadian government, rejecting its request for them to meet with Bishop while he was in the country. Nonetheless, Bishop met briefly with White House officials to reaffirm the PRG's oft-stated desire for normal, peaceful relations with the U.S. government.

Above all, however, Bishop took advantage of his U.S.

trip to speak directly to as many people as possible about the Grenada revolution, its social gains, and its importance for the oppressed and exploited in the United States and around the world. The high point of Bishop's U.S. tour was his speech to an overflow crowd of 2,000 at New York City's Hunter College.[81]

Not long after Bishop's return to Grenada, a six-day Central Committee meeting was held from July 13 to 19. Coard's supporters were unable to make much headway at this meeting. Coard was not satisfied with its outcome and raised his displeasure with members of his faction. A one-day Central Committee meeting, on August 26, thus opened with a report by Coard supporter Leon Cornwall on "the concern expressed by a senior party member" that "some conclusions of the [July meeting] are not correct." These "concerns" were immediately seconded by a couple of more recent recruits to Coard's clique—Ian St. Bernard, who explained what "he had picked up," and Tan Bartholomew, who reported on "what had reached him."

Liam James then spoke, urging that another Central Committee meeting be convened in September, since the "last assessment was not deep enough." Labeling the committee's July decisions "opportunist," Selwyn Strachan added that while the October 1982 meeting had "held back the party from a social democratic path, the situation is now qualitatively worse." He too urged the rapid convening of another meeting.

Speaking at the conclusion of the meeting, Bishop stated that it was clear that the party was facing a serious internal situation, and that another Central Committee discussion was called for. Warning of the dangers of secret factional activity behind the backs of the NJM's leadership bodies, Bishop expressed "the concern that many key decisions of the party, if not the majority have been made informally outside of higher organs."[82]

Bishop's warning was fully justified. The decisions being made by Coard's clique were not only bypassing party bodies, they were above all affecting the course of the government, the unions and other mass organizations, and the lives of tens of thousands of Grenadian working people. The revolution was being weakened and endangered by Coard's bureaucratic course.

The NJM's next Central Committee meeting was scheduled for September 13–15.

The 'joint leadership' proposal

It was at this September 1983 Central Committee meeting that the Coard faction made its open move to displace Bishop from party leadership. The meeting opened with an orchestrated challenge to the agenda proposed by Bishop.[83] One after another, Liam James, John Ventour, Ewart Layne, Selwyn Strachan, and Phyllis Coard each raised objections. Bishop expressed willingness to alter the agenda, and the meeting agreed to a counterproposal by Ventour. The proceedings then got under way with a report by Layne on "the present state of the party and revolution."

Layne's report was apocalyptic in its evaluations. The revolution "now faces the greatest danger since 1979," he said. The "party is crumbling." All the "mass organisations are to the ground." The "organs of people's democracy are about to collapse." The internal state of the party "is very dread." Members say that "democracy is dead in the party."

All these developments, Layne said, indicate that the Central Committee "has proven its inability to give leadership to the process." Openly rejecting Bishop's view that the primary immediate tasks of the party and government still remained anti-imperialist and democratic in character, Layne said that the Central Committee had shown that it "cannot determine the stage the revolution is at."

The Central Committee, Layne said, "is on a path of right opportunism." If not corrected, he concluded, these problems "will lead to the total disintegration of the party and the collapse of the revolution." One by one, other Coard supporters then took the floor to repeat Layne's charges.

The dire picture painted by the Coard faction was grossly overdrawn. Grenadian workers and farmers certainly faced big problems. Grenada's centuries of colonial oppression had bequeathed a legacy of lopsided agriculture, little industry, ramshackle transport and communications, and poor living and working conditions. The U.S. government's international campaign to deny loans and aid to Grenada, and to cripple its tourism, put a squeeze on national income. Washington kept escalating its military pressure and aid to local counterrevolutionary forces.

Nonetheless, the PRG's social and economic advances were winning the revolution broadening support among workers and farmers on the island. Grenada's economic growth rate was among the highest in the Caribbean, and joblessness had fallen sharply. The island's first international airport—the revolution's largest single development project and a source of great patriotic pride—was only a few months from completion. When completed, the airport would have represented a big step forward in trade prospects, as well as tourism, and would have lessened Grenada's isolation from the rest of the Caribbean and the world. In mid-1983 the PRG had set in motion the drafting of a new constitution to further institutionalize the workers' and farmers' democratic gains and lay the basis for island-wide elections.

Despite these big advances, there had been erosion in the organization and mobilization of workers and farmers during the year prior to the September 1983 Central Committee meeting. And the NJM—too narrow to reflect new popular forces being drawn to the revolution—clearly was in crisis. On both counts, however, the bureaucratic practices and secret factional activity of the Coard group bore heavy responsibility.

AT THE SEPTEMBER MEETING, the exaggerations in Ewart Layne's opening report were challenged by George Louison and Maurice Bishop. While acknowledging big difficulties, Louison contested the claim by Coard's supporters "that the ideological levels of the masses have gone backwards." He said that "sufficient weight has not been given to the objective situation and problems in the economy." Some comrades, Louison concluded, "give a panicky impression in the way they make their points."

Bishop, too, pointed to many serious problems, but cautioned that some of the proposed conclusions were "a bit premature." Bishop's remarks reflected his conviction that problems facing the party could be dealt with only as part of confronting the broader relationship between the government, the mass organizations, and the workers and farmers. Unlike Coard and his followers, Bishop saw party cadres as leaders, not administrators, of the masses.

The Central Committee's main problem, Bishop said, was that it was "paying no significant attention to the views of the party and the masses." Due to this, he said, "we became bureaucratic and formalistic in our approach." He cited the fall-off in participation by NJM leaders in village and neighborhood council meetings, visits to workplaces, and public political activities. These problems, Bishop said, have "been compounded by the weakness in the material base" of Grenadian society.

But the Coard faction did not back off. Liam James opened the next agenda item (a "collective and individual analysis of the C[entral] C[ommittee]") with the judgment that "this is the last chance for the C.C. to pull the party out of this crisis and onto a firm M[arxist-] L[eninist] path." The "most fundamental problem," James said, "is the quality of leadership of the Central Committee and the party provided by Cde. Maurice Bishop."

James hypocritically praised Bishop's "great strength, his ability to inspire and develop" party members, his capacity "to raise the regional and international respect for the party and revolution," his "charisma to build the confidence of the people." Nonetheless, James said, Bishop lacked the "qualities which are essential" for leadership of the party. These qualities were: "A Leninist level of organization and discipline"; "Great depth in ideological clarity"; and "Brilliance in strategy and tactics."

James's report, too, met with universal acclaim from others in the Coard faction.[84] Like the agenda challenge and choreographed speeches following Layne's report, the sudden "consensus" that Bishop's leadership was *the* root of all problems had obviously been discussed and decided behind the scenes by Coard's faction and then unloaded on the rest of the Central Committee.

The third agenda item ("the role of the Central Committee") was initiated by Bishop. Once again he cited as the Central Committee's main problem its distance from the workers and farmers. "To develop and maintain links with the masses," Bishop said, "the leadership must personally get on the ground among the people, step up participation in zonal and parish councils, visit schools, monitor and push production." The Central Committee, he said, had to develop "mechanisms for accountability," "review constant feedback from the membership," and "ensure channels of communication with them."

It was at this point in the meeting, on its third and final day, that Liam James sprang the secretly prepared proposal—in the form of a plan for "joint leadership" of the NJM—to remove Bishop from central leadership responsibilities in the party. Coard's backers had no choice but to push for Bishop's removal. Two political lines—one fought for most consistently by Bishop, the other advanced systematically by Coard—were coming into irreconcilable conflict in the day-to-day, week-to-week practice of the NJM and the PRG.

ACCORDING TO the Central Committee minutes, Liam James proposed "a model of joint leadership, marrying the strengths" of Bishop and Coard. He defined the division of responsibilities as follows:

> *Cde. Maurice Bishop*
> (i) Direct work among the masses, focus on production and propaganda.
> (ii) Particular attention to the organs of popular democracy, working class, youth masses, visits to urban and rural work places.
> (iii) Militia mobilisation
> (iv) Regional and International work
> *Cde. Bernard Coard*
> (i) Party organisation work Chairman of the

O[rganising] C[ommittee]
(ii) Party organisational development and formation [education] of Cdes.
(iii) Strategy and tactics.

Coard's supporters voiced unanimous and unhesitating agreement with James's seemingly sudden recommendation. On the other hand, Louison spoke against it, as did Unison Whiteman, and Fitzroy Bain raised serious doubts. Louison later recalled that he had pointed out that "proposals of that character must be given weeks in advance, so that they really could be studied." Yet the so-called joint leadership proposal "was only sprung half way into the last day of the discussion. . . . They rushed a vote on this that very same day."[85]

The minutes of the September 1983 meeting record a sharp exchange when Louison pressed for at least a little time for the members of the party to consider and debate the proposal before voting on it. Liam James retorted that "Cde. Louison is seeking to disturb the proceedings of the meeting for opportunist reasons."

Bishop himself said he had never had any problem with sharing leadership rights and responsibilities in the Central Committee and Political Bureau, including with Bernard Coard. (The entire history of the NJM proved that Bishop was speaking the truth in this regard. Bishop had consistently sought to draw Bernard Coard, along with others, into the leadership of the party and the government. It was Coard who had always had trouble working with Bishop. Coard was jealous of Bishop, unable to accept that he was not Bishop's political equal.)

Bishop said that he needed time to think about the political and organizational ramifications of James's proposal, and he too objected to trying to settle the matter that day. The vote was rammed through, nonetheless. The motion was adopted with Louison voting against and Bishop and Whiteman abstaining. (Hudson Austin also abstained, explaining that he had not been present for most of the meeting.)

Coard's supporters then proposed that the Central Committee meeting—originally scheduled to adjourn that evening—continue the following day with Bernard Coard's participation. Bishop said that he felt that the Central Committee's new leadership proposal was going to be "counterproductive." Given the situation, he said, he would not attend another meeting the next day, since he needed time to consider the matter. Despite Bishop's objections, however, the meeting was scheduled to reconvene on September 17.

THE CENTRAL COMMITTEE remained in session throughout much of the following week, with Coard now openly functioning as its leading figure. Bishop did not attend. Neither did George Louison, who left for Czechoslovakia and Hungary to prepare a visit scheduled for Bishop later in the month to discuss important aid and trade arrangements.

The September 17 meeting opened with a rehash of the previous three day's proceedings by Strachan, Layne, James, Cornwall, and others. Then Bernard Coard took the floor.

Coard opened with the same doomsday prognoses with which he had primed his supporters. "Within six months," he said, "the party will disintegrate totally unless a fundamental package of measures are done." The "loss of state power is only a few months away."[86]

Coard then turned to the question of his resignation

from the Central Committee in October 1982. He said that he had become "tired and sick of being the only hatchet man and critique" in the leadership. No one else had been willing "to speak up freely" about the "total absence of making decisions" under Bishop's leadership. Coard pointed to three examples:

(1) the *Torchlight* issue;

(2) the "Gang of 26" (that is, the dispute over how to respond to the launching of the *Grenadian Voice*); and

(3) the delay in "when the position was taken to put [Ewart] Layne over Einstein [Louison]" in the top army officer corps.

DURING THIS PERIOD, Coard said, Bishop had "found himself vacillating between the M[arxist-] L[eninist] trend and the petty bourgeois trend in the party." By October 1982, Coard said, he had become convinced "that the party and revolution [would] disintegrate within 24 months," but that, "It had reached to a stage where he realized that his ability to influence the process was no longer possible."

Coard said that he "has noted a Petty Bourgeois Revolutionary trend becoming greater in Cde. [George] Louison over the last year," as well. Coard said that he had been planning "to raise it with him."

Coard protested that he "would not like to return" to the Central Committee and Political Bureau. He was afraid that comrades "will think that he is fighting for leadership." Even after resigning from the party's leadership bodies, Coard said, "he had tried to give the party his best support in strategy and tactics," but he still "would prefer to operate as in the past year."

Coard said he would reconsider, however, if assured

that it will not "be left for him to manners" [discipline] Bishop. In the past, he said, the Central Committee has never "consistently crushed petty bourgeois characteristics and trends as soon as [they] rise." Unless the Central Committee is now "prepared to manners all petty bourgeois responses," Coard said, "he will withdraw." Following Leon Cornwall's assurance that the Central Committee would begin showing "consistency," Coard agreed to return to the body.

The September 17 meeting called a gathering of the party's full members for Sunday, September 25, to discuss the decisions of the Central Committee. Bishop was scheduled to report his further thinking on the "joint leadership" proposal to the Central Committee the afternoon prior to the general membership gathering. Bishop showed up, but the meeting had been canceled. When Unison Whiteman brought this incident to the attention of party members the next day, Liam James replied that "the meeting was specifically to discuss and agree on the Central Committee report to the [membership] but the document was not yet rolled off. Thus it was not possible for the meeting to be held."[87] Instead, the Coard faction prepared a written report without any prior consultation and delivered it to Bishop on the morning of September 25.[88]

Falsifying the history of the Grenada revolution, the report sought to portray Bernard Coard as having played the decisive leadership role in the party from its origins. "It was Cde. Coard who formed the first M[arxist] L[eninist] study group in 1974," the report stated, "who provided the ideological guidance for the NJM party manifesto, and who struggled for the formation of the O[rganising] C[ommittee] in 1977, which lifted the party's level of organization, a key factor for the winning of state power."[89]

But such a record did not and could not qualify Bernard Coard, or anyone else, to serve as the central leader of the New Jewel Movement. The NJM was an organization that had led tens of thousands of Grenadians in a popular struggle against a hated dictatorship and that was now standing at the head of a revolutionary government. Its leadership had been earned through those mass struggles and was recognized by Grenada's workers and farmers, who valued the courage, integrity, and clarity of Maurice Bishop, Unison Whiteman, and others. Heading an internal party committee or guiding a Marxist study group was no substitute.

FIDEL CASTRO has aptly characterized Bernard Coard as an "alleged theoretician of the revolution who had been a professor of Marxism in Jamaica." Coard sought to establish himself and his faction as "a kind of a priesthood of the doctrine, guardian of the doctrine, theoretician of the doctrine, philosopher of the doctrine," Castro explained.

The Coard group "didn't work with the masses; it worked among the party members . . . and with the cadres of the army and the Ministry of the Interior," Castro said. Coard "was the scholar of politics, the professor of political science; while Bishop was the man who worked with the masses, worked with the people, worked with the administration, and was active internationally."[90] That was what established Maurice Bishop as the central leader of the Grenada revolution and of the New Jewel Movement.

The demagogic atmosphere of the September 25 general membership meeting was set by Ewart Layne. In his opening report, Layne sought to blackmail the membership with the following ultimatum: "He had spoken to all C.C. members who voted for the Majority position," and all of them "agreed that if the road of opportunism is chosen, they would have no alternative but to resign from the C.C. on the ground of principle. The membership is then free to choose a new Central Committee." The issue before the meeting, Layne said, was

> Are we going to build a petit bourgeois social democratic party with one man above everyone, where people fulfill decisions they like and do not fulfill those they do not like, where there is one discipline for some and a next set for others, where some can be criticised and others are above criticism? . . . What faces us is the road of opportunism or Leninist principles.[91]

At the opening of the meeting, Bishop was not in attendance. After a visit from a delegation elected by the meeting, however, he agreed to attend and present his views. Bishop expressed serious reservations about the way the Central Committee decision had been arrived at, its workability, and its impact among the Grenadian people. During the discussion, however, only Whiteman and Fitzroy Bain spoke in opposition to "joint leadership."

Under intense political and personal pressures, and wanting to hold the party together and preserve the equilibrium of the leadership, Bishop said at the conclusion of the meeting that "his desire now is to use the criticism positively and march along with the entire party to build a Marxist-Leninist Party that can lead the people to socialism and communism." He "pledged to the party that he would do everything to erode his petit bourgeois traits." Bishop repeated that "he had never had difficulties in working with Cde. Coard," and said that "joint leadership would help push the party and revolution forward."[92]

Bishop maintained his doubts about the workability of the proposal, however, and these were to mount as the true objectives of Coard and his backers became unmistakable over the next several weeks.[93]

Overthrow of the revolutionary government

On September 26, Bishop and Whiteman left for Hungary and Czechoslovakia on the aid and trade visit that Louison had gone there to prepare the previous week. Three of Bishop's aides traveled with him: Don Rojas, press secretary; Shahiba Strong, chief of protocol; and Cletus St. Paul, chief of security.

In Bishop's absence, the Coard faction took a number of steps to consolidate its power base. Coard's own political mentor, Jamaican WPJ leader Trevor Munroe, came to Grenada for two days during this period to advise his cothinkers.[94]

Coard began disarming the militia. The pay of soldiers in the People's Revolutionary Army was raised. In addition, according to George Louison:

> During those two weeks Maurice was overseas, they called in all party members, did full assessments of their personal situations, financial positions, and other things. They made big promises to help them solve personal situations.
>
> When I looked at what was done in those two weeks with party members, I saw that we ran the danger of creating a real elite in the society. A number of party members already had relatively good incomes, in the Grenadian context. And these people [the Coard faction] were discussing

> with them their personal situations, to give them even more benefits, so that the party was going to get more benefits than the average person among the masses.[95]

On the way back from Eastern Europe, the Grenadian government delegation spent a few days in Cuba for meetings with Fidel Castro and other Cuban leaders. When Bishop returned to Grenada on October 8, only one other NJM leader, Selwyn Strachan, was on hand at the airport. This was contrary to the well-established practice of sending a substantial government leadership delegation to meet the prime minister and exchange information about the results of his visit and developments in Grenada during his absence. Over the next three days, Bernard Coard—who had been acting prime minister during the trip and was supposedly now Bishop's co-chairman in the NJM—made no effort to contact Bishop to brief him on party and government affairs.

Coard, in his August 1986 trial statement, sought to explain away this behavior by stating that Bishop's chief security guard, Cletus St. Paul, had phoned from Havana the night before the delegation's return and "issued a number of threats against Cde. Bernard Coard personally." Coard first raised this charge in October 1983. Four years later, however, he chose to tailor the original story rather drastically.

The initial story was that St. Paul—*acting on Bishop's instructions*—had plotted Coard's assassination as far back as October 1982. At an October 13, 1983, NJM membership meeting, for example, Liam James charged that a year earlier St. Paul approached Coard's personal security guards about the planned assassination. "But it was not taken seriously" at that time, James said, due to St.

Paul's "strange behavior."[96]

The Coard faction's original story is also recounted in an October 17, 1983, letter by Vincent Noel to the NJM Central Committee. Noel reported that on October 12 he had been told by Selwyn Strachan that "it was Maurice who had been planning to kill members of the C.C. He said that within the past few days a lot of evidence had come to light. For instance, last year St. Paul had approached another security man to kill Bernard after he resigned from the C.C." Noel wrote that John Ventour had also told him that "Maurice was a psychopath and last year tried to kill Bernard after he resigned."[97]

Today, however, this lie that Maurice Bishop was a bloodthirsty conspirator and assassin no longer serves Coard's aims, since he is now portraying himself as Bishop's dearest comrade and friend. So Coard has simply put that part of his tale back in a drawer. He now charges Bishop's chief of security, but not Bishop himself, with the assassination plot.

Bishop's views of the situation shortly after his return to Grenada are described in the letter by Vincent Noel:

> We spoke first of all about his trip to Eastern Europe and then my trip to Jamaica. We also spoke about the local and regional Trade Union situation and especially the upcoming C.C.L. [Caribbean Congress of Labour] Congress. Finally I introduced the discussion of the Party stating that I had picked up from various comrades that he had not accepted the decision of the Party on Joint Leadership.
>
> Maurice denied that he had any problems with Joint Leadership and went into a long history of his acceptance of that principle dating back to the formation of the Movement. He stated he himself

> had voted for Joint Leadership at the [September 25] meeting of full members of the Party, but at that time and at the meeting of the Central Committee he had expressed certain reservations. These reservations were reinforced during his trip and by certain developments since his return.[98]

Bishop had already informed the Political Bureau of these reservations and asked that they be placed on the agenda of a meeting previously scheduled for October 12. Beginning in the earliest hours of that morning, however, the Coard faction set in motion the first steps in a coup d'etat. Some twenty-four hours later, Bishop was placed under house arrest.

FIRST, AT 1:00 A.M. ON OCTOBER 12, selected members of Bishop's security detail were awakened and brought to a meeting. Cletus St. Paul was not informed. Maj. Keith Roberts told the guards that Bishop was "becoming a dictator" and that "their responsibility was to protect the working class, not the life of any one leader." They should no longer take orders from Bishop, they were told, but only from the Central Committee.[99]

At 7:00 a.m. NJM members in the army were called together. They were presented with a resolution condemning "cultism, egoism, the unreasonable and unprincipled desires of one man." Those reraising the question of "joint leadership" were "endangering the party and revolution and holding our country to ransom," the resolution said. It called "on the Central Committee . . . to expel from the Party's ranks all elements who do not submit to, uphold and implement in practice the decision of the Central Committee. . . ."[100]

At 9:00 a.m. the Political Bureau met. Bishop attended the meeting. On his way there, Bishop had stopped briefly at the Cuban embassy to provide information to the Cuban leadership for the first time about the divisions within the NJM. This visit was reported in the October 20, 1983, statement of the Cuban government and Communist Party:

> On Wednesday, October 12, our embassy in Grenada reported the surprising and disagreeable news that deep divisions had surfaced in the Central Committee of the party in Grenada. During the morning of that day, Bishop himself communicated [to the embassy] regarding the differences that had arisen some time before. He said that they were being discussed and that efforts were being made to resolve them, but that he had never imagined the seriousness they were going to take on during his absence. He simply stated the differences and did not request any opinion or cooperation on our part in trying to overcome them, once again showing great respect for Cuba's international policy and for the internal affairs of his own party.[101]

At the Political Bureau meeting, the resolution presented a few hours earlier to NJM members in the army was read and referred for action to the Organising Committee. The next major item placed on the agenda by Coard's faction was a proposal to expel George Louison from the Central Committee. Louison was charged with violating democratic centralism by taking his opposition to "joint leadership" outside the party's leadership bodies. The meeting adjourned at noon without taking any decision on Louison, and a meeting of the Central Committee was set for 3:30 p.m.

DURING THE DAY or so prior to the October 12 meetings, a rumor had begun to circulate that Bernard and Phyllis Coard were plotting the assassination of Maurice Bishop. There was ample basis for such concerns, given the vilification campaign against Bishop that the Coard faction had been promoting over the previous few weeks. According to Vincent Noel, for example, Political Bureau member and Coard supporter John Ventour had told a rank-and-file party member "that there would be a solution like Afghanistan if the Chief fucked around on the question of Joint Leadership." (Two presidents of Afghanistan, Noor Mohammad Taraki and Hafizullah Amin, were murdered in the space of a few months during a faction fight in late 1979.) Bishop, too, had heard rumors about "an Afghanistan solution" upon his return to Grenada, Noel wrote. Bishop told Noel "that in his case he had picked it up as coming from [Coard security guard] Ram Folkes."[102]

When the Central Committee convened on the afternoon of October 12, the Coard faction placed the assassination rumor at the top of the agenda. They charged that Bishop was the source of the rumor, and that he had ordered Cletus St. Paul and another security guard, Errol George, to spread it to a list of selected individuals. Bishop flatly denied the charge, as did St. Paul, but Errol George backed up Coard's story. When St. Paul was hauled before the Central Committee for interrogation about the rumor, he was also accused of the alleged assassination plots against Coard the previous week and in October 1982. Despite his denial of all charges, St. Paul was then arrested and thrown in jail. The atmosphere at this Central Committee meeting was described by Bishop to Vincent Noel. "Maurice gave me a blood chilling account of what happened at the C.C. meeting the day before," Noel wrote. "He said that members of the C.C., particularly Chalkie [John Ventour], kept pulling out their weapons threateningly during the whole meeting. . . ."[103]

Following a decision to expel George Louison from the party, the Central Committee majority voted to demand that Bishop make a statement over Radio Free Grenada to rebut the rumor that Bernard and Phyllis Coard were plotting to assassinate him. Bishop agreed to do so, while still denying that he had anything to do with spreading the rumor. His brief statement was broadcast three times over Radio Free Grenada between midnight and 2:00 a.m.

After Bishop returned home in the predawn hours of October 13, he was placed under house arrest. His phones were cut off, and security guards loyal to him were disarmed.

Coard had carried out a coup d'etat. The workers' and farmers' government established on March 13, 1979, had been overthrown.

Coard faction vilifies Bishop

The next day, October 13, Coard's faction called together a meeting of all full, candidate, and applicant members of the NJM—about 350 people in all. Bishop was brought to the meeting from house arrest.

"Given the extremely serious nature of what we were there to discuss," Vincent Noel wrote in his October 17 letter to the Central Committee, "one would have thought that the discussions and decisions would have taken place in a calm and sober way. Instead, led by members of the

Political Bureau, the meeting was a horrendous display of militarism, hatred and emotional vilification. Never before have I witnessed this trend within our party and on no ground can this conduct be justified."[104]

Bernard Coard painted quite a different picture of this October 13 meeting in his trial statement last year. "When Comrade Bishop come in to the meetings," Coard said, "everybody rises and applauds. This is how Cde. Maurice Bishop is treated who is supposed to be under *house arrest!* This is what always happened, including on October 13, *after* the rumour of October 12. There is tremendous love for him." Coard asked "how a man under house arrest" could be "given a standing ovation at the beginning of the meeting."[105]

How does Coard's loving account square with what actually happened at the October 13 meeting?

The meeting opened with a report by Selwyn Strachan on the Political Bureau and Central Committee decisions from the day before. Strachan accused George Louison of having "played a key role in poisoning the mind" of Bishop against the so-called joint leadership plan. Louison had once done "fantastic work and was in the Leninist trend," but he had now joined Kendrick Radix and "the r[igh]t opp[ortunist] elements."[106]

Strachan then turned his fire against Bishop. "We struggled against one-manism, cultism [i.e. against Gairyism] for 28 years and would not allow this in our party (applause)," the account of the meeting records him saying. "Can we allow one man to hold up the party? (No) Can we allow a minority to hold the party to ransom? (No)" Strachan announced that the Central Committee had placed the army on alert.

Liam James addressed the meeting next. James reported on Cletus St. Paul's alleged assassination plots and reported the allegation about Bishop's rumor. According to the written account of the meeting, James said: "There have been threats on the lives of CC comrades as a result of the crisis—B[ernard] & P[hyllis] C[oard] and other cdes who took the Leninist position. . . . All of these are as a result of p[etty] b[ourgeois] opp[ortunism] of a tiny minority, esp. M[aurice] B[ishop]." Liam James reported to the October 13 meeting that "the security forces" had decided earlier that day to "confine MB indefinitely (long applause)" and to have the "phones of MB cut off (applause)."

James also reported that Major Einstein Louison—who had vigorously opposed the house arrest of Bishop—had been "suspended and confined (applause) for his opp[ortunism] and p[etty] b[ourgeois] behavior on this issue. He tried to influence cdes. in A[rmed] F[orces]."

Bishop spoke next. He once again denied spreading the rumor about Bernard and Phyllis Coard or being involved in any threats against their lives. Bishop acknowledged that he maintained reservations about the Central Committee majority's "joint leadership" proposal and said that these concerns had been reinforced by events since his return. He could not accept the Central Committee decision to confine him on the basis of the false charges against him, Bishop concluded.

Liam James then responded to Bishop. According to the written account of the meeting, James said that

> he finds it very difficult to understand how MB could be treated in the normal way when MB defies the decision of CC & entire membership (appl). . . . It is fully correct to treat him so & consider his expulsion from the party (appl). . . . [Bishop] had given an order to A[rmed] F[orces] to liquidate CC

> members. This is why measures were adopted. The interests of the party is higher than any individual interests (appl).

Toward the end of the meeting, Ewart Layne spoke in the discussion. Grenada's "bourg[eoisie] know where M[aurice] B[ishop] is coming from," Layne said. "They see him as the chosen one to defend [their] class interest." Layne continued: "We have lived for 28 yrs. under Gairy & cultism and not prepared to tolerate one single day more (appl & chants). We won't tolerate it even with a Bishop face (appl). If you want to rule with a minority go to S[outh] A[frica]."

Layne explained that he was "firmly of the view as a minimum [Bishop] has to be expelled from the party, dismissed from every state position he holds (appl chants). . . . If MB is not dismissed we would have departed from soc[ialism]. . . . Let us not be fooled by those who could make pretty speech and talk revolutionary," said Layne, "because Gairy did this in 1951."

"The only question then," Layne concluded, "is whether [Bishop] be allowed to operate as a private citizen or arrested & court martialled for stirring up counter[revolution] against the revo[lution]. (ovation)."

Coard attended this October 13 meeting and never once took the floor to disassociate himself from any of the scurrilous attacks against Maurice Bishop. Yet today Coard claims that "tremendous love" for Bishop was shown at this meeting!

Coard faction's campaign to smear Cuba

Even prior to October 1983, the Coard faction in the NJM had sought to portray Maurice Bishop's political collaboration with Fidel Castro and other Cuban Communist Party leaders as somehow improper. Leon Cornwall, Grenada's ambassador in Havana and a Coard supporter, had complained for months that he was not being kept properly informed of top-level party-to-party and state-to-state relations. At the September 13–16, 1983, Central Committee meeting, Coard's majority voted to accept Cornwall's demand to be relieved of the position on these grounds and rejected replacing him with another Central Committee member.

At that Central Committee meeting, Cornwall said that "his time is seriously wasted as Ambassador to Cuba because the work is carried out in spite of him." Phyllis Coard agreed, saying that the "party should be blamed for what has happened to Cde. Bogo [Cornwall] in Cuba." George Louison and Unison Whiteman spoke against withdrawing Cornwall as ambassador. Louison called this decision "a mistake that will further strain the relations between the two countries."

Cornwall defended this decision at the September 25 general meeting. He said that it was "unnecessary for a CC member to be based in Cuba as ambassador since a lot of information was being channelled from Grenada to Cuba by our party and government without his knowledge." Cornwall cited two meetings between Bishop and Cuban leaders that he said had been arranged without his prior knowledge.[107]

FOLLOWING BISHOP'S STOP in Cuba on his way back from Eastern Europe, innuendo gave way to outright vilification of Fidel Castro by Coard's supporters. They began peddling the lie that Bishop and Castro had discussed the divisions inside the NJM and that the Cubans pledged to use military power to back Bishop.

The Coard faction, George Louison reports, "went around spreading the rumor that Maurice Bishop and myself had met with Fidel Castro on Friday, October 7, that Fidel Castro had agreed to give us the support of Cuba and to use the Cubans who were in Grenada to get rid of Coard."[108] Coard's supporters "went so far as to say Fidel had made himself a little god in Cuba," Louison said, and they would not permit Bishop to do the same in Grenada.[109]

According to Vincent Noel, Selwyn Strachan told him shortly after Bishop's return "that Maurice had now compounded the problem by taking the party's business to the Cubans in an unfraternal and unprincipled way using his personal friendship with Fidel. Selwyn claimed that Maurice had spent two extra days in Cuba just for this, and, that as a show of support to Maurice, Fidel had given a reception for Maurice at which eight members of the Political Bureau had been present including Fidel and Raoul [Raúl Castro]."[110]

Fidel Castro responded to similar charges in a letter dated October 15 to the NJM Central Committee:

> I send you this message motivated by certain references which, in their conversations with our Ambassador, have been made by several Grenadian leaders in relation to Cuba.
>
> The supposed notion that on passing through our country Bishop had informed me of the problems inside the Party is a miserable piece of slander. Bishop did not mention a single word to me, nor did he make the slightest allusion to the matter. Completely the opposite. He expressed to me in general terms and with great modesty that there were deficiencies in his work which he

> thought he would overcome in the next few months.
>
> In reality, I am grateful to Bishop for that discretion, and for the respect he showed to his Party and to Cuba by not touching on such matters.
>
> We are indignant at the very thought that some of you would have considered us capable of meddling in any way in the internal questions of your Party. We are people of principle, not vulgar schemers or adventurers.

Having rebutted the slanders against Cuba and Bishop, Castro went on to express his views on the events unfolding in Grenada:

> Everything which happened was for us a surprise, and disagreeable. In our country, the Grenadian Revolution and Comrade Bishop as its central figure were the object of great sympathies and respect. Even explaining the events to our people will not be easy.
>
> In my opinion, the divisions and problems which have emerged will result in considerable damage to the image of the Grenadian Revolution, as much within as outside the country.
>
> Cuba, faithful to its moral values and its international policy, will pay strictest attention to the principle of not interfering in the slightest in the internal affairs of Grenada, fulfilling the promises made in the field of cooperation. Our promises are not to men. They are to the peoples and to principle.[111]
>
> History and developments yet to come will judge what has happened in these last few days.
>
> I wish for you the greatest wisdom, serenity,

> loyalty to principles, and generosity in this difficult moment through which the Grenadian Revolution is passing.[112]

Castro commented further on Bishop's relations with the Cuban leadership in a 1985 interview with Mervyn M. Dymally, a U.S. congressman, and Professor Jeffrey M. Elliot, published under the title *Fidel Castro: Nothing Can Stop the Course of History*. Castro once again emphasized that

> when Bishop returned to Cuba [in October 1983], he didn't say a single word about this problem. As I see it, this was for two reasons. First, he underestimated the problem and second, he may have been embarrassed by the idea of raising an internal problem of his party.

Castro then posed the question, "If we had known at the time of the discussions which had taken place [inside the NJM], could we have done something? Could we have helped to prevent what happened there?" Castro answered as follows:

> Perhaps not. . . . [Bishop] himself was not aware of the importance and the potential gravity of the charges, in the form of criticism, that were being addressed to him. But the fact is he went back, and by that time, Coard and his group—who by then had gained control of the majority of the leadership bodies—had already made some major decisions. . . .
>
> It might have been possible to do something if the gravity of the problem had been known two months earlier—perhaps a month before the events—and some delegation of ours could have

> talked with them. It's possible that we might have been able to do something to avert the catastrophic outcome. But no one can guarantee this.
>
> Coard's conspiracy, his intrigues, and his demagogic behavior had already undermined Bishop's authority within the party almost irreversibly.[113]

'No Bishop, No Revo!'

While Coard had used demagogy, deceit, corruption, and terror to capture a majority in the narrow New Jewel Movement, he quickly discovered that he faced mass opposition among the workers and farmers of Grenada. As news of Bishop's house arrest began to spread, walls around the island began to be covered with the slogan, "No Bishop, No Revo!"

On October 14, as Coard's supporters started trying to justify their actions publicly, they began to get a taste of the popular response to their counterrevolutionary coup. George Louison reports:

> They went out and said, "Principle is principle, if you were in our organization and the majority decided on something, could you as one person go against that decision?" People were not impressed with this childish way of presenting it. The people asked, "Well, what was it everybody wanted to decide on?" Which is what party members should have asked on their own—what was the issue?[114]

To this day, Coard and his supporters continue to seek to justify their counterrevolutionary course in the name of "democratic centralism." This is a constant theme of Coard's apologists such as Richard Hart (Bishop violated "a fundamental principle of the NJM—democratic centralism") and Trevor Munroe (Bishop's error was his "reluctance to accept collectivism, majority decision and democratic centralism").[115]

And in an April 4, 1986, letter smuggled out of prison in Grenada, Coard faction leader John Ventour insists that there "was no power-struggle, no ideological split, within our Party. The issue which precipitated the crisis was that . . . the entire Party leadership and membership was deeply concerned by the flouting by P[rime] M[inister] Bishop (pushed by a tiny group of opportunists) of decisions taken at General Meetings of the NJM in September, by the *unanimous* vote of all NJM members."[116]

True, the Coard faction had captured a majority in the NJM. But they used this majority against the Grenadian people and their revolutionary government. "Democratic centralism" is nothing to the Coard faction but a slogan (like "Marxism-Leninism") invoked to justify their criminal course. And that course stripped the NJM of all its political authority. It lost the right to speak in the name of the Grenadian people. Nor did Coard view the support of the people as a decisive question—the people, after all, followed a "herd psychology," in Coard's own contemptuous words.

But Grenadian working people were not the passive, obedient, depoliticized souls that Coard and his accomplices hoped they were. When Selwyn Strachan tried to hold a public meeting in downtown St. George's on October 14 to announce that Bishop had been replaced by Coard as prime minister, a crowd gathered and chased Strachan off the streets. As such incidents awakened Coard to how badly he had misjudged the ease of consolidating the coup, he and his backers began to panic. Later on October 14, Radio Free Grenada announced that Coard had resigned all government posts in order to "clear the air."

Bernard Coard had gone underground, refusing to face the Grenadian people. He carried out a coup and then hid from the workers and farmers. What a profile in political cowardice! What a contrast to Maurice Bishop, who had been placed under house arrest in order to prevent him from explaining the truth to the people of Grenada and leading them in defense of their revolution.

Nothing further was heard from Coard publicly until his arrest by the U.S. invading forces some two weeks later. Nonetheless, he continued to operate behind the scenes as the leader of the counterrevolutionary forces.

On October 15 Kendrick Radix and Fitzroy Bain led the first street demonstration demanding the release of Bishop. According to Radix:

> We confirmed to the people that Bishop had been placed under house arrest, since no formal announcement had been made, and alerted them to the impending catastrophe we foresaw—the collapse of the revolution. We called for Bishop's release by 6:00 p.m. that day, and warned the Coard group that unless Bishop was released, the people would go on strike and there would be continuous mass demonstrations to try to pressure a solution to the problem.
>
> Later that day, I was arrested as a counterrevolutionary and locked away until two days after the invasion.[117]

The following night, Gen. Hudson Austin, who had thrown in his lot with Coard's faction in September, spoke over Radio Free Grenada. Hoping to defuse the growing mass opposition, Austin sought to assure the population that Bishop remained prime minister and was "at home and quite safe." At the same time, however, Austin stated that the NJM Central Committee had expelled Bishop from the party in order "to stop the steady growth of one-man rule in our party and country."[118] (Coard, in his August 1986 trial statement, indignantly denies that Maurice Bishop was ever expelled from the NJM Central Committee, contradicting Austin's announcement over the radio that Bishop had been expelled from the party. Since neither Coard nor any of his followers did anything to correct the broadcast statement at the time, however, his claim now is somewhat less than credible.)

On October 18 street protests against Bishop's house arrest spread to Grenville, the island's second largest town. During this period, George Louison and Unison Whiteman were holding meetings with Coard, in a last-ditch effort to find some way to resolve the situation. Coard and his group "were completely contemptuous of the Grenadian people," Louison later recalled. "They believed that no matter what action they took, they could eventually explain it away."[119]

Coard was operating under the bureaucratic delusion that he could successfully con the Grenadian workers and farmers—and ultimately the entire world—with the same demagogy he used in the limited confines of the NJM. He was so accustomed to operating inside a clique that he was completely out of touch with the Grenadian people. According to George Louison:

> We pointed out [to Bernard Coard] that the situation could easily develop into a civil war because the people were so incensed they would

> do anything to get back their leader, and therefore the party had a responsibility to ensure that no violence took place in the country. Bernard said that he didn't buy that scenario because the situation was that he could permit the people to demonstrate for any amount of weeks, that they could demonstrate over and over.
>
> To use his exact words, "They could stay in the streets for weeks, after a while they are bound to get tired and hungry and want peace." He said [Prime Minister] Eric Williams did it in 1970 (in Trinidad) and survived. Gairy did it in '73 to us in St. George's and it could be done again.[120]

Coard now claims that as of October 18 "it looked like a solution was about to be reached, the crisis about to be solved."[121] George Louison, who was directly involved in the negotiations, has described the "compromise" that the Coard group offered Bishop that day. Bishop was to publicly accept responsibility for the crisis. He was to remain prime minister, but be stripped of powers as commander-in-chief of the army and of his membership in NJM leadership bodies, attending Political Bureau meetings on a consultative basis only.[122]

In other words, Coard was offering Bishop the opportunity to capitulate entirely and give his blessing to the coup. Neither Bishop, his closest supporters, nor the Grenadian people were prepared to do so.

At the end of the day on October 18, the Coard faction placed George Louison under arrest. By that time, Bishop's supporters had become convinced that there was no way to reverse Coard's coup and restore the workers' and farmers' government to power short of the uprising that more and more Grenadian working people were now demanding. Bishop's supporters knew that Washington was moving in for the kill, and that only the immediate restoration of the revolutionary government could have a chance to forestall a U.S. invasion.

SO, ON OCTOBER 19, as many as 30,000 Grenadians poured into the streets of St. George's. The country's working people went on strike; schools and workplaces were shut down. Unison Whiteman and Vincent Noel led part of the crowd to Bishop's home and freed him.

Don Rojas, Bishop's press secretary, is among the last persons still alive to have spoken with Bishop that day. Rojas reported that Bishop told him that "those criminals up on the hill" were going to turn their guns on the people and that the people "must disarm them" first.

Bishop then asked Rojas to lead a contingent to the central telephone exchange and communicate several messages to the world. He asked Rojas to call on Grenadians overseas and on trade unions and progressive forces throughout the Caribbean to make known their support for the mass outpouring that day. Bishop was concerned by efforts on the part of pro-imperialist forces both inside and outside Grenada to exploit the events there to spread anti-Cuban and anticommunist propaganda. According to Rojas, Bishop "wanted the point made very clearly that President Fidel Castro and the Cuban people had absolutely no involvement in this crisis," and that nothing that might happen in Grenada that day should serve as a justification for U.S. military intervention.[123]

Bishop remained an uncompromising internationalist and anti-imperialist up till the very end. He gave top priority to the interests of the Grenadian people and of the world revolution, which he recognized as inseparable.

And he sought to lead a popular insurrection to restore the revolutionary government necessary to defend and advance those interests.

Bishop and the crowd that liberated him then marched to Fort Rupert, the army headquarters. They appealed to the soldiers there to turn over their weapons, and many did so. Bishop organized a small security squad from members of the militia in the crowd. He dispatched a detachment under the command of Peter Thomas, an immigration officer, to the central telephone exchange with orders to "get the lines connected to speak to Radio Grenada and to the rest of the World."[124] Bishop wanted to appeal to working people, including members of the armed forces, to refuse to cooperate with the illegitimate Coard regime so that the revolutionary government could be restored to power.[125]

THOMAS SUCCEEDED in opening the lines at the telephone exchange and returned to Fort Rupert with additional arms to defend Bishop and the others.

Coard and his backers, already in a state of panic, responded to these developments with confusion, cowardice, and murderous repression. Three armored personnel carriers with soldiers under the command of officers loyal to the Coard faction were ordered to Fort Rupert and arrived on the scene before any broadcast by Bishop could be organized. These forces began to fire automatic weapons into the crowd, killing many demonstrators (including Vincent Noel) and wounding others. "Oh my god, they have turned the guns against the people," Bishop said, according to a nurse who was at the fort attending him at the time.[126]

Given the heavy firepower in the hands of Coard's backers, Bishop decided to surrender without resistance.

He recognized that the battle to reverse the counterrevolutionary coup and head off an imperialist invasion would not be advanced by a massacre by the better-armed forces under Coard's command. According to Peter Thomas:

> I remember, among the people who actually had rifles, I was the first to cock my rifle and put a bullet up in the [breech] and I removed the safety catch and when Maurice heard these sounds he commanded us "don't fire back." He said, "Do not fire back." So as a matter of fact nobody from the fort building actually fired back into the attackers.

Coard's troops stormed the fort and reoccupied it. Bishop—together with Whiteman, Fitzroy Bain, Norris Bain, and Jacqueline Creft—were then separated from the rest of the crowd and taken to an inner courtyard in the fort. There they were summarily murdered.

Coard's political defenders have tried to sidetrack the debate surrounding Coard's responsibility for destroying the Grenada revolution onto the question of whether or not the NJM Central Committee met and voted on October 19 to order Bishop's murder. Whether the Central Committee voted or not for such a motion is utterly irrelevant. The bloodbath that day was the culmination of the Coard faction's counterrevolutionary coup.

Coard's faction had overthrown the revolutionary government. But they had not yet destroyed the morale of Grenadian workers and farmers. In fact, the working people went into action that week—culminating in the largest revolutionary mobilization in Grenada's history—in an attempt to reconquer power. But instead of accepting the verdict of the people, Coard's supporters fired on them. Then, by declaring a four-day, round-the-clock curfew, they locked the entire population up in their homes.

"Anyone who seeks to demonstrate or disturb the peace will be shot," Gen. Hudson Austin announced over the radio on the evening of October 19. "No one is to leave their house. Anyone violating the curfew will be shot on sight."[127]

The next day a new Revolutionary Military Council (RMC) was announced to the terrorized and disoriented population. Of the twelve cabinet members in the People's Revolutionary Government as of the beginning of October, four had been murdered and another three placed under arrest. Still in hiding from the Grenadian people, Bernard Coard took no formal position in the RMC, which was composed entirely of army officers loyal to his faction.

George Louison has described the days following Coard's October 19 massacre:

> The four-day shoot-to-kill curfew was in a sense an act of the greatest treachery and terror, which struck fear into a large section of the Grenadian population.
>
> You have to recognize that [people] . . . had no stocks of foodstuffs. Also, because the country is agricultural, many people have small animals and crops in the fields to take care of.
>
> So the curfew imposed the greatest hardship and provided a material base for the fear and the terror that developed with an around-the-clock curfew, with no food, no water for most; they had to hide to go to the toilet.
>
> In addition, the Coard clique had deployed teams of party members around the country, fully armed, who shot all over the place, to run people back into their homes whenever people under this

> great hardship attempted to break the curfew.
>
> They also compiled what they called assessment sheets of each village, in which they listed who were for the RMC and who were against it. And those lists struck fear in the people because they saw them as virtual death lists.[128]

The crushing of the attempted mass insurrection on October 19 and the days of terror that followed left the Grenadian people demoralized, without hope or perspective. Coard's faction demobilized the workers and farmers and drove them out of politics. In doing so he destroyed the only social force in Grenada that stood in the path of a U.S. invasion.[129]

Coard's new slander campaign

In his trial statement, Bernard Coard pretends that the assassination of Maurice Bishop and his supporters on October 19 was a terrible loss to him. When he first learned of Bishop's death, Coard states, "It was not only a stunning blow for me, but an event which I personally have yet to recover from, if indeed I will ever recover from it. . . . The memories of that afternoon and evening and of the days following are painful ones for me, tragic ones. No greater blow could have been struck than that."

"The death of Cde. Maurice Bishop," Coard says, "is the most tragic, most devastating event—not only for the people of Grenada but for the Caribbean region—in this century. That was my assessment at the time, and it is still my assessment. . . . It is my belief that his death still remains to be investigated."[130]

Coard made no such statements at the time, however. Nor did anyone in his RMC. Just the opposite.

The murder of Maurice Bishop, now called a "tragic"

and "devastating" event by Coard, was publicly justified by the RMC at the time, on the grounds that Bishop was a counterrevolutionary right opportunist plotting to wipe out the NJM leadership to restore power to Grenada's bourgeoisie.

Military officers directly involved in the Fort Rupert massacre were among the fifteen-member Revolutionary Military Council appointed just a few hours after the bloodbath.

Coard now portrays Bishop as a well-intentioned revolutionary, but a weak and subjective individual who fell under the evil personal influence of those surrounding him. "On his own," Coard said in his trial statement, "there is no way Cde. Maurice Bishop would have taken such a decision [to go to Fort Rupert on October 19]. It was completely out of character, both for him personally and for the NJM.[131]

Whispering in one ear, according to Coard, were the power-mad George Louison and Kendrick Radix, who swayed Bishop to resist Central Committee decisions. Whispering in Bishop's other ear were CIA agents who, having wormed their way into his confidences, lured him into a provocation on October 19. These CIA agents, Coard charges, were Don Rojas, Shahiba Strong, and Cletus St. Paul—Bishop's press secretary, chief protocol officer, and chief security guard.

"Some do it because of personal reasons—because they have an axe to grind," Coard says. "Others do it for bribes, others because they are professional agents." But whatever their motivations, this cabal "surrounded him, they bombarded him. All but one were present on the trip [to Eastern Europe] with him. They pushed plot and conspiracy lines at him constantly." As a result, Coard claims, these individuals were able "to greatly aggravate the situation and turn it into a crisis of monumental proportions, which it was not. . . .[132]

Bishop was under "tremendous stress and strain" as a result of his son's illness, according to Coard, as well as his concerns about "whether the joint leadership proposal really represented a vote of no confidence." Given this personal situation, "one can understand that George Louison and others had fertile ground to work on," Coard says. Bishop was "at his most vulnerable; in a period of the greatest self-doubt regarding his capabilities, deeply worried about his son."[133]

COARD SAYS he tried "to persuade Cde. Bishop against this conspiracy obsession which was being pushed at him" and urged him to become part of "the monumental task of the reorganization of the Party at all levels to stave off Party disintegration, and invasion. . . . That was my aim."[134]

But Coard just couldn't get Bishop's ear, he says. As a result, Coard claims, by October 18 he and his supporters were ready to give in to Bishop's refusal to accept the party's majority decision. "Better to have a situation where the Revolution has a chance of survival, and that can only be with Maurice Bishop leading the process, even if it means breaking all the rules and decisions of the Party. Because the Revolution must come first." Coard was even planning "to leave the country" in order "to put to rest the tremendous propaganda campaign" that he was trying to grab power.[135]

But Louison, Rojas, and others intervened with Bishop on October 18 to block this peaceful solution, according to Coard.[136] They organized the demonstration on October 19 and convinced Bishop, once released, to go to Fort Rupert. According to Coard, the crowd that poured into the streets that day was composed of "three elements": (1) "many decent, law-abiding supporters of the revolution," some of whom "got carried away with excitement"; (2) those such as Vincent Noel who "were not *consciously* acting as agents" of the CIA but were "acting as they saw best for whatever their reasons"; and (3) the CIA agents "which the United States had in place" and right-wing, pro-imperialist Grenadians.[137]

"We have to examine closely the real possibility," Coard states, "that on October 19 the link between the Vincent Noel group in the demonstration and the 'God Bless America', 'We love America', C.I.A. group, could be an individual working on the one hand for the C.I.A.—Don Rojas—and ingratiating himself with the Party and Revolution. He may very well be the chemistry that led to the attack and seizure of Fort Rupert. It is worth careful study and investigation."[138]

"The only thing the U.S. government and its agents didn't do on October 19 was to pull the trigger," Coard states. "They did everything else."[139]

Coard and his supporters invoke the charge of CIA responsibility for the October 19 events for a reason. They hope to gain a hearing among radical-minded fighters around the world, who know that the CIA is the deadly enemy of workers and farmers everywhere, and that it expends vast resources to destabilize governments that refuse to do Washington's bidding.

But Coard's new version of events is only a more subtle slander against Bishop himself. It was Bishop's "weaknesses" that caused him to surround himself with CIA agents and other suspect types, Coard suggests, thus opening the road to destruction of the revolution.

Coard's account is riddled with lies and contradictions from start to finish. We've already recounted many of these. But the lie on which Coard rests his entire case is that Don Rojas, Shahiba Strong, and Cletus St. Paul were CIA agents. The practice of defaming political opponents as police spies is a poison to the worldwide struggle for national liberation and socialism. It was used by the Social Democratic enemies of the Bolshevik-led revolution in Russia to smear Lenin and other communist leaders of the working class. Agent-baiting later became standard operating procedure for Stalin's regime, which used it to justify murderous purges and assassinations in the 1930s and 1940s.

Coard's story is a frame-up, pure and simple. He offers no proof to substantiate his agent-baiting of these three revolutionaries, all of them close aides chosen by Bishop. Instead, Coard builds a case based on innuendo and outright fabrication.

WE HAVE ALREADY SEEN what kind of justice Cletus St. Paul received at the hands of Coard's Central Committee majority. Coard does him no better several years later. Coard offers no evidence against him. Instead, Coard insinuates that St. Paul was in it for the money. The only other "evidence" against St. Paul is that, under the threat of imprisonment and death, he refused to be broken and to turn against Bishop and the Grenada revolution in October 1983. That's it—the entire case against Cletus St. Paul!

And Coard's evidence against Shahiba Strong? First, she lived in the United States for several years prior to the revolution. Second, following the U.S. occupation of Grenada she was not detained by the invading forces. (Nor were many others. Coard does not mention that in 1984 Strong was deported by the U.S.-installed regime and permitted to return to Grenada only following a protest campaign led by the Maurice Bishop Patriotic Movement.)

Coard says in his trial statement that the alleged CIA agents Strong, St. Paul, and Rojas had access to "the private offices and even bedrooms" of some of the leadership. Why mention "bedrooms"? Coard himself doesn't elaborate. But the answer is contained in a document being publicly circulated by Coard's supporters, entitled "Grenada 1983: Whose Struggle for Power?" This document is a simple rehash of Coard's testimony. In the case of Shahiba Strong, however, it sheds some additional light on Coard's smears. It reports an interview with a PRG security officer, who states that "we were fairly certain [!] this woman was working for the CIA." This individual then says that Bishop knew that Strong was a CIA agent, but permitted her to infiltrate the party and government nonetheless because he could not resist her sexual advances. "She kept after him, and after a while he just couldn't resist her."[140]

WHAT ABOUT DON ROJAS? Where is the proof that Rojas was a CIA agent? First, Rojas lived in the United States prior to the revolution. Second, Rojas led a contingent to Grenada's central telephone exchange on October 19. Third, Rojas was not jailed after the U.S. invasion and was flown out of Grenada. That's the *entire* case.

Suggesting that something sinister must have been involved, Coard asks,

> What precisely did Don Rojas send out to the world media by telephone at the time he seized the telephone company, in the heart of things, and what did he send out to the media after the

> invasion? There are records of this and what do they tell us about the activities of Don Rojas prior to, during and after the invasion.[141]

Coard is right about one thing—there are records of what Rojas did and said. But these records belie Coard's implication that Rojas's behavior was somehow suspicious. Rojas was carrying out his duty as Bishop's press secretary, and as a Grenadian revolutionary.

What "did Rojas send out to the world media by telephone" on October 19? Rojas himself has explained many times, but we don't have to rely on his account alone. We can cite the Caribbean News Agency (CANA) dispatches from that day. According to CANA:

> In a telephone conversation with CANA from St. George's shortly after Bishop was freed, his press secretary Don Rojas quoted the prime minister as saying that Cuba was not in any way involved in the trouble here.
>
> He said it was "the work of militarists and anarchists led by Bernard Coard," and he called on the army "not to turn their guns on the people."
>
> "The guns are to defend the interest of the people and not to be used against them," Rojas quoted Bishop as saying.[142]

Another CANA dispatch the same day reported further on Rojas's telephone message:

> Gunshots were heard in the vicinity of Grenada's army headquarters Fort Rupert, where Prime Minister Maurice Bishop had taken refuge after being freed from house arrest by a large crowd of

> supporters, Bishop's press secretary, Don Rojas, said in a brief telephone call to CANA's Bridgetown [Barbados] headquarters this afternoon.
>
> "From where I am standing I could see smoke and fire and the people are scattering," a frenzied Rojas told CANA. Rojas said Bishop was still in the midst of the huge crowd when truckloads of troops arrived and opened fire.
>
> "We don't quite know what's going on, but we know the prime minister was among the people," Rojas said.[143]

Coard states, as if there is something fishy, that a few days after the U.S. invasion, Rojas was "not detained but flown out [of Grenada] in a U.S. military aircraft to Barbados, where they set up a press conference for him." Coard calls this being "taken out of Grenada in VIP style."[144]

What are the facts? After Don Rojas, his wife Karen, and son Maceo were rounded up by U.S. authorities on October 29, 1983,

> we were ordered to go to the site of the Point Salines airport, then controlled by the invading forces. I was separated from my family and interrogated at gunpoint. My family was sent to Barbados on a U.S. military transport plane. Some hours later I, too, was expelled and sent to Barbados.[145]

Rojas has been barred from returning to Grenada ever since by the U.S.-installed government there.

Was there something suspicious about Rojas being "flown out in a U.S. military aircraft"? No. Rojas, born on the island of St. Vincent, was deported from Grenada along with many others who were not Grenadian-born. The invading forces had stopped all commercial flights. The only way to get off the island on October 29 was aboard U.S. military aircraft.

What about Rojas's press conference in Barbados? It was not "set up" by the U.S. government. What did Rojas say? An October 30 dispatch by a Manchester *Guardian* correspondent reported the following:

> Rojas predicted that Grenada would now be "rapidly colonized" with the building of a large U.S. embassy and a lot of aid money.
>
> "I think they will move very quickly to wipe out all vestiges of the revolution," he said. "The local councils and other democratic structures we put in place will be dismantled and kept that way by military force. But I can't think that any honest, patriotic Grenadian is going to accept that situation in the end."[146]

In fact, Rojas was the first prominent NJM member who had been on the island during the October events to be quoted in the world press condemning the U.S. invasion. That was a welcome voice to opponents of Washington's aggression around the world. In his press conference Rojas also exposed Coard's counterrevolutionary actions, pointing out that these crimes "gave the Grenadian revolution on a platter to the U.S. with all the trimmings."

How the Cuban leadership responded

The Cuban leadership immediately condemned the massacre of Maurice Bishop and other Grenadian revolutionaries. In an October 20 statement they emphasized:

> No doctrine, no principle or position held up as revolutionary, and no internal division, justifies atrocious proceedings like the physical elimination of Bishop and the outstanding group of honest and worthy leaders killed yesterday. . . . No crime must be committed in the name of the revolution and freedom.

The Cuban revolutionaries warned that these crimes would embolden Washington to invade Grenada and "subject it once again to neocolonial and imperial domination." In this situation, the statement said,

> no step must be taken that would aid imperialism in its plans. . . . Though profoundly embittered by the events, we will take no precipitate step with regard to technical and economic collaboration that could affect essential services or economic interests vital to the people of Grenada, for whom we have sincere and deep feelings of admiration and affection. . . . But our political relations with the new figures in the Grenadian leadership will have to be subjected to serious and profound analysis.[147]

The NJM Central Committee adopted a motion the following day labeling the Cuban statement "a *personal* and not a *class* approach" based on Castro's friendship with Bishop, and charging that "the Cubans' position creates an atmosphere for speedy imperialist intervention."[148]

In his interview with Mervyn Dymally and Jeffrey Elliot, Castro elaborated further on Cuba's response to Coard's counterrevolution:

> What kept us from withdrawing? We might have had to withdraw in a week, in view of the tenseness of the relations between us. What kept us from doing so was the news that U.S. intervention forces were sailing toward Grenada. That was the one moment when we couldn't withdraw from the country.[149]

Given the clear danger of U.S. military intervention, Castro sent a message to the Cuban embassy in Grenada on October 22 instructing that Cuban construction workers and other personnel on the island should fight invading forces only if directly attacked. "I repeat: only if we are directly attacked," Castro wrote. "We would thus be defending ourselves, not the [new Grenadian] government or its deeds."[150]

THE FOLLOWING DAY, October 23, Castro sent another message to Cuba's embassy in Grenada, explaining that the Cuban government had rejected a request by the Revolutionary Military Council for military assistance. The members of Grenada's new military council "themselves are the only ones responsible for the creation of the disadvantageous and difficult situation" confronting them militarily, the statement said.[151]

In his 1985 interview with Dymally and Elliot, Castro commented further on the decision to limit combat by Cuban construction volunteers strictly to self-defense. "To fight against U.S. troops would have called for a different type of personnel, different weapons, and a different kind of war," Castro said. "Above all, there would have had to be a government worth defending, one supported by the people."[152]

In the interview, Castro called the U.S. invasion "one

of the most inglorious and infamous deeds that a powerful country, such as the United States, could ever commit against a small country." Pointing to the political crimes of the Coard group, Fidel said that the RMC

> could not have endured. We wouldn't have offered any support to that government after it murdered Bishop and fired on the people. After we had assumed that attitude, it would have been difficult for any other socialist or progressive country to support that group, because Bishop actually had great authority and great international prestige. . . . The whole world thought highly of Bishop; that Pol Pot-type group that murdered him would never have been forgiven. . . .
>
> Despite everything that happened, the United States had no right to invade that nation. Nor does it even have the right to keep that extremist group in prison or to try them, because no invading force has the right to run the courts and enforce the laws. I think all that is illegal.[153]

IV. A LESSON FROM THE CUBAN REVOLUTION

THERE ARE STRIKING SIMILARITIES between the campaign organized against Maurice Bishop by the Coard faction and that waged against Fidel Castro during the early years of the Cuban revolution by a secret faction led by Aníbal Escalante.

The Cuban workers and peasants triumphed over the U.S.-backed Batista dictatorship in January 1959 under the leadership of the July 26 Movement. The victory created both the need and the opportunity for a new, mass political party of Cuba's working people, qualitatively different from the political organization that had led the fight for power.

Looking back at this turning point, in a March 1962 speech, Castro explained:

> I, too, belonged to an organization. But the glories of that organization are the glories of Cuba, they are the glories of the people, they belong to all of us. And there came a day that I stopped belonging to that organization. Which day? The day when we had made a revolution greater than our organization, the day we had a people with us, a movement far greater than our organization . . . at the time of the victory, when the entire people joined us and demonstrated their support, their sympathy, their strength.[154]

If ever there was an organization that had established the political authority in struggle to proclaim itself the undisputed vanguard of a revolutionary people, that organization was the July 26 Movement. But Fidel Castro correctly saw that the task was to put this political authority to work to build a mass vanguard party of the Cuban working people much broader than the July 26 Movement.

In the March 1962 speech, Castro continued:

> As we moved through towns and cities, I saw lots of men and women, hundreds and thousands of men and women with the red and black uniforms of the July 26 Movement. But many more thousands wore uniforms that weren't black and red but were the workshirts of workers and farmers and other men and women of the people. And since that day, honestly, in my heart, I left the movement that we

> loved, under whose banners we had fought, and I joined the people. I belonged to the people, to the revolution, because we had truly accomplished something that was greater than ourselves.[155]

The New Jewel Movement, too, accomplished something in March 1979 much greater than itself. Its glories, too, became the glories of the Grenadian workers and farmers. But unlike what happened in Cuba, the NJM in Grenada was blocked by the Coard faction from acting on this reality to begin the construction of a mass revolutionary proletarian party.

At the end of 1961, the July 26 Movement fused with two other organizations that had participated in the anti-Batista struggle and supported the new revolutionary government. These were the Popular Socialist Party (PSP)—the prerevolution Communist Party in Cuba—and the Revolutionary Directorate, a largely student-based revolutionary group. The new organization took the name Integrated Revolutionary Organizations (ORI).

Castro's aim was to forge a united membership and leadership, regardless of any individual's political origins or past political positions. "We feel that from this moment on," Castro said, "all differences between the old and the new, between those who fought in the Sierra and those who were down in the lowlands, between those who took up arms and those who did not, between those who studied Marxism and those who did not study Marxism before, we feel that all differences between them should cease."[156]

Castro opposed those who claimed favored rank for July 26 cadres over those from the other groups. "We always told the people," Castro said, "that all those who did not have the opportunity to fight before should not be discouraged, that ahead of them there were many opportunities, that all of history before them waited to be written, that the revolution had barely begun and a long road lay ahead of us."[157]

The opposite course, however, was pursued by Aníbal Escalante, a longtime PSP leader elected as organization secretary of the ORI. Escalante's backers gossiped that a personality cult was developing around Fidel Castro. They doled out posts in the embryonic new organization and Cuban state apparatus almost exclusively to former PSP cadres, often pushing out those from other political backgrounds. They employed bureaucratic methods and fostered privilege and corruption, leading to widespread discontent among workers and peasants who fell victim to these policies.

To justify these practices, Escalante claimed that those who had not been trained in Marxism as PSP cadres had too "low a political level" to serve in most responsible positions. On this basis, he began to purge army commanders who had played leading roles in the guerrilla struggle against Batista and in combating the abortive, U.S.-backed Bay of Pigs invasion. "How could they be removed from their commands for being of a 'low political level'," Castro asked, "and then put in his place some bachelor of arts who can recite from memory a Marxist catechism even though he doesn't apply it? . . . Is this Marxism? Is this Leninism?"[158]

The Escalante group also undermined the worker-farmer alliance in Cuba. In 1961–62, when the new Cuban government ordered expropriation of the land of anyone engaged in counterrevolutionary actions, Escalante's backers began to seize the holdings of small and middle farmers, including those of many who supported the revolution. "Poor and rich were hit indiscriminately, without taking into consideration all the circumstances in each case," Cuban CP leader Carlos Rafael Rodríguez wrote in a 1963 article.[159]

As the ORI National Directorate found out about the bureaucratic abuses being carried out around the country, it held a series of discussions to reverse these practices. In a televised speech in March 1962, Castro explained to the Cuban people how the party had responded to the actions of the Escalante faction. Castro pointed out that under Escalante, the ORI was developing not toward a party "of the workers' vanguard," but was being transformed into a "nest of privilege," "favoritism," and "immunities." The working people, Castro said, were beginning to ask whether the ORI was "a nucleus of revolutionists" or "a mere shell of revolutionists, well versed in dispensing favors."[160]

Escalante was removed from his position and steps were taken to guard against the degeneration of the organization into a morass of favoritism, privilege, and bureaucratic methods. The ORI was reorganized from top to bottom. It was this reorganization that made possible the construction of a vanguard party of Cuba's exploited producers.

The majority of nominees were now accepted into party membership only after having been selected as model workers by an assembly of their co-workers—party members and non-party members alike. Party membership was to be the product of disciplined work, self-sacrifice, and leadership, not a stepping stone for careerists and privilege-seekers. "The best workers in the country should be members of [the] party," Castro said.[161] He continued:

> How could we keep the masses out? How could we divorce ourselves from the masses? There are

> many model workers among the old revolutionists who are recognized as such by the masses. There are others who are not model workers. There is no reason why there should be disagreement with this because being a communist does not endow one with a hereditary title nor with a title of nobility.
>
> To be a communist means that one has a certain attitude towards life and that attitude has to be the same from the first day until the moment of death. When that attitude is abandoned, even though one has been a communist, it ceases to be a communist attitude towards life, towards the revolution, towards one's class, towards the people.[162]

As a result of this reorganization in the early 1960s and subsequent measures, the weight of workers, peasants, and volunteers for internationalist missions has grown in the Cuban party.[163]

ESCALANTE SHARED Coard's contempt for working people. As we've seen, Coard's explanation for why masses of Grenadians poured out October 19 to support Bishop is that they were susceptible to a "herd psychology." Escalante's attitude toward the Cuban workers and peasants was explained in an April 1962 speech by Castro to the ORI leadership in Matanzas province. Castro pointed out that the Escalante grouping exhibited

> the real petty-bourgeois spirit, because the petty bourgeois, when the people are disgusted as a consequence of his errors, does not take the blame himself, he blames the people. . . . He ends up accusing the masses of being counterrevolutionary

> when they are not turning against the revolution but rather against his arbitrary acts.[164]

Castro explained that the actions of the Escalante grouping fueled anticommunism, which was a legacy from the island's decades of domination by U.S. imperialism. The leaders of the revolution were making steady progress in countering anticommunism in the population through experience and patient education, Castro said. But the bureaucratic abuses of Escalante and his supporters, Castro explained, caused many Cubans to ask, "'Is this communism? . . . Is this socialism? This arbitrariness, this abuse, this privilege, all this, is this communism?'"[165]

ESCALANTE WAS "serious in making his bid for power," Castro said. His bureaucratic course weakened the revolution in the face of imperialism and the Cuban exploiters. If not reversed, Castro emphasized, this course may well have led not to power for the Escalante grouping, but "to the destruction of the revolutionary power," to "power by the counterrevolutionaries, to a type of defeat such as that of the Paris Commune, with the general beheading of revolutionaries that the triumph of the counterrevolution would signify."[166] That is just what happened in Grenada as a result of Coard's counterrevolutionary coup.

Following the removal of Escalante as the ORI's organization secretary, he worked in Cuba's diplomatic service for several years in its embassy in Czechoslovakia. In 1964 he returned to Cuba and began organizing renewed secret factional activity inside the party. Escalante and his supporters "maintained that the petty bourgeois line was the prevailing current in the policy of the Revolution and that the petty bourgeoisie had made attempts to seize all power in its hands," Cuban leader Raúl Castro explained in 1968. They said that Escalante "was the one who most firmly defended the ideological positions of the working class."[167]

The Escalante faction condemned the Cuban government's policy of allowing all those who wanted to emigrate from the island to do so. They belittled Cuba's encouragement of volunteer labor from the cities to help out during harvest time. They disagreed with the Cuban leadership's political positions that differed from those of the governments of the Soviet Union and Eastern European workers' states over such questions as aid and solidarity with the Vietnamese revolution, support for Palestinian national self-determination, and other international issues.[168] Escalante and his supporters urged personnel in the Soviet, Czech, and East German embassies in Havana to get their governments to bring pressure on the Cuban leadership—including withholding economic and military aid—to change its course.[169] Some officials from these embassies cooperated with Escalante's factional maneuvers and were later ordered to leave the country.

In 1968 Escalante and the core of his grouping were tried for violations of Cuban law committed in the course of their factional activity, especially their dealings with embassy personnel behind the backs of government bodies. They were convicted and imprisoned for a number of years.

In his speech at the trial of Escalante in 1968, the special prosecutor outlined the internationalist perspective that Lenin had advanced right up to his death:

> Lenin's internationalist ideal was the close alliance of the revolutionary elements of every

> country, and he proclaimed that to renounce insurrection and assistance to the people in rebellion was "tantamount to going back on the idea of the Revolution." He sustained the thesis that the international proletariat must actively support the uprisings of exploited people against their oppressors. And, as a corollary, in June 1920 he summed up proletarian internationalism as follows:
>
> 1. Subordination of the interests of the proletarian struggle in one country to the interests of that struggle on a worldwide scale.
>
> 2. That a nation which has triumphed over the bourgeoisie must be able and ready to make the greatest national sacrifices for the sake of overthrowing international capital.

"Our country," the Cuban prosecutor said, "has never attempted to subordinate international interest to national interest. Its national existence has been threatened, and yet it has not temporized a single moment."[170]

That revolutionary internationalism, steadfast but without bravado or adventurism, has remained the greatest strength and inspiration of the Cuban revolution to this day.

V. FROM STALIN TO COARD

BOTH ANÍBAL ESCALANTE and Bernard Coard were trained in the political school of Stalinism, which triumphed over Lenin's course in the Soviet Union, Soviet Communist Party, and Communist International some six decades ago.

The ground for Stalinism's consolidation in the leading bodies of the Soviet Communist Party was laid by the economic and human toll of years of civil war and imperialist intervention and by the defeats and setbacks suffered by the world revolution during that period. The Soviet working class was decimated, dispersed, and politically exhausted by the ravages of war, and its alliance with the exploited peasants was placed under severe strains.

In the final year of his life, Lenin waged a battle in the Communist Party of Soviet Russia to combat the corrosive political effects of these developments by increasing the mobilization and politicization of the workers and peasants, and expanding their control over the economy and state affairs.[171]

Following Lenin's death, however, the majority of the Communist Party leadership succumbed to the mounting pressures and ultimately abandoned Lenin's internationalist and communist policies. The prospects of countering these pressures through new victories over imperialism were dashed by defeats of revolutionary upsurges in Germany (1923), China (1927), and elsewhere.

The new majority in the Soviet leadership came to rely on administrative means of rule. It increasingly spoke for a bureaucratic layer in the state and party apparatus who drew material privileges from their positions of command. Joseph Stalin emerged as the most powerful representative of this bureaucratic social caste. Under his leadership the Communist Party broke decisively with Lenin's communist course.

Stalin and his backers subordinated the interests of working people, both internationally and in the Soviet Union, to the consolidation of the caste's own political power and material comforts. While some members of this bureaucratic stratum were working people by origin, it was a petty-bourgeois social layer. Its caste interests were alien to those of the workers and peasants. Stalin's regime shattered the worker-peasant alliance, imposing a forced collectivization that cost millions of lives from famine and brutal repression and that set back Soviet agriculture to this day. Stalin sought to eliminate all resistance to this course, organizing the murder of the central Bolshevik leadership team assembled by Lenin—Bukharin, Kamenev, Radek, Tomsky, Trotsky, Zinoviev—and executing or jailing millions of cadres at all levels of the party, state, and mass organizations. This culminated on the eve of World War II with Stalin's beheading of the Red Army; nearly one-quarter of its officer corps was arrested and thousands were executed.

The leaderships of Communist parties around the world were purged to bring these organizations under the control of officials who would implement each new political line propounded by Stalin. The Stalinists veered from ultraleft adventures to opportunist accommodation with the capitalists and landlords.

As the Stalinists transformed the Communist International from a revolutionary force into a foreign policy instrument of the Soviet bureaucracy, more and more of its cadres on every continent were trained in this approach to politics. Stalin's *Foundations of Leninism* and his *Dialectical and Historical Materialism,* used by Coard to "raise the ideological level" of NJM cadres, served as handbooks throughout the world. These pamphlets, packaged as "orthodox Marxism-Leninism," falsified the history of the Bolshevik Party, the October 1917 revolution in Russia, and the early years of the Communist International under Lenin's leadership, and presented a political program that is the opposite of communism.

This is the common political root of so many policies, implemented in the name of communism, that have actually dealt heavy blows to the worldwide struggle for national liberation and socialism. Among these are: the "Great Leap Forward," the forced march toward "rural people's communes," and the bureaucratic upheavals of the "Cultural Revolution" under Mao Zedong; the post–World War II purge trials and forced collectivization policies in the Eastern European workers' states; the postwar murders of Vietnamese revolutionaries who resisted Stalin's deal to return the country to French imperialism; the Soviet government's invasion of Czechoslovakia in 1968; the anti-Vietnamese xenophobia and barbaric treatment of Kampuchean workers and peasants at the hands of Pol Pot; and the brutal administrative methods and bloody bureaucratic in-fighting of the Peoples Democratic Party of Afghanistan.

All these policies, carried out in the name of socialism, have resulted in the demoralization and depoliticization of working people. Their common root is Stalinism and its false claim to "Marxist political orthodoxy" and "Leninist organizational methods."

This was the origin of Salvador Cayetano Carpio's secret factional maneuvers to block progress toward fusion of the five organizations that make up the Farabundo Martí National Liberation Front in El Salvador, going so far as to organize the assassination in 1983 of Mélida Anaya Montes (Commander Ana María), who had broken politically with Carpio's sectarianism and was helping to lead the fight for unity. Carpio had never overcome the Stalinist political and organizational conceptions learned as a central leader of the Salvadoran Communist Party in the late 1940s and 1950s.

STALINISM DESTROYED the Grenada revolution. Bernard Coard was trained in its brutality, rigidity, and bureaucratic "decisiveness." Like all Stalinists, he confused political clarity with dogmatism, centralism with commands, flexibility with softness, discipline with submission, firmness with harshness. The faction he was building in Grenada was truly petty bourgeois—the nucleus of an administrative caste trained in giving orders and wielding authority, not of a political vanguard of the working class relying on the revolutionary organization, mobilization, and political education of the exploited producers.

Maurice Bishop, not Bernard Coard, was the communist educator of Grenadian working people. Through Bishop's speeches, workers and farmers gained a deeper understanding of the class struggle in Grenada, the Caribbean, and worldwide. Through working to deepen the Grenadian people's involvement in the revolution, Bishop helped promote their class-struggle experience and politicization. Bernard Coard was not a "brilliant master of Marxist strategy and tactics." He was a Stalinist phrasemonger.

Although Stalinism remains a powerful obstacle to workers' and peasants' struggles, as shown by the events in Grenada, its hold over the international working-class movement has been irreversibly weakened by the advance of the world revolution since the closing years of World War II. Above all, a corner was turned in 1959 with the victory of the Cuban revolution under the leadership of a revolutionary internationalist leadership. Revolutionary-minded workers, peasants, and youth throughout Latin America and many other parts of the world have been attracted to and influenced by the example of the Cuban Communist Party.

This example had been reinforced since 1979 by the Sandinista-led revolution in Nicaragua. The Nicaraguan workers' and peasants' government is inspiring emulation through programs such as the Atlantic Coast autonomy plan, aimed at overcoming the legacy of racial and national oppression of the country's minority Indian and Black populations and forging a united Nicaraguan nation for the first time. It is setting a positive example of how a revolutionary government can approach the church and religious believers. Its commitment to barring the death penalty, building a humane prison system, and advancing human rights has set a new standard of state morality that challenges every government in the world.

As a result of political advances such as these, growing numbers of democrats, anti-imperialist fighters, and communists in the Americas and worldwide have come to reject apologies for Stalinist policies and practices, including lies and bloody methods, such as those of Bernard Coard and his accomplices.

VI. MAURICE BISHOP'S POLITICAL LEGACY

CONTRARY TO Bernard Coard's supporters, the bonds between Fidel Castro and Maurice Bishop were not based on personal friendship. That turns cause and effect on its head. The close friendship they forged was the product of their shared communist political perspective and the common values that flowed from it.

Like the leadership of socialist Cuba, Maurice Bishop was a revolutionary internationalist. "We see the importance of progressive forces worldwide joining together," Bishop said. "We see that struggle as being *one* struggle, indivisible. And what happens in Grenada, we recognize its importance for all struggles around the world."[172]

Bishop understood that for Grenada, internationalism began by working to break down the barriers erected by imperialism to keep the peoples of the Caribbean and Central America divided and weak. "One of the greatest curses of colonialism," Bishop explained in his June 1983 speech in New York City, "was that they divided the region according to different metropolitan centers. They taught us different languages. And then they made a great play of the fact that you are Dutch-speaking, you are Spanish-speaking, you are French-speaking, and, more recently, you are American-speaking.

"And based on this linguistic nonsense," Bishop said, "they taught us to hate each other. . . ."

"We see it therefore as one of our historic duties and responsibilities," Bishop told the New York audience, "to pull down these artificial barriers of colonialism and to develop that oneness and unity that we nearly lost."[173]

BOTH FIDEL CASTRO and Maurice Bishop based their political strategies on the recognition that revolutions are made by the working people and can survive and advance only with their growing class consciousness and direct involvement in the political life of their country and of the world.

Coard's apologists are dead wrong in seeking to portray Bishop as solely a mass leader and agitator, while Coard excelled at party and organizational work. Maurice Bishop *was* a party builder. The New Jewel Movement that led the March 1979 revolution was built around the political course that he advocated. Following that victory, Bishop's political leadership helped create the broad popular base among Grenada's workers and farmers on which a mass communist party could have been constructed.

Bernard Coard didn't build a party. He maintained a tiny secret faction that *blocked* the transformation of the

NJM into a mass revolutionary party. Bishop and Coard had opposite organizational conceptions, flowing from their conflicting political perspectives.

Contrast what happened to the New Jewel Movement in the years following the March 13, 1979, victory to the course of the Sandinista National Liberation Front after the triumph over Somoza on July 19, 1979.

The FSLN recognized that the establishment of a workers' and peasants' government in Nicaragua created both the opportunity and need "to make qualitative organizational changes in order to carry out the revolutionary changes required in all aspects of society: economic, social and military."[174] The FSLN began reaching out after July 1979 to draw into its ranks those who were now leading other Nicaraguan working people on myriad fronts to defend and advance the revolutionary process. The FSLN reached out to those who were being tested in struggle and looked to for political guidance by other working people.

FSLN cadres are initiated into membership at public assemblies of those they work alongside of in factories, on the farms, in the Sandinista army and militia, in the schools, and working-class neighborhoods. At a meeting in August 1986 launching several months of celebrations of the FSLN's twenty-fifth anniversary, Commander Carlos Nuñez announced a recruitment drive aimed at taking "a qualitative leap forward" for the FSLN. He explained that the organization "will affirm its class character with the workers, poor peasants, and other sectors and demand of all its members the qualities characteristic of the working class: selflessness in our work, a combative disposition, fraternity, initiative. . . ."[175]

This is the political course that Maurice Bishop set out on during the Grenada revolution. In his radio speech to the Grenadian people at the opening of 1983, Bishop emphasized that

> our people must develop in the new year a mental grasp of the true nature of the international capitalist crisis which is holding back the progress of our revolution and the development of all poor countries in the world. . . . They must see clearly the link between politics and economics, between imperialist exploitation and persistent poverty, between the mad buildup of arms by imperialism and the economic crisis.
>
> With their political consciousness raised and broadened our people will better understand the necessity to join and strengthen those mass organizations and trade unions that already exist.
>
> Political education will help to identify from the ranks of our working people the future leaders of the revolution, and it will help to prepare the working class to assume its historic role of transforming Grenada from backwardness and dependency to genuine economic independence.[176]

It was along these lines that Maurice Bishop sought to build a revolutionary party of Grenada's working people throughout the four-and-a-half years of the workers' and farmers' government. And it was to the mobilized workers and farmers of Grenada that Bishop turned on October 19, 1983, to restore the revolutionary government that Coard had overthrown.

Coard and his supporters showed their fear of and contempt for Grenada's working people that day—firing on them, murdering their leaders, and then imposing a round-the-clock, shoot-to-kill curfew on the entire population. Those political crimes were the culmination of the political course carried out by Coard throughout the history of the New Jewel Movement and the Grenada revolution.

Maurice Bishop and Bernard Coard personified two irreconcilable political courses for the Grenada revolution. Bishop is part of a revolutionary continuity that encompasses the Bolshevik Party led by Lenin, the Cuban Communist Party under the leadership of Fidel Castro, and the leadership of the Sandinista National Liberation Front. Coard shares the heritage of Stalin, Mao, Escalante, Pol Pot, Carpio, and the practitioners of the "Afghanistan solution."

Maurice Bishop's uncompromising refusal to back off from a revolutionary course made it inevitable that Coard would not stop short of house arrest and murder. Those are the methods that Stalin, Mao, Pol Pot, and Carpio have used. Had Escalante's faction triumphed, he would have employed such repressive measures against Fidel Castro and other Cuban revolutionaries.

What was not inevitable in Grenada, however, was the outcome. Bishop and his supporters were correct to lead a popular insurrection on October 19. That was the only chance to restore the revolutionary government to power.

THE COARD FACTION portrayed itself as the proletarian communist current inside the New Jewel Movement. But the opposite was the case. Bernard Coard's political course was based on a rejection in practice of what Lenin called "one of the most profound and at the same time most simple and comprehensible precepts of Marxism."

"The greater the scope and extent of historical events,"

Lenin said in 1920, "the greater is the number of people participating in them, and, contrariwise, the more profound the change we wish to bring about, the more must we rouse an interest and an intelligent attitude toward it, and convince more millions and tens of millions of people that it is necessary.

"In the final analysis," Lenin said, "the reason our revolution has left all other revolutions far behind is that . . . it has aroused tens of millions of people, formerly uninterested in state development, to take an active part in the work of building the state."[177]

That is the communist perspective that Maurice Bishop died fighting to advance.

NOTES

1. The best guide to Maurice Bishop's political legacy is the collection of his speeches published in Bruce Marcus and Michael Taber, eds., *Maurice Bishop Speaks: The Grenada Revolution 1979–83* (New York: Pathfinder Press, 1983). All page references for it in the notes that follow are to the 2011 printing.

2. Gen. Hudson Austin, transcript of statement broadcast over Radio Free Grenada, October 19, 1983.

3. Main Political Department of the People's Revolutionary Armed Forces, "Revolutionary Soldiers and Men of the People's Revolutionary Armed Forces," October 19, 1983.

This document and many others cited in this article are part of the enormous quantity of party, government, and personal files stolen by U.S. occupation forces following the invasion of Grenada. A tiny portion of these documents were released to the media in several batches in late 1983 and early 1984. Many of these were subsequently photographically reproduced in a large U.S. government collection: *Grenada Documents: An Overview and Selection* (Washington, D.C.: Department of State and

Department of Defense, September 1984). A vast number of other stolen documents are stored in Washington, D.C. and can be read at the National Archives. A 533-page listing of the available documents can be ordered for $20 by writing: National Archives, Machine-readable Branch, Washington, D.C. 20408. The minutes and other records that are part of these files have been used as sources by writers on all sides of the political disputes in the New Jewel Movement.

The most complete record of the New Jewel Movement and of the People's Revolutionary Government of Grenada was contained in Maurice Bishop's personal files, all of which were seized by the U.S. invaders. Bishop's family has demanded that the U.S. government return this stolen personal property, but Washington has refused to do so. The Maurice Bishop Patriotic Movement in Grenada has pointed out that Washington's theft of this enormous archive is a violation of the country's national sovereignty and has demanded that it be returned to Grenadian soil and made available to the people of that country.

In addition, among the many violations of democratic rights during last year's trial of Bernard Coard and seventeen others in the U.S.-imposed court in Grenada, the defendants were denied access to documents from this archive that they wanted to consult and introduce into evidence.

4. Main Political Department of the People's Revolutionary Armed Forces, "Their Heroism is an Example for Us," October 20, 1983.

5. Bernard Coard, statement from the dock at 1986 trial, August 13–20, 1986. This has been reproduced in the United States by the *Friends for Jamaica Caribbean Newsletter* and all page numbers cited hereafter refer to this edition.

6. Chief among these apologists in the United States are former U.S. Attorney General Ramsey Clark and Doris Kitson, editor of the *Friends for Jamaica Caribbean Newsletter*. In Britain, one of Coard's most outspoken political supporters is Richard Hart; Hart, a Jamaican by birth, was attorney general

of Grenada in October 1983. The editors of the British daily *Morning Star,* reflecting the views of one wing of the Communist Party of Great Britain, have also remained firm political backers of the Coard faction. Leaders of a few organizations in the English-speaking Caribbean have also lined up politically alongside Coard; among the most prominent of these have been spokespeople for the Workers Party of Jamaica such as its general secretary, Trevor Munroe.

7. Coard, statement from the dock, pp. 25–26.

8. Jeffrey M. Elliot and Mervyn M. Dymally, *Fidel Castro: Nothing Can Stop the Course of History* (New York: Pathfinder Press, 1986), pp. 144, 147; see also "Fidel Castro on the Events in Grenada," in *Maurice Bishop Speaks,* p. 549.

9. Bishop, "Three Years of the Grenada Revolution," in *Maurice Bishop Speaks,* p. 448.

10. Bishop, "The Fighting Example of Sandino Lives!" in *Maurice Bishop Speaks,* p. 173.

11. Bishop, "Imperialism Is Not Invincible," in *Maurice Bishop Speaks,* p. 147.

12. Bishop, "Two Years of the Grenada Revolution," in *Maurice Bishop Speaks,* p. 263.

13. Bishop, "Three Years of the Grenada Revolution," in *Maurice Bishop Speaks,* p. 464.

14. Elliot and Dymally, *Fidel Castro,* pp. 145–46.

15. Richard Hart, "Introduction," in Chris Searle, ed., *In Nobody's Backyard: Maurice Bishop's Speeches, 1979–1983; A Memorial Volume,* (London: Zed Books Ltd., 1984), p. xxi.

16. Coard, statement from the dock, p. 6.

17. "Extraordinary Meeting of the Central Committee of the NJM, 14–16 September, 1983," in *Grenada Documents,* pp. 112:44, 112:45. The September 17 session was scheduled during this meeting and the minutes of it are included in this document.

18. Grenada and other Caribbean islands are different from most South Pacific islands in this respect, as are the character and tasks of revolutions in these two parts of the world. This

reflects a more general reality in the degree of capitalist development throughout Latin America and the Caribbean in comparison to many countries in Asia and Africa.

Manuel Piñeiro, a member of the Cuban Communist Party's Central Committee, commented on this broader question in an April 1982 speech translated and printed under the tide "Imperialism and Revolution in Latin America and the Caribbean" in a previous issue of *New International.* Piñeiro said:

"The revolutions for national and social liberation in Latin America and the Caribbean . . . embody characteristics that are significant in relation to the present liberation process in Africa and Asia. Our revolutions, like those of Africa and Asia, are also advancing along the world historical path that began in October 1917. They form part of the three underdeveloped continents that are confronting imperialism. But the material premises created by capitalist domination in our countries (a level of development that on average is superior to that of Asia and Africa) have created better conditions for a more intense and radical advance of our revolutions. These revolutions, in their dialectical course, take on tasks of a democratic, popular, and anti-imperialist content in their first stage. As they develop, they tend to carry out clearly socialist tasks—as an indissoluble part of their own process and in accordance with their general historical character." (*New International* 1:3 [1984], pp. 104–5.)

19. "Forward to Socialism and Final Victory," *New Jewel,* March 11, 1983.

20. "Grenada's Revolution: an Interview with Bernard Coard," *Race and Class* XXI:2 (1979).

21. "Bishop Trial Report," *The Nation* (Barbados), December 1986.

22. Whiteman, Radix, and Louison were central leaders of the popular uprising on October 19 that liberated Bishop from house arrest and sought to reverse Coard's counterrevolutionary coup. Whiteman and Creft were murdered along

with Bishop that day. Radix and Louison were imprisoned but survived Coard's days of terror. They are currently leaders of the Maurice Bishop Patriotic Movement (MBPM) in Grenada. Austin and Strachan were accomplices in Coard's coup.

23. For a short popular history of the New Jewel Movement by a Cuban journalist, see Arnaldo Hutchinson, "The Long Road to Freedom," in *Maurice Bishop Speaks,* pp. 70–90.

24. Bishop, "The Struggle for Democracy and Against Imperialism in Grenada," in *Maurice Bishop Speaks,* p. 100.

25. "Manifesto of the New Jewel Movement for Power to the People and for Achieving Real Independence for Grenada, Carriacou, Petit Martinique and the Grenadian Grenadines (1973)," in Tony Martin, ed., *In Nobody's Backyard: The Grenada Revolution in its Own Words—Volume I: the Revolution at Home* (Dover, Mass.: The Majority Press, 1983), pp. 3–46.

26. *George Louison and Kendrick Radix discuss . . . Internal Events Leading to the U.S. Invasion of Grenada,* (New York: Grenada Foundation, Inc., 1984), p. 7.

27. All of these early OREL cadres emerged as leading participants in Coard's counterrevolutionary coup in October 1983.

28. June 1984 interview with OREL leader Basil Gahagan, cited in Tony Thorndike, *Grenada: Politics, Economics and Society* (London: Frances Pinter Publishers, 1985), p. 50.

29. Report by Ewart Layne for the NJM Central Committee to the September 25 membership meeting.

In a 1977 pamphlet Trevor Munroe, Coard's close political collaborator in Jamaica, spoke of "the New Jewel Movement, which has a Marxist wing." See Trevor Munroe, *The Marxist 'Left' in Jamaica: 1940–1950* (Mona, Jamaica: University of West Indies, Institute of Social and Economic Research, 1977), p. 71.

30. Kendrick Radix and George Louison, interview with author, St. George's, Grenada, March 29, 1985.

31. Ibid.

32. Bishop recalled this conflict during the September 14–16, 1983, meeting of the Central Committee, whose ma-

jority was by then held by Coard's backers. According to the minutes of that meeting, Bishop pointed out that when Coard was accused of "wanting to grab power," Bishop had opposed Coard's expulsion.

33. Two of Coard's political supporters—Trevor Munroe and Richard Hart—have publicly stated, after Bishop's murder, that Bishop voted against the proposal to carry out the March 13 insurrection. See, Trevor Munroe, *Grenada: Revolution, Counter-revolution* (Kingston, Jamaica: Vanguard Publishers, 1983), pp. 133–34; and Hart "Introduction," in Searle, ed., *In Nobody's Backyard,* p. xxiii. Not a single piece of evidence has ever been presented by Hart or Munroe to back up this assertion.

In my March 1985 interview with Kendrick Radix he emphasized that this story is not true. Radix labelled it "a story that has been put about by Bernard Coard that he and his handful of people made the Grenada revolution. That is totally and completely untrue."

34. Bishop's opposition to shutting down the *Torchlight* remained internal to the New Jewel Movement at the time; references to these differences appear in subsequent Central Committee and Political Bureau minutes cited later in this article.

35. Lyden Ramdhanny, interview with author, Grenville, Grenada, March 27, 1985. Ramdhanny was a supporter of the revolution and PRG cabinet member who did not belong to the NJM. Shortly after the March 1979 victory, Ramdhanny—a member of a leading Grenadian capitalist family and former president of the Grenada Chamber of Commerce—had been asked by the *Torchlight*'s publishers to join its board of directors. With Bishop's encouragement, Ramdhanny accepted. He placed the motion on the floor at the *Torchlight* shareholders' meeting to invite Bishop to address the meeting. Ramdhanny is currently a supporter in Grenada of the Maurice Bishop Patriotic Movement.

36. Bishop, "Organize to Fight Destabilization (Radio Free

Grenada broadcast, May 8, 1979)," in Searle, ed., *In Nobody's Backyard,* p. 19.

37. See for example, Bishop, "Beat Back Destabilizers (Radio Free Grenada broadcast, September 18, 1979)," in Searle, ed., *In Nobody's Backyard,* p. 28.

38. Coard's comment on the *Torchlight* events at a meeting of the NJM Political Bureau two years later; see Minutes of Political Bureau, June 24, 1981.

39. "Out the Torchlight," *Free West Indian,* October 20, 1979.

40. Thirty-seven detainees were released from prison in December 1979, including some of those initially picked up in connection with the arms cache and assassination plot. No formal charges were brought until July 1981, when two of those arrested—Teddy Victor and Wilton De Raviniere—were arraigned under the Terrorism Law. Others arrested in the fall of 1979 were held without charges until their release in 1981 and 1982.

41. In November 1982 four people arrested in connection with the bombing were convicted and sentenced to death; the sentences had not been carried out in October 1983. One defendant was acquitted.

42. Radix and Louison, interview with author.

43. Ramdhanny, interview with author. This incident is also referred to briefly in Thorndike, *Grenada: Politics, Economics and Society,* p. 73. Thorndike's reference is based on an interview with Barbadian political activist Bobby Clarke.

44. "Interview with George Louison," *Intercontinental Press* (April 16, 1984), p. 217.

45. Bishop, "Freedom of Press and Imperialist Destabilization," *Maurice Bishop Speaks,* pp. 296–308.

46. "Minutes of Political Bureau, Meeting on Wednesday, 24th June, 1981," in *Grenada Documents,* pp. 57:1–57:2.

47. "Minutes of Central Committee Meeting Held on Wednesday, 24th June, 1981," in *Grenada Documents,* pp. 97:1–97:2.

48. According to a December 1982 report on detainees, some 100 were released over the course of that year, but there is no indication as to how many of these may have been individuals picked up in the June–July 1981 Rasta roundup. This incident raises the broader question of the NJM leadership's handling of the question of political detentions.

The PRG clearly had both the need and the right to take measures to forestall armed resistance by the ousted police and paramilitary squads of the Gairy dictatorship and to combat counterrevolutionary crimes such as the June 1980 Queens Park bombing and other terrorist acts. In the days and weeks following the March 1979 revolution, a few hundred of Gairy's cops, army officers, and members of his goon squads were picked up; only some twenty remained in prison by mid-1981.

Aspects of the PRG's detention policy, however, were unjustifiable and unnecessarily damaged the revolution's political authority and standing both at home and abroad.

The PRG's emergency Terrorism Act of 1980, for example, was explicitly modeled on the reactionary Prevention of Terrorism Act imposed by British imperialism on its colony of Northern Ireland. The article announcing the law on the front page of the *Free West Indian* explained that, "The experience of other countries has shown that in jury trials involving terrorists, the jurors lives are endangered. Therefore, as under the British law which applies to Northern Ireland, trial will be by regular High Court judges, sitting alone. . . . The report of the British Commission on Terrorist Activities in Northern Ireland in 1972 states: 'The main obstacle to dealing effectively with terrorist crime in the regular courts of justice is intimidation.' The lives of witnesses were threatened, and they were therefore afraid to come forward with evidence, or to appear in court." By publicly presenting its emergency measures as patterned on those of the British colonial oppressors, the PRG evidently sought to undercut hypocritical condemnations by London and other imperialist governments. The political price, however, was identification of its own justice system with London's bloody and arbitrary repression of freedom fighters in Northern Ireland—an oppressive policy hated by workers and farmers around the world.

Bishop commented on the PRG's preventive detention policy in his speech on the "Line of March of the Party" to the NJM membership in the fall of 1982. "Consider how people get detained in this country," Bishop said. "We don't go and call for no votes. You get detained when I sign an order after discussing it with the National Security Committee of the Party, or with a higher Party body. Once I sign it—like it or don't like it—it's up the hill for them."

Nonetheless, Bishop had begun to take steps more than a year earlier to deal with evident problems being created for the revolution by its detention policy and the slowness in holding trials of those detained. Lyden Ramdhanny, in the March 1985 interview, said that he had expressed concerns to Bishop "over the number of detainees that we were holding."

In mid-1981, Bishop established a special committee to review the detainee situation and bring in recommendations. Progress in dealing with this problem, however, was clearly set back by the detention without charges of sixty-one Rastas just as the review process was getting under way.

A September 1981 report to Bishop recommended the release of nearly fifty detainees:

• nineteen being held for nonpolitical crimes such as burglary;

• nineteen held since "the early stages of the revolution" but for whom there was not "sufficient evidence to bring charges successfully against them in the Courts"; and

• ten "for alleged involvement in the November 1979 plot" but on whom there was "absolutely no evidence of an incriminating nature available and it is therefore difficult to lay charges against them."

An article in the January 9, 1982, issue of the *Free West Indian* reported on the establishment of the special committee in the course of announcing the release of twenty-four detainees. According to the article, committee member Miles Fitzpatrick explained that "the PRG has been reviewing the position of the detainees, both as a group and individually," and that "previously there were problems in quickly bringing charges against the detainees," but that "this problem has now been solved and since June 1981, some 40 detainees have been formally charged."

Over the course of 1982, some 100 detainees were released, according to a year-end report to Bishop that cited the "unavailability of sufficient evidence for successful prosecution" in these cases. An additional 31 had been detained in 1982. There were some 118 detainees in all as of the beginning of 1983.

Clearly, scores of Grenadians were jailed for indefinite periods by the PRG for no reason other than their political views. Some were released after a number of months or years, but others were not.

The Nicaraguan government presents a striking contrast in this regard. As much as the U.S. government and Nicaraguan counterrevolutionaries have searched for issues to discredit the Sandinista-led government, they have never been able to make a credible case that political opponents of the regime, on the right or the ultraleft, disappear from their homes and languish in Nicaraguan prisons without charges and trials. During the first year of the revolution, certain ultraleft opponents of the government were detained for short periods of time, but all were released and such arrests have not been repeated. Apparently the Sandinistas concluded that these measures had been in error.

In subsequent years, those arrested and jailed in Nicaragua have been suspected on solid grounds of having participated in illegal acts against the people and government of the country. They have been tried and sentenced or released on the basis of the evidence. This policy has been adhered to despite the U.S.-backed *contra* war and despite the temporary suspension of the right of habeas corpus under the State of

Emergency declared by the government last year. Inevitable individual abuses by police or other government officials in this regard have been remedied and those who committed them have been disciplined.

49. The NJM's Workers Committee was responsible for the party's activity in the trade unions and among workers.

50. Coard was a past master at the use of the Stalinist practice of individual "criticism and self-criticism" to advance the goals of his secret faction within the NJM leadership. To justify this practice, Coard supporter Ewart Layne cited the following passage from Lenin at a September 1983 meeting of the NJM membership:

"A political party's attitude towards its own mistakes is one of the most important and surest ways of judging how earnest the party is and how it fulfills *in practice* its obligations towards its *class* and the *working people.* Frankly acknowledging a mistake, ascertaining the reason for it, analysing the conditions that have led up to it, and thrashing out the means of its rectification—that is . . . how it should perform its duties; and how it should educate and train its *class* and then the *masses.*" [The quotation is from Lenin's 1920 article, "'Left Wing' Communism—An Infantile Disorder," in Lenin, *Collected Works,* vol. 31, p. 57.)

Contrary to the misuse to which Layne put this quotation, however, Lenin's view of the need for a revolutionary workers' party to be self-critical—as shown by this passage itself—had nothing to do with confessions of personal failure and shortcomings by individual members at party meetings, followed by penance (and, if you're lucky, by absolution). To the contrary, Lenin was talking about the party's *collective* responsibility to assess its errors, correct them, and go forward on that basis. This obviously also requires the capacity of individual members and leaders to function objectively in assessing and correcting their own mistakes. Within that framework, all revolutionaries are responsible for their conduct and are held accountable by the party to function in a loyal and disciplined manner.

The Bolshevik Party under Lenin's leadership never had this kind of institution of personal "criticism and self-criticism." The institutionalized practice of confessional "criticism and self-criticism" was begun under Stalin as one method to purge those in the party who resisted his headlong flight from Lenin's internationalist and communist course, and was further honed by Mao Zedong. It is the method of a self-perpetuating leadership cut off from democratic accountability to the membership and to the masses of working people.

This kind of "criticism and self-criticism" was put to similar uses by Coard's faction in the New Jewel Movement. Coard's Organising Committee and its subcommittee, the Discipline Committee, chaired by Selwyn Strachan, oversaw this practice. Supporters of Coard's faction sometimes acknowledged mild and innocuous failings, occasionally being subjected to a slap on the wrist. Meanwhile, others in the membership and leadership were mercilessly "criticized," bullied into self-deprecation, and then meted out harsh penalties, including expulsion from party bodies.

51. "Central Committee Minutes Held on 22nd July, 1981," in *Grenada Documents,* p. 99:3.

52. "Minutes of the Political Bureau Meeting Held on Wednesday, 23rd Sept. 1981," in *Grenada Documents,* p. 67:1. See also Coard's reference back to this dispute at the September 17, 1983, meeting of the NJM Central Committee. ("Extraordinary Meeting," in *Grenada Documents,* p. 112:43.) Also, Einstein Louison, interview with author, April 5, 1987.

53. Three other OREL cadres—Basil Gahagan, Leon Cornwall, and Chris Stroude—had been advanced to the rank of major by 1983, along with others who had been drawn into the Coard faction, such as Tan Bartholomew, Ian St. Bernard, and Keith Roberts. In October 1983 the only top PRA officer who did not support Coard's coup was Maj. Einstein Louison. He was placed in detention by the Coard faction on October 12 when he refused to go along with plans for Bishop's house arrest.

54. Don Rojas, interview with author, May 1987.

55. "Meeting of the Central Committee of the New Jewel Movement Held on the 21st April 1982," in *Grenada Documents,* p. 102:7.

56. Ibid., p. 102:8.

57. "Line of March for the Party, presented by Comrade Maurice Bishop, chairman, Central Committee, to General Meeting of Party on Monday 13th September 1982," in *Grenada Documents,* pp. 1:1–1:49.

58. Ibid., p. 1:2

59. Ibid., pp. 1:10–1:11.

60. Ibid., p. 1:9

61. Ibid., pp. 1:33–1:34.

62. Ibid., p. 1:37.

63. Ibid., p. 1:48.

64. Thorndike, *Grenada: Politics, Economics and Society,* p. 79.

65. "Line of March for the Party," in *Grenada Documents,* p. 1:42.

66. *George Louison and Kendrick Radix discuss,* p. 32; "Louison in London," *Grenada Update* 4 (Spring 1985), p. 6.

67. Don Rojas, "Open Letter on the Sixth Anniversary of the Grenada Revolution," 1985. The open letter was published widely. In the Caribbean it was serialized in *The Vanguard,* newspaper of the Oilfields Workers' Trade Union of Trinidad and Tobago, beginning in the April 26, 1985 issue. In the United States it was run, among other places, in the March 20 issue of *The City Sun,* the March 27 issue of the *Guardian,* and the April 1 issue of *Intercontinental Press.* In Britian it was run in the November 1986 *New Beacon Review.*

68. George Louison, interview with author, March 29, 1985, St. George's, Grenada.

69. In the Communist Party (Bolshevik) in Soviet Russia, for example, the percentage of peasants rose from 7.5 percent at the time of the revolution in 1917 to just over 25 percent by 1921–22. (Marcel Leibman, *Leninism Under Lenin* [London:

Merlin Press, 1980], p. 304.)

70. This is an entirely different question from the need for separate mass organizations of urban and rural wage workers (trade unions) and of farmers (including separate organizations for the most exploited farmers).

71. George Louison, interview with author.

72. Lenin, *Collected Works* (Moscow: Progress Publishers, 1966) vol. 31, pp. 152–164. See also the amended version adopted by the congress in *Second Congress of the Communist International* (London: New Park, 1977), vol. 2, pp. 286–95.

73. Lenin, *Collected Works,* vol. 31, p. 250.

74. Ibid., p. 249.

75. "Central Committee Minutes Held on 22nd July, 1981," in *Grenada Documents,* pp. 99:1–99:2. Minutes of the NJM's September 1983 Central Committee meeting record Ewart Layne's assertion that "in practice [Coard] has been giving ideological and organisational leadership, and elaborating strategy and tactics . . . e.g. the land question."

76. "Minutes of Central Committee Meeting Held on Wednesday, 19th August, 1981," in *Grenada Documents,* pp. 100:1, 100:3.

77. "Central Committee Resolution on Agriculture," January 1983.

78. Not all property is capital. In the *Communist Manifesto,* Marx and Engels contrast the "hard-won, self-acquired, self-earned property" of "the petty artisan and of the small peasant" to "capital, *i.e.,* that kind of property which exploits wage-labour, and which cannot increase except upon condition of begetting a new supply of wage-labour for fresh exploitation." Karl Marx and Frederick Engels, *Selected Works* (Moscow: Progress Publishers, 1977), vol. 1, pp. 120–21.

79. All quotations are from "Minutes of Extra-Ordinary Meeting of the Central Committee of NJM From Tuesday 12th–Friday 15th October, 1982," in *Grenada Documents,* pp. 105:1–105:9.

80. Just prior to this meeting of the Central Committee, in

September 1982, two correspondents for the English-language magazine *Intercontinental Press*—Flax Hermes and Baxter Smith—were ordered to leave the island by the PRG's immigration authorities. *Intercontinental Press* was the English-language publication that, from 1979, had carried the most regular news coverage on the revolution and its gains, including the greatest number of interviews with NJM and PRG leaders.

Besides covering the revolution for *Intercontinental Press,* Smith and Hermes had worked as volunteer construction laborers at the international airport site. Despite this work in solidarity with the revolution, they were denied extensions of their visas and ordered to leave the island without any explanation. They were once again told to leave the island after being there only a few days when they returned to cover the first congress of the National Women's Organisation in early December.

After the destruction of the revolution, reports from supporters of both Bishop and Coard revealed that members of the Coard faction had frequently engaged in "Trotskyist-baiting," especially of the U.S. Socialist Workers Party and publications edited by SWP leaders. This fact sheds additional light on the political motives behind the expulsion of the *Intercontinental Press* correspondents, an action that seemed inexplicable at the time.

81. See Bishop, "Maurice Bishop Speaks to U.S. Working People," in *Maurice Bishop Speaks,* pp. 486–523.

82. "Minutes of Emergency Meeting of N.J.M. Central Committee Dated 26th August, 1983," in *Grenada Documents,* pp. 111:1–111:7.

83. Bishop had proposed the following major agenda items: Feedback from members, work committees, and masses; Evaluation of the Central Committee's collective work; Evaluation of the Central Committee members' individual work; Implementation of past Central Committee decisions (regional work, literacy program, militia); and Proposed new responsibilities, tasks, and meeting schedule of the Central Committee.

The agenda and the quotations from this meeting given below are from "Extraordinary Meeting of the Central Committee NJM, 14–16 September, 1983," in *Grenada Documents,* pp. 112:1–112:47.

84. These statements by James and other NJM Central Committee members refute Bernard Coard's shameless lie in his August 1986 trial speech that George Louison was "the only CC member that said Maurice Bishop is the number one problem."

85. "Interview with George Louison," *Intercontinental Press* (April 16, 1984), p. 210.

86. This and the quotations from the September 17 meeting given below are from "Extraordinary Meeting of the Central Committee NJM, 14–16 September, 1983," in *Grenada Documents,* pp. 112:38–112:47.

87. "Extraordinary General Meeting of Full Members, Sunday 25th of September," in *Grenada Documents,* p. 113:9.

88. Ibid., p. 113:12.

89. Report by Ewart Layne for the NJM Central Committee to the September 25 membership meeting, p. 10.

90. Dymally and Elliot, *Fidel Castro,* pp. 143, 145, 154.

91. "Extraordinary General Meeting," in *Grenada Documents,* p. 113:5.

92. "Extraordinary Meeting of Full Members of the NJM," in *Caribbean Review* 12:4 (Fall 1986), p. 58.

93. At an October 13 NJM membership meeting, Bishop is recorded as saying that at the September 25 meeting "he was at high emotion when he accepted the position [on 'joint leadership']. . . . He was concerned with the operationalising of ['joint leadership'] but because of the G[eneral] M[embership] position he voted for the resolution. He had made up his mind to go along." (Account from handwritten notes by a participant in the October 13, 1983, NJM membership meeting.)

94. Munroe reported this trip in October 1983 and his remarks were reprinted in the November 11, 1983, issue of the WPJ's newspaper, *Struggle.* Munroe said that on Septem-

ber 23 he received two telephone calls: "One from Comrade Bernard saying take the next flight, we have serious problems that we need to discuss with you and get your opinion. And the other from Comrade Maurice in which he also asked me to come. I said to Maurice, look, if the thing is so serious and you can't tell me on the phone, send your private plane up to Barbados for me so that I could get in on Sunday [September 25]. He agreed.

"For reasons which are still not clear to me, the plane did not come, and I got into Grenada on the morning of Monday the 26th, at the very same time that Maurice was leaving for Hungary and Czechoslovakia. So that nobody feels it more than me when I did not have a chance to speak with him fully. If I had gotten in Sunday night it would have been possible, the Monday morning it was not possible."

Munroe said that during the two days he was there in Bishop's absence, he looked into "the full extent of the crisis" in the NJM and gave "my advice on how the crisis was to be solved." He made suggestions "to overcome the weaknesses that were identified in Comrade Maurice which he agreed with, that he wasn't sufficiently organised in terms of keeping appointments and fulfilling the work and the tasks that were set. On the other hand, I proposed that as Bernard's weakness was insufficient contact with the ordinary people, some of the work in relation to visiting work centers he should also do."

Also recounted in Munroe's December 1983 pamphlet, *Grenada: Revolution, Counter-revolution,* pp. 100–102.

95. "Interview with George Louison," *Intercontinental Press* (April 16, 1984), pp. 211–12.

96. From handwritten notes by a participant in the October 13, 1983, NJM membership meeting; released with captured NJM minutes and other materials by the U.S. government. This document corresponds to accounts of the meeting by others who attended it, including George Louison, Vincent Noel, and Don Rojas.

97. Vincent Noel letter, "Comrades of the Central Committee and Party," October 17, 1983. Noel wrote this letter—two days prior to being murdered—to protest being placed under house arrest by the Coard faction. Much valuable information about the final weeks of the Grenada revolution is contained in Noel's letter.

98. Ibid., p. 1.

99. George Louison, quoted in "Introduction," in *Maurice Bishop Speaks,* p. 50; also "Interview with George Louison," *Intercontinental Press,* April 16, 1984, p. 212. Bishop referred to this ominous step in his remarks to the October 13 general meeting of the NJM membership.

100. "Resolution of the People's Revolutionary Armed Forces Branch of the New Jewel Movement," October 12, 1983.

101. "Statement by the Cuban Government and the Cuban Communist Party," in *Maurice Bishop Speaks,* p. 525.

102. Vincent Noel letter, p. 3.

103. Ibid. Noel had been allowed by Coard's guards to visit Bishop on October 13 following Bishop's house arrest. As he left Bishop's home, however, Noel himself was seized by the guards and taken to his home where he was placed under detention.

104. Vincent Noel letter, p. 9.

105. Coard, statement from the dock, pp. 49, 92. Coard and his supporters now flatly deny that Bishop was ever placed under house arrest. At a February 1987 meeting in New York City, for example, Weldon Brewer—law partner to Ramsey Clark—insisted that Bishop had simply been placed under "protective custody" for his own safety. ("New York Meeting Covers Up Truth About Grenada," by Steve Clark, *Militant,* February 20, 1987.) Ramsey Clark himself, in a November 1986 statement, refers euphemistically to "the temporary confinement to quarters of [Grenada's] popular Prime Minister." ("Statement of Ramsey Clark, former U.S. Attorney General, on the Illegal Trial of the Grenada 18, November 24, 1986.")

106. This and the quotations below are from the previously cited handwritten notes by a participant in the October 13,

1983, NJM membership meeting.

107. "Extraordinary General Meeting," in *Caribbean Review*, p. 53. Cornwall's model of a political leader seems to have leaned more toward Trevor Munroe of the Workers Party of Jamaica than Maurice Bishop or Fidel Castro. Grenadian students living in Cuba at the time report that Cornwall had a picture of Munroe on his desk in the PRG's Havana embassy.

108. "Interview with George Louison," *Intercontinental Press*, April 16, 1987, p. 212.

109. Cited in "Introduction," in *Maurice Bishop Speaks*, p. 50.

110. Vincent Noel letter, p. 5.

111. The Cuban government was providing substantial assistance to Grenada. The largest project was the new international airport at Point Salines. The Cuban government had also sent doctors and dentists to Grenada, provided scholarships for Grenadian students to attend Cuban universities, and aided the revolution in numerous other ways.

112. Fidel Castro, "A Miserable Piece of Slander," *Intercontinental Press*, April 16, 1984, p. 214.

113. Elliot and Dymally, *Fidel Castro*, pp. 156–57.

114. "Interview with George Louison," *Intercontinental Press*, April 16, 1984, p. 213.

115. Hart, "Introduction," in Searle, ed., *In Nobody's Backyard*, p. xxxvi; Trevor Munroe's report to the WPJ's Third Congress, December 1984.

116. "NJM (Grenada): An Appeal to the International Community," circulated by the London Committee for Human Rights in Grenada.

117. *George Louison and Kendrick Radix discuss*, pp. 11–12.

118. Cited in "Introduction," in *Maurice Bishop Speaks*, p. 53.

119. Cited in "Introduction," in *Maurice Bishop Speaks*, pp. 53–54.

120. Cited in Gordon Lewis, *Grenada: The Jewel Despoiled* (Bal-

timore: The Johns Hopkins University Press, 1987), pp. 50–51.

121. Coard, statement from the dock, p. 20.

122. Cited in *Grenada: Whose Freedom?* (London: Latin America Bureau, 1984), p. 74. Also Hugh O'Shaughnessy, *Grenada: Revolution, Invasion and Aftermath* (London: Sphere Books, 1984), pp. 130–31.

Coard also insisted that Bishop acknowledge the "subordination of the state to the party." This is a revealing insight into Coard's perversion of Leninism. Coard viewed the party as a tight apparatus to run the state from the top down. Bishop, on the other hand, saw the party as a growing political vanguard of the workers and farmers to *lead* the masses in deepening *their* participation in, and assuming greater control over, the administration of all state bodies and agencies. Coard demanded the subservience of the state to the party. Bishop wanted the subservience of the state to the working people, led by a vanguard communist party that drew them into political activity and helped raise their political consciousness. The difference is fundamental.

123. Cited in "Introduction," in *Maurice Bishop Speaks,* pp. 54–55. Rojas has presented this account on many occasions. Also see "Behind the Revolution's Overthrow," *Intercontinental Press,* December 26, 1983; and "Open letter by Don Rojas on Slander Campaign," printed among other places in the United States and the Caribbean in the *City Sun,* December 3–9, 1986; *Carib News,* December 9, 1986; *Guardian,* December 3, 1986; *Militant,* December 12, 1986; *The News* (Aruba), December 8, 1986; and *The Outlet* (Antigua), December 19, 1986.

Coard in his August 1986 statement from the dock makes much of the presence in the crowd on October 19 of some individuals carrying anticommunist placards, suggesting that this "proves" CIA instigation of the uprising that day. Coard himself acknowledges, however, that Vincent Noel and others in the leadership of the protest were outraged by these posters and had them removed.

George Louison has correctly placed responsibility on the

Coard faction for opening the door in 1983 to a revival of anticommunist agitation in Grenada. "Through their ultraleftism," Louison said in a 1984 interview, "they whipped up the worst anticommunist sentiments in the country. Whatever sentiments of anticommunism have emerged, I think the Coard clique has to take full responsibility for them. American propaganda has further reinforced that.

"People were going around describing themselves as the hardest communists, Ventour and others were going around saying that Maurice Bishop was a petty-bourgeois who cannot bear Marxism. . . . That created grave problems among the people, and affected their consciousness. How could you murder the leader of the country, how could you murder a number of people without the least warning, how could you close down the whole society and put the entire nation under house arrest . . . and then turn around and say you are doing it in the name of an ideology to benefit the people." ("Interview with George Louison," *Intercontinental Press,* April 16, 1984, p. 215.)

124. Interview with Sylvia Belmar in the *Trinidad Guardian,* November 12, 1983, p. 8. Belmar was with Bishop at Fort Rupert. Her account is confirmed by Peter Thomas. (Interview with Thomas in the Barbados *Sunday Sun,* November 6, 1983, p. 9.) Thomas says that Bishop also ordered the detachment to disconnect the telephone lines of Bernard Coard and others involved in the counterrevolutionary coup.

125. According to Belmar's account, when Bishop arrived at Fort Rupert he "called to the chief man up in the army who was Christopher Stroude, the major and he told him, 'Well, the masses are here and I would not like the soldiers to shoot at them. My reason for coming here, as you know Radio Free Grenada is off the air; the telephone is also off and I would like to contact my people of Grenada and the rest of the world and when I finish speaking to them, I can die.' So he then asked Christopher what he thinks: if the soldiers going to shoot at the crowd. Christopher assured him that they will not. So he

said, 'Christopher, that may be your wish, but I'm afraid they might shoot at the masses and I would not like it.'"

126. Reuters dispatch, November 10, 1983.

127. Gen. Hudson Austin, transcript of statement broadcast over Radio Free Grenada, October 19, 1983.

128. *George Louison and Kendrick Radix discuss,* pp. 35–36.

129. The enormity of these counterrevolutionary crimes explains why many in the audience at a February 1987 meeting in New York City were outraged by Ramsey Clark's statement that Bernard Coard "reminds me of Nelson Mandela." Clark said of Coard: "You look at that man and you say, 'My God, what grace and beauty'." (See Steve Clark, "New York Meeting Covers Up Truth About Grenada" the *Militant,* February 20, 1987, p. 3.)

The Grenada revolution did produce one figure whom fighters against oppression and exploitation around the world look to as comparable in political stature to Nelson Mandela. That was Maurice Bishop, whose murder was organized by Bernard Coard.

130. Coard, statement from the dock, pp. 85–86, 106.

131. Ibid., p. 25.

132. Ibid., pp. 47, 69.

133. Ibid., p. 81.

134. Ibid., p. 81.

135. Ibid., pp. 83–84.

136. The "peaceful solution" proposed by Coard has been described above.

137. Coard, statement from the dock, p. 27.

138. Ibid., pp. 42–43.

139. Ibid., p. 34.

140. "Grenada 1983: Whose Struggle?" (typescript circulated by the New York-based Friends for Jamaica), p. 35.

141. Coard, statement from the dock, pp. 37–38.

142. Caribbean News Agency dispatch, October 19, 1983.

143. Ibid.

144. Coard, statement from the dock, pp. 32, 79.

145. "Open Letter by Don Rojas on Slander Campaign," *Militant,* December 12, 1986, p. 10.

146. Cited in "New Jewel Leaders Speak to Press," *Intercontinental Press,* November 14, 1983, p. 654.

147. "Statement by the Cuban Government and Cuban Communist Party," in *Maurice Bishop Speaks,* pp. 527–28.

148. From two handwritten accounts by participants in the October 21, 1983, meeting of the NJM Central Committee.

This charge was stated publicly at the time by Coard's Jamaican apologist, Trevor Munroe. In remarks in October 1983 reported in the November 11 issue of *Struggle,* newspaper of the Workers Party of Jamaica, Munroe said: "I believe, looking back at it, that [the Cuban government and Communist Party] would have given the imperialists a signal when they said that they would be reexamining their political relations with the rulers in Grenada who followed on the killing of Bishop. . . .

"A serious mistake was made [by the Cubans]," Munroe said. "Over the three days especially the Friday and the Saturday, October 28 and 29, it was possible to send in reinforcements, but this was not done. Whereupon the American imperialists seized the opportunity and sent in their submarines by the Sunday. At this point it was impossible for the Cuban comrades to send in reinforcements.

"While mourning, mourn, but also understand that an attack is imminent," Munroe said. "Do something to reinforce those who were going to be under attack. . . . We feel that our comrades in the Cuban leadership made an error which had meant the comrades [in Grenada] have not been able to hold out longer than they have done so far." (Reprinted in Munroe, *Grenada: Revolution, Counterrevolution.*)

A year later, in his December 1984 report to the Workers Party of Jamaica's third congress, Munroe stated that the WPJ "and its leadership committed errors in relation to the Grenadian crisis—mainly the erroneous criticism of and the publication of the criticism of Cuba; and most generally, insufficient independent assessment, analysis and criticism of the NJM majority." Nonetheless, Munroe still refused to place responsibility for the destruction of the revolution clearly on the shoulders of the Coard faction, stating that "the revolution was mortally wounded by the gravest errors committed by the entire leadership of the revolutionary process."

While quick to parrot the Coard group's charges about Bishop's "one-manism," Trevor Munroe has been less inclined to root out sycophantic adulation of leaders in his own organization. The three-and-a-half page biography of Munroe at the opening of his 1983 pamphlet on the Grenada events, for example, reports that: "Trevor Munroe, the Jamaican Rhodes Scholar of 1966, represents in our country and in our region, one of the finest examples of intellectuals getting their education through the hard work and sacrifices of the working people, and putting that education and training to the service of the people and against imperialism. . . . As the [WPJ's] General Secretary, Trevor Munroe has led the Party through the twists, turns, and difficulties of our peoples' struggles."

The December 19, 1983, issue of *Struggle* featured an article headlined, "Happy Birthday Trevor." The article reported on a surprise birthday party thrown for Munroe. The article stated that, "Party Headquarters staffers, urban and rural Party organisers and individual Party members sent many birthday cards expressing warm and fraternal greetings to Comrade Trevor. 'Continue communist staunchness', 'Good health and most of all long life', 'In recognition of your commitment, devotion and selfless contribution in the interest of workers', 'To a nice and lovely person', 'looking forward to continued enjoyment of your political lectures' were just some of the sentiments expressed in these birthday cards. . . . The singing of the Internationale marked the end of Comrade Trevor's surprise party."

149. Elliot and Dymally, *Fidel Castro,* p. 160.

150. "The Truth About Cuba's Role," in *Maurice Bishop Speaks,* p. 532.

151. Ibid., p. 536.

152. Elliot and Dymally, *Fidel Castro,* p. 158.

153. Ibid., pp. 146–48.

154. Cited in Marta Harnecker, *Fidel Castro's Political Strategy: From Moncada to Victory* (New York: Pathfinder Press, 1987), p. 66. The speech was given on March 26, 1962, and is published in *Historia de la revolución cubana (Selección de discursos sobre temas historicos),* (Havana: Editora Política, 1980).

155. Ibid.

156. Fidel Castro, "Against Bureaucracy and Sectarianism," in *Selected Speeches of Fidel Castro* (New York: Pathfinder Press, 1979), p. 76.

157. Ibid., p. 60.

158. Ibid., p. 65.

159. Carlos Rafael Rodríguez, *Four Years of Agrarian Reform* (Havana: Ministry of Foreign Relations, 1963), p. 18; cited in Jack Barnes, "The Workers' and Farmers' Government in the United States," *New International* 2:1 (Spring 1985), p. 166, which describes this episode.

160. Castro, "Against Bureaucracy and Sectarianism," p. 57.

161. Ibid., p. 71.

162. Ibid., pp. 72–73.

163. Fidel Castro's December 1980 report to the Cuban Communist Party's second congress emphasized the progress in bringing more workers, more small farmers, more women, more veterans of internationalist missions into the party's membership and leadership. This "means that our Party has become more proletarian," Castro said, "and, therefore, more Marxist-Leninist and more revolutionary." (*Granma Weekly Review,* December 28, 1980; cited in *Intercontinental Press,* February 9, 1981, p. 104.)

164. Fidel Castro, speech in *Cuba Socialista* (May 1962); cited in Barnes, "The Workers' and Farmers' Government."

165. Castro, "Against Bureaucracy and Sectarianism," p. 68.

166. Fidel Castro, speech in *Cuba Socialista* (May 1962).

167. Raúl Castro, "Meeting of the Central Committee of the Communist Party of Cuba, January 24, 1968," in *Informa-*

tion from the Central Committee of the Communist Party of Cuba on Microfaction Activities (Havana: Ediciones Políticas, 1968), pp. 9–10.

168. In his January 1968 report to the Cuban CP's Central Committee, Raúl Castro said the members of the Escalante faction were "always arguing in defense of the USSR when topics such as the Middle East Crisis, relations with Latin American countries, or aid to Viet Nam were discussed." Ibid., pp. 25–26.

169. Ibid., pp. 13–14, 157.

170. Cited in "Prosecutor's speech before the Revolutionary Tribunals," in *Information from the Central Committee,* p. 153.

171. For articles by Lenin from this period, see John Riddell, ed., *Lenin's Unfinished Fight* (New York: Anchor Foundation, A Pathfinder Book, 1987).

172. "The Class Struggle in Grenada, the Caribbean, and the USA," in *Maurice Bishop Speaks,* p. 239.

173. Bishop, "Maurice Bishop Speaks to U.S. Working People," in *Maurice Bishop Speaks,* pp. 513–14.

An important advance along that road, made possible in large part by the Grenada revolution and Maurice Bishop's political contributions, was the formation in June 1984 of the Anti-Imperialist Organizations of the Caribbean and Central America at a conference in Havana. For more on this important political development in the Americas, see the "In This Issue" column preceding this article.

174. See the article by the head of the FSLN's Department of Organization, Lea Guido, "The Sandinista National Liberation Front's 25th Anniversary: At the forefront of change," *Barricada International,* November 6, 1986, p. 8.

175. Harvey McArthur, "Sandinista Party Launches Recruitment Drive," the *Militant,* October 17, 1986, p. 9.

In the Managua region, for example, 705 candidate members—most of them workers—became full members on November 7, 1986. Another layer became candidate members. All were taken into membership at public ceremonies attended by their co-workers. At the Cotexma textile plant, which employs 260 workers, 5 candidate members became full members (there were 21 candidate members in all, including 6 taken in that day); at the IMEP metal fabrication plant 15 new candidates were taken in, for a total of 2 full and 22 candidates in that factory of some 280 workers. (Cindy Jaquith, "FSLN Admits Hundreds of New Workers," the *Militant,* November 21, 1986, p. 7.)

176. Bishop, "The Year of Political and Academic Education," in *Maurice Bishop Speaks,* pp. 470–71.

177. V.I. Lenin, "The 8th All-Russia Congress of Soviets," in Lenin, *Collected Works,* vol. 31, p. 498.

New from Pathfinder!

Voices from Prison

The Cuban Five

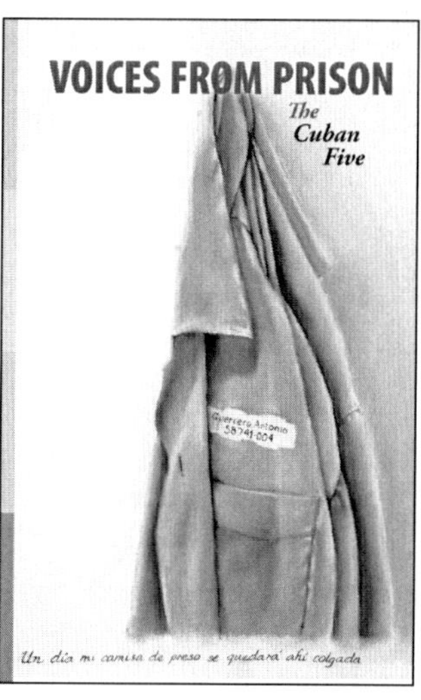

The unbending dignity, truthfulness, and integrity of the five Cubans framed up by the US government and today serving draconian sentences in federal prisons has won them the admiration and respect of prominent figures around the world and thousands of their fellow prisoners as well. Here two who have known them in prison speak out. Also includes accounts of prison life and resistance by Gerardo Hernández and Ramón Labañino, and Elizabeth Palmeiro. Puerto Rican independence fighter Rafael Cancel Miranda, who himself spent more than 27 years in US prisons, pays tribute to the example of the Cuban Five. $7. Also in Spanish.

"I will die the way I've lived"

15 watercolors by Antonio Guerrero on the 15th anniversary of the imprisonment of the Cuban Five

Fifteen paintings that graphically portray the 17 months Antonio Guerrero, Gerardo Hernández, Ramón Labañino, Fernando González, and René González spent in the "hole" at the Miami Federal Detention Center after their 1998 arrests on trumped-up charges including espionage conspiracy. The integrity, creativity, and humor displayed by the Five strike a deep chord with working people in the US and elsewhere determined to resist the system of capitalist "justice." With text by Antonio Guerrero, Gerardo Hernández, Ramón Labañino. $7. Also in Spanish.

www.pathfinderpress.com

The Cuban Five

The Cuban Five

Who They Are
Why They Were Framed
Why They Should Be Free

Presents the facts on the worldwide struggle to free Gerardo Hernández, Ramón Labañino, Antonio Guerrero, Fernando González, and René González. Shows how this battle to defend the Five is part of the class struggle in the US, where millions of working people know how the courts and prisons are used to punish those who refuse to accept the conditions imposed on us by capitalism. $5. Also in Spanish and French.

Cuba and Angola
Fighting for Africa's Freedom and Our Own

1975–91

The story of Cuba's nearly 16-year internationalist mission to aid the people of Angola, in the words of those who made that history, including Fidel Castro, Nelson Mandela, and Raúl Castro. With a special feature by Gabriel García Márquez. Also includes accounts by three of the Cuban Five who fought in Angola. $12. Also in Spanish.

LAND, LABOR, AND THE CANADIAN SOCIALIST REVOLUTION

by Michel Dugré

FARMERS IN CANADA face today the worst economic crisis since the 1930s. Thousands have been driven off their land and stripped of their means of livelihood. Tens of thousands more fear they will suffer the same fate. Farmers in Québec have been the hardest hit; in 1984 the bankruptcy rate was twice the Canada-wide average.

Net agricultural income has fallen sharply since the mid-1970s. This has led to a significant fall in the living standards of farmers and their families. In order to meet rising costs of production, farmers have had to mortgage an increasing portion of their land. The capitalist government on a federal and provincial level contributes to the ruin of farmers by restricting agricultural credit and dismantling aid programs such as subsidies for grain transportation.

This economic squeeze has deepened class divisions in the countryside between a relatively small number of wealthy capitalist farmers and the big majority of farmers, who are exploited and rely on the labor of family members.

All these factors have pushed a significant layer of exploited farmers toward militant actions in recent years.

In several cases, the trade unions have supported the

struggles of farmers. The Canadian Labour Congress (CLC) supported the farmers' movement against the abolition of the Crow's Nest grain transport subsidy, the worst government attack against farmers in Canada since the Second World War. In 1985, the United Auto Workers endorsed the National Farmers Union recruitment drive and held a joint rally with the farmers' union in Ontario to help it win new members. In Québec, farmers are fighting alongside workers against national oppression and for Québec's independence. The Union of Agricultural Producers in Québec has joined Québec's major labor federations in a campaign to defend Law 101, a law protecting the linguistic rights of Québécois.

The conditions for building an alliance of Canada's workers and farmers are therefore better today than they have been at any time since the Second World War.

This article will examine the economic, social, and political weight of farmers in Canada, the history of the struggles over the land, and the crisis facing farmers today. It will also look at how the labor movement can participate in the struggles farmers are now waging in order to build the alliance the working class needs to defend its interests and advance toward replacing the current government of the capitalist exploiters with a workers' and farmers' government.

I. THE SOCIAL AND POLITICAL WEIGHT OF AGRICULTURE AND FARMERS IN CANADA

CANADA IS AMONG the world's top agricultural producers and exporters. The food sector—farming and related industries—represents 17 percent of the gross national product. Sales of agricultural products rose to $20 billion in 1984.

Canada is a major world producer of grains, above all wheat but also barley, oats, and rye. These are the main commodities grown in the Prairie provinces of Saskatchewan, Alberta, and Manitoba. Ontario is a major center of corn and soybean growing and, together with Québec and—on the Pacific Coast—British Columbia, a big source of vegetables and fruits. The Maritime provinces along the Atlantic Coast are important in potato production.

About half of Canadian farm output is accounted for by cattle, hogs, and dairy and poultry products. Québec and Ontario produce some two-thirds of the hogs and are also the main dairy and poultry centers. Some 70 percent of the cattle are raised in Alberta, Saskatchewan, and Ontario.

Agriculture in Canada directly employs a half million people. But a much larger number work in related activities such as transportation of food, preparation of fertilizer and seed, production of machinery, retail sales. Those directly involved in agricultural production represent about 5 percent of the economically active population. In the heavily agricultural province of Saskatchewan, some 20 percent of the population live and work on farms. Farmers and farm workers account for about one out of seven working people in Canada who are involved in the production of commodities—that is, those working in manufacturing, construction, mining, forestry, agriculture, fishing, hunting, and transportation.

The social weight of farmers among the producers in Canada can be clearly seen by examining Canadian agriculture's place in the world market. Agricultural goods account for about 10 percent of Canadian exports. Close to 50 percent of Canadian agricultural production is exported.

Canadian wheat makes up some 20 percent of the wheat sold on the world market, and Canada is second only to the United States as a world wheat exporter. With a total population of 25 million, Canada produces more than three times as much wheat per capita as the United States. Canada supplies close to one half of the Soviet Union's wheat imports.

THE RULING CAPITALIST families, who own and run Canadian big business, dominate agricultural production and export. Their goal is to enhance their profits, not to meet human needs for food and fiber—either in Canada, or anywhere in the world. The federal government in Ottawa uses its international food aid programs as one more commercial and political weapon in the hands of the Canadian bourgeoisie.

First, only a paltry 3 percent of Canadian agricultural exports goes to feed the hungry around the world. This food aid, which is taken from agricultural surpluses, is directed not toward humanitarian goals, but to developing additional markets for Canadian products among colonial and semicolonial countries.

Canadian food aid often results in an influx of agricultural products into these countries that undermines the market for the local small producers, often driving them into ruin and off the land. The Canadian government almost always uses this aid to change the eating habits of the local population in recipient countries toward consuming more wheat and thus become more dependent on Canadian imports. Many countries that were previously self-sufficient in cereal production are now dependent on wheat from Canada and the United States.

Canadian food aid is also used as a political weapon

by Ottawa against governments and peoples who stand up to imperialist oppression and fight back. Food aid to the Socialist Republic of Vietnam, for example, was stopped in 1978. Repressive right-wing regimes that are subservient to imperialist interests, however, come in for better treatment. The Canadian government provided an example of this double standard in 1985, when it resumed its bilateral aid to the imperialist-backed regime in El Salvador, while sharply cutting the quota on beef imports from revolutionary Nicaragua.

Agriculture and farm policy in Canada have substantial repercussions on the world market. Farmers in Canada have considerable social weight, in the international arena as well as at home. Moreover, they are directly affected by international political developments and vicissitudes in the world market.

Canada's importance in the world market for agricultural products has grown at the same time that the number of farms in Canada has declined enormously—by nearly one-half during the past thirty years. Today there are only about 315,000 farms in Canada.[1]

Despite the sharp decline in the number of farmers and in the proportion of the working population they represent, farmers maintain a very important place in economic production in Canada. In fact the decline in the farming population in Canada has been accompanied by a major increase in agricultural production. From 1959 to 1983, for example, there was a 56 percent increase in output per acre (an acre = 0.4 hectares) of cereal grains in the Canadian west; total production more than doubled during this period. Canadian wheat exports tripled. Given the increase in production and the decline in the number of farmers, each grain farmer can today feed more than three times as many people as a quarter century ago.

Class structure of agriculture in Canada

To understand what is happening to farmers today it is essential to begin with a description of the different social classes in the countryside. Not all farmers have the same class interests. The conflicting interests of different classes in the farming population is an important source of deep-going economic and political struggles in the countryside.

It is somewhat difficult to precisely distinguish classes in the countryside, since there is substantial overlap among various social layers. Some farmers hire agricultural wage workers during certain periods of the year although they themselves work in a factory part of the year. And there are many other examples of farmers who exploit some wage labor while being exploited themselves in various ways by capital.

Several major class divisions can be distinguished in the countryside.

First, there is the sector of agricultural production often referred to as agribusiness. Some of these farms are directly managed by big corporations and are operated entirely by exploiting hired labor. Some corporations employ landless farmers to operate company-owned farms. Other corporations do not themselves own or operate farms, but instead sign contracts with landholding farmers committing them to sell their products to be marketed by these large capitalist outfits.

In addition, a small percentage of farm families are themselves capitalists who depend in whole or in large part on exploiting the labor of wage workers.

Altogether, this capitalist sector of farm production accounts for enormous yields. In 1981, the top 1 percent of the farms in Canada (in sales) sold 19 percent of all agricultural products. The largest farms, 2.3 percent of the total, accounted for 36 percent of all the wages paid to agricultural workers. These farms, which operate on the basis of wage labor, are veritable factories in the fields.

The exploiters in the countryside also include landowners who rent out their land, either for use by capitalist farmers or by working farm families. More than 30 percent of the acreage used for agriculture in Canada is rented.

The proprietors who rent out land are themselves very heterogeneous. They include the government and government agencies, banks and other financial institutions, certain agribusiness companies, as well as individuals, many of whom are agricultural producers who are still farming or are retired. As landlords, however, they all extort a portion of the value produced by the labor of either the farmers or wage laborers who work the land.

In addition to these exploiting layers in the countryside (the agribusiness-owned farms, capitalist farm families, and landlords), there is a range of middle layers in the farming population, as well. On the top end are small capitalist farmers who hire agricultural workers but also rely substantially on their own labor and the labor of their families. Their situation is generally more precarious than that of wealthier capitalist farmers. Some are deeply in debt. But their interests remain counterposed to the interests of the workers they exploit.

On the bottom end of the range among these middle layers are farmers who rely first and foremost on family labor and who only use a small amount of wage labor to a very limited extent—at the high point of the harvest season, for example. Most of these working farmers are also victims of capitalist exploitation. Some of these farmers must themselves work off-the-farm jobs for wages to make a decent living. These farmers have interests that conflict with the workers they employ, but also share many of the conditions of exploited farmers who rely solely on family labor. These farmers can be more easily drawn into struggle and won to the side of the labor movement in battles against the big exploiters.

THE MAJORITY OF FARMERS own their means of production (in whole or in part) but do not exploit agricultural workers. They rely exclusively on their own labor and that of their families. In 1981, 203,000 of the 318,000 farms in Canada—some 64 percent—did not employ agricultural workers. These independent farmers are responsible for more than 36 percent of total agricultural production. A very high proportion of the value that these exploited farmers produce goes to the banks, landlords, and big capitalist marketing and processing corporations.

To support themselves, one or more members of these farm families frequently work off their farms as well. Many are industrial workers. Nearly a third of these farmers held down jobs for more than 97 days in 1981.

Finally, wage laborers make up an important component of the agricultural producers. Some of these are themselves exploited farmers who also work for wages on other farms in order to earn needed income. Many other agricultural workers, however, are producers who own no land and can only support themselves and their families by selling their labor power. In 1983 there were 158,000 agricultural wage workers in Canada. These workers are the most exploited and most oppressed producers in the countryside. Among Canadian workers, these farm laborers have the worst working conditions, receive the lowest wages, are the least well organized, and are the least protected by government health, safety, and other labor laws.

Attempts to organize agricultural workers have exposed the atrocious conditions under which they are often compelled to work and live: pay below the minimum wage, fifteen-hour workdays, extremely dangerous working conditions and health hazards, inadequate and unhealthy housing, firings at the slightest attempt to organize.

Among these farm laborers there are a large number of immigrants and a significant number of Québécois working outside Québec, particularly in British Columbia and Ontario. Each year, the federal government provides for the temporary entry of thousands of workers from the Caribbean and Central America who are subject to extreme exploitation. Many of these workers are brought into Canada under contract labor agreements that subject them to almost slavelike conditions as part of labor gangs. These workers have no rights while in Canada, and the contracting outfits ship them back to their home countries as soon as their supercheap labor is no longer needed.

In January 1983 the federal government changed the unemployment compensation rules to cover temporary agricultural workers, but these changes were later reversed by Ottawa as a result of pressure from capitalist farmers. Whether Québécois, Sikh, or Caribbean, agricultural workers are targets of open racism as well as superexploitation.

These, then, are the main class layers in the Canadian farming population.

The sharp decline in the total rural population since

the Second World War has been accompanied by a deepening of the social differentiation: the rich farmers have become richer and the poor poorer. At the same time that the small farmers were subjected to growing exploitation by the owners of the big companies and banks, the capitalist farmers were hiring more and more agricultural workers. From 1961 to 1981, the average yearly number of weeks of wages paid by those farmers who employ labor jumped from 26.2 to 39.4, an increase of 50 percent. The proportion of agricultural labor performed by wage workers therefore rose during this period.

Exploited independent commodity producers

The proportion of Canadian farmers who do not exploit wage labor rose slightly between 1961 and 1981, going from 62 percent to 64 percent of all farmers. These farmers account for more than a third of total farm sales in Canada. Together with their families, they provide a significant portion of the hours of labor that go into the production of food. This is an indication of the social and political weight of working farmers as part of the toiling population in Canada.

The exploited commodity producers must pay much more for land costs, machinery, fuel, and fertilizer today than in the past—even after allowing for inflation. The value of the average farm's stock of machinery and equipment, for example, rose seventeen times (in current dollars) between 1951 and 1981. As a result, the small farmers must take greater risks. Despite these big expenditures—which cause their "net worth" to be calculated as seemingly very large—these family farmers remain exploited producers. The income that these farm families live on is comparable to that of workers and has generally declined during the farm crisis of recent years.

It should be noted that large-scale capitalist farms have penetrated a few sectors of agricultural production to a far greater extent than most others. For example, independent commodity producers still predominate in grains, dairy, and livestock, while large-scale capitalist enterprises have established greater sway in poultry raising and fruit and vegetable production. In many arenas of farming, big capital has found it more profitable to leave the actual production process—with all its accompanying expenses and risks (both natural and economic)—to individual producers, while establishing capitalist dominance over these farmers through loans and its monopoly over processing and distribution.

Given Canada's relatively short planting and harvesting seasons and the perishable nature of most agricultural products, farming that is dependent on wage labor is particularly vulnerable to last-minute strike action. The larger the number of farm workers and the greater their concentration, the greater becomes their bargaining power in relation to the bosses—for example, by striking on the eve of the harvest. This is an additional reason for big business to invest in marketing and processing rather than directly in production of many agricultural commodities.

Thus, contrary to a widespread misconception, capitalism's growing domination of agriculture in Canada has not taken place primarily through the transformation of the lands of independent farmers into vast factories in the fields employing agricultural workers. In fact, the exploitation of working farmers has remained a central feature of capitalist domination of agriculture.

The exploitation of these working farmers, as Marx explained, "differs only in *form* from the exploitation of the industrial proletariat. The exploiter is the same:

capital."[2] Capitalist exploitation in Canada today is not limited to a single form: wage labor. The class structure of modern capitalist society cannot be reduced solely to bosses and wage workers. On a world scale, the form of exploitation that the small farmer is subjected to is still a predominant way in which wealth is extorted from the toilers, and—as we have seen—it remains a vital source of profits today for capitalists in Canada, as well.

Exploitation of working farmers

Working farmers are exploited differently from wage workers. Wage workers, having no other means of making their living, are forced to sell their labor power—their ability to work—to a capitalist. Wages received by workers represent only a portion of the total value they produce during their hours of labor. They produce a value equivalent to their total wage during one part of their work day; during the rest of the day they work for free for the capitalist. The products workers produce do not belong to them but to the employer. After the sale of the product on the market, the capitalists pocket the value produced by this unpaid labor in the form of profit. This is the fundamental method of the exploitation of workers under capitalism.

Farmers, by contrast, generally possess some means of production with which to make a living. They do not have to rely solely on the sale of their labor power to a capitalist. Many hold title to the land on which they work, and even if they rent the land, they own some farm machinery and livestock. The majority of farmers also possess the product of their labor, which they then sell on the market.

Nevertheless, after the sale of their products, the working farmers do not realize the entire value they produced.

The capitalists take a portion of that value from these farmers; they reap profits from a portion of the farmers' labor time.

This exploitation of farmers takes place in two principal ways. The first is through the gap between their production costs and their minimum living expenses, on the one hand, and, on the other, the price they receive from the capitalist "middlemen"—whether government marketing boards or private corporations—who purchase, process, and market agricultural products. And the second is through the system of rents and mortgages.

The gap between costs and prices flows from the farmers' exploitation by capitalists at both ends of the food production chain. They are exploited both by those capitalists who sell them the goods they need in order to produce, and by those to whom they sell their products.

When they come to the market to buy or to sell, farmers find themselves in a situation similar to that facing the underdeveloped countries vis-à-vis the imperialist powers: they confront unequal terms of trade. The farmers confront powerful monopolies capable of imposing prices and terms. They must pay inflated monopoly prices for the commodities they need (machinery, fuel, fertilizer, fodder, etc.), while they receive far less for their products than they are worth from the government marketing boards and the big processing and marketing concerns. The wealthy capitalist families who own the monopolies pocket the difference.

Four corporations selling agricultural machinery control practically the entire market in Canada. Cominco and Imperial Oil control 55 percent of the market for chemical fertilizers. Kraft controls 60 percent of the canning industry in Québec. Kraft and Aulds control the sales of 90 percent of the cheese produced in Ontario. A handful of companies control the entire market in Canada for red meat. In 1983, five big chains of stores controlled 86 percent of the retail food trade. Two rail giants share the entire rail transportation of agricultural products.

The meat-packing industry provides a good example of how these monopolies function. Since the 1930s, this industry has been completely dominated by three giants: Canada Packers, Swift, and Burns. On at least two occasions—in the 1930s, and again in 1959—these companies have been cited by Royal Commissions of Inquiry for their price-fixing practices. In 1969, they were found guilty of collusion in price-fixing over a five-year period, but the matter was settled out of court. Investigations revealed a similar situation in the sugar refining industry.

The capitalist government in Canada, far from suppressing the development of these monopolies, encourages them. This was recently revealed once again by the Canadian government's support to companies that claim the right to exclusive possession of new genetic lines of plants.

One of the most direct expressions of this exploitation of working farmers through the monopolies' control over the prices of farm inputs and farm products is contract farming. Farmers sign contracts committing them to sell their products only to a specific company at a set price. Sometimes companies concentrating in one sector of agricultural production branch out into others in order to build up a guaranteed market for their products among farmers. Grain companies, for example, sign contracts with independent pork producers. The companies agree to buy the farmer's entire production on the condition that the farmer buy feed grain only from them. In 1981 a majority of the pork producers in Québec operated under such contracts. Farmers placed in that situation become almost employees of the company. While they lose nearly all control over their production, however, the farmers continue to take all the risks.

System of rents and mortgages

Farmers are also exploited by capital through the system of rents and mortgages.

With the decline of feudal social relations and the development of the capitalist mode of production, land began to take on the character of a commodity, that is, it began to be bought and sold. The land itself *did not become* a commodity, however, since land is not a product of human labor. While land, or rather the right to *use* of the land, comes to have a market price (regulated by a combination of factors not discussed in this article), the land itself has no value.[3]

Marx explains in volume 3 of *Capital* that "the purchase and sale of land, the circulation of land as a commodity . . . is the practical result of the development of the capitalist mode of production, in as much as here the commodity becomes the general form of every product and of all instruments of production."[4]

Under capitalism, therefore, the farmers have to either buy land or rent it from a landowner. They have to pay rent or interest on a mortgage loan to cover a land purchase, simply to get access to grazing land or a field to till.

The October 1985 issue of *Union Farmer,* the monthly newspaper of the National Farmers Union, reported the case of two farmers from Dawson Creek, British Columbia, Carl and Joyce Torio. "The Torios, who have been farming for 38 years in the community, started to get into trouble in 1977. A year in which, ironically, their farm was virtually debt-free."

"The Bank of Montreal encouraged the Torios to use

their equity towards investing in the feedlot business and supplied a major loan." Eight years later, after a fall in beef prices and a rise in interest rates, the Torios had their backs to the wall. "After having paid the bank in excess of $700,000 in interest payments since 1977, the Torios are still $400,000 in debt and face foreclosure proceedings," the *Union Farmer* commented.

The Torios' case is typical. The pressures that the Bank of Montreal exerted on the Torios to switch sectors of production are a common practice. The bankers' aim is to keep the farmers in debt. That is how the banks make their money.

When a bank lends money to industrial capitalists for expansion of their factories, the interest on the debt is the bank's share in the overall surplus value that the industrial capitalists take from the unpaid labor of workers. When a bank lends money to a working farmer, on the other hand, the interest paid by that farmer on the loan constitutes the bank's *direct* expropriation of part of the value produced by the farmer. The bank therefore is directly involved in exploiting the farmer.

Several governmental bodies and programs also work to increase the farmers' indebtedness. Legal proceedings that Québec farmers brought against the Québec Office of Agricultural Credit in March 1985 revealed that the credit office actually exaggerated the assets of some farmers as part of pressuring them to take higher loans than they themselves had initially requested.

The capitalists also expropriate a portion of the value produced by the farmers through land rents. In Canada, nearly 37 percent of the farmers rent at least some of the land they work. Land rents in 1981 represented an expense to farmers of at least $630 million.

At least 45 percent of this rent is paid either in kind or

as a share of production or revenue. This modern version of sharecropping is increasingly widespread. In a typical agreement, the farmer will pay a rent of one-third of the total revenue from sales of the crop, while the landowner pays the land tax.

THE RENTING OF LAND is an obstacle to the development of agriculture. Landlords try to negotiate relatively short leases with farmers, so that they can quickly renegotiate them with higher rents. As a result, farmers are discouraged from making lasting improvements on the land. Farmers know that any benefits from these improvements—which they have had to pay for in higher production costs—will end up in the pockets of the landlords, who will use such improvements in order to raise rents when the next lease comes around.

This system of renting, whose most grotesque form is sharecropping, illustrates the parasitical character of the capitalist landlords. The landlords make no contribution to production. They acquire the right to profit from the labor of others simply by the possession of a land title.

To complete the picture, another layer of exploiting parasites must be mentioned: the land speculators. These speculators, who in no way participate in production, accumulate fortunes simply by profiting from variations in land prices. This form of profiteering has emerged as a growing aspect of the exploitative practices of big capital in Canada.

In addition to these particular forms of exploitation, many farmers are exploited as wage workers, as well. These semiproletarian farmers must take jobs in a factory, as farm hands, or elsewhere in order to make a living income. Farmers, like other exploited working people, are also victims of the other evils of capitalist society: imperialist wars, inflation, racism and national oppression, women's inequality and subjugation, nuclear power and other environmental destruction, and so on.

II. THE STRUGGLE FOR CONTROL OF THE LAND

TO UNDERSTAND the importance to the working class of forging a fighting alliance with exploited working farmers, it is useful to look at the struggle for control of the land in the history of Canada. This includes the relationship between the struggle for land and the national oppression of many minorities, as well as farmers' collaboration with workers in this century in building the Co-operative Commonwealth Federation (CCF) and later the New Democratic Party (NDP), two labor political parties.

Prisonhouse of peoples

Canada has an area of nearly four million square miles (10 million square kilometers). This immense territory had been occupied by indigenous peoples for more than 20,000 years. They numbered about a quarter of a million when the first permanent European colonists arrived at the beginning of the seventeenth century. The form of social organization of these indigenous peoples was communal, with no private ownership of land.

The arrival of the European colonizers unleashed a ferocious struggle for control of the land. This struggle for land was at the heart of the process that led to national oppression of the Native peoples, the Acadians, the Québécois, and the Métis. Step by step Canada was transformed into the prisonhouse of peoples that it is today.

The first victims of this struggle were the indigenous peoples themselves. In the course of more than two centuries, their land was stolen from them by merchants, seigneurs (semifeudal landlords), the French and then the British crowns, the church, speculators, and capitalists. Today more than one million Native Indians, Inuit, and Métis live in Canada. Some 200,000 Native Indians live on more than 2,200 reservations with an area totaling less than 0.3 percent of Canadian territory. As for the Inuit, they too were for all practical purposes dispossessed of their immense territories in the northern reaches of what is today Canada.

With the arrival of growing numbers of colonists, the French colony of New France was initially developed primarily as a commercial territory for the profit of merchants, principally in the fur trade. The latter first exploited the labor of the Indians, giving them only a pittance in return for their pelts, and then increasingly intensified their exploitation of the new colonists, as well.

Agriculture originally served to feed those involved in commerce. As more colonists arrived, agriculture itself gradually developed into the main economic activity, involving the vast majority of the population.

The French colonizers imposed on New France a modified form of the feudal relations on the land that, although disintegrating, still prevailed in France (the colonization began more than a century and a half prior to the bourgeois-democratic French revolution of 1789–95). Almost eight million acres were taken from the Indians and distributed as landed estates to 375 seigneurs, who operated them in part for profit. A quarter of these newly established estates were granted to the Catholic hierarchy.

The peasants were subjected to semifeudal forms of

exploitation: various forms of rent (both in money and in kind); compulsory unpaid labor on the seigneur's personal fields at planting and harvest time (the corvée); compulsory milling of their grain in the landlord's mill for a high fee; and compulsory tithes to the church.

Expulsion of the Acadians

In its rivalry with France over control of North America, Britain conquered the main French settlements in Acadia, on Canada's Atlantic coast, in 1710. To maintain control over their new conquest, British merchants needed a rapid increase in the British population of the region. The presence of French-speaking Acadians on the most fertile land constituted an obstacle to this colonization. That is how the small farmers of Acadia became the second victims of the struggle for the land.

In 1755, 6,000 Acadians were deported from what is now Nova Scotia. All their houses and belongings, including 118,000 head of cattle, were expropriated. Other deportations followed, and in 1763 only some 1,000 Acadians were still living in Nova Scotia. In the years following this brutal mass deportation, Acadians settled in almost all the thirteen American colonies of Britain. Many ended up in Louisiana, where their descendants are referred to as "cajuns," derived from the word *Acadians.*

Today, more than two centuries after these deportations, the Acadians in Canada—who make up 30 percent of the population of New Brunswick—are still fighting for the recognition of their linguistic and cultural rights.

Britain concluded its military conquest of New France in 1760; by the Treaty of Paris of 1763, Britain acquired all French possessions on the North American continent. Unlike France, feudal relations on the land had not predominated in England for some four centuries, and a bourgeois-democratic revolution in the mid-1600s had limited the power of the monarchy and concentrated power in the hands of an alliance of urban merchants and emerging capitalist landowners. By 1760 a growing layer of capitalist manufacturers was also expanding its economic power in Britain, and that country was on the threshold of its industrial revolution.

Nonetheless, the victory of Britain's more advanced merchant capitalism did not lead to the rapid abolition of the semifeudal forms of agricultural production in New France. In fact, the semifeudal rents extorted from the French-speaking peasantry were exacted with new rigor in the years that followed the conquest, with the British colonial authorities and commercial interests making the task easier for the landlords.

Britain, threatened by the revolt of its thirteen colonies to the south and aware that colonists of British origin were still very few in its newly conquered lands, sought to establish a reactionary alliance with the seigneurs of Québec and with the Catholic church. This alliance was formalized in the Québec Act of 1774, which codified maintenance of the seigneurial system of landed property, the privileges of the Catholic hierarchy, and the French civil code.

This alliance enabled the British conquerers to consolidate their domination of Canada. Over time a large majority of French seigneurs abandoned their lands and returned to France. British merchants and army officers took over the best landed estates, continuing to operate them along traditional lines. Immense territories were ceded to British companies, particularly in the Eastern Townships of Québec. These were in turn sold to Loyalists who had fled the thirteen colonies during the American revolution, especially following the defeat of the British colonial power there. English and American small farmers who began to come to Canada in larger numbers and established themselves on this land were never subjected to seigneurial land tenure.

French-speaking peasants had little or no access to these new lands. Instead, they were confined to the seigneurial lands; the population on these lands jumped by 234 percent between 1784 and 1831. Unable to survive under these conditions and too poor to purchase land elsewhere in Québec, many of these peasants emigrated to the United States. In 1900, more than 500,000 Québécois were living in the New England states.

Maintenance of semifeudal relations on the land had a disastrous effect on the development of agriculture in Québec. The oppressive conditions of the peasants, burdened by multiple rents and duties, sapped initiative in raising agricultural production; their subsistence level of existence restricted the development of an internal market to spur manufacturing and commerce, as well.

THE CONFINEMENT OF the French-speaking peasants to the seigneurial lands also accelerated the subdivision of farms with each generation. Peasant land increasingly took on the form of longer and narrower strips. This system hindered the rotation of crops, sapped the land's fertility, and made it difficult to employ new techniques. It slowed down the development of roads and communication in the Québec countryside.

Seigneurial forms of land tenure in Canada, however, were never purely feudal. From the beginning, the brutal, semifeudal forms of exploiting the peasants served as a mighty engine to promote the accumulation of capital in the hands of wealthy landowners and merchants—a newly rising commercial bourgeoisie. This process, already in motion under French rule, gained momentum under the rule of Britain, which by the time of the conquest was the leading commercial power in the world.

The legacy of the seigneurial system disappeared very slowly in Québec. It suffered major blows between 1822 and 1854 through the adoption of partial reforms reflecting both the national and democratic struggles in Canada and the impact on Canada of bourgeois-democratic movements in Europe. While the semifeudal rents and duties were abolished by the mid-nineteenth century, however, they were replaced by other, more purely capitalist methods of exploiting the peasants.

For example, semifeudal rents were replaced by straight money rents—unless the peasants were somehow able to come up with enormous sums to purchase their plots from the landlord. Over the next century, those peasants who remained on the land became in essence small independent landholders. Nonetheless, it was not until 1940 that the final residual rent payments to the seigneurs were abolished by act of the federal parliament. At that time, 60,000 farmers (44 percent of the farms of Québec) were still paying a total of $212,000 each year to 242 seigneurs. Even then, the farmers had to continue payments for several more decades to a government bank that assumed the remaining rent payments to the landowners.

The American revolution of 1775–83 constituted the first serious threat to the domination of the intertwined class of British merchants and landowners in Canada. The revolutionaries, gathered around a new American merchant and landed bourgeoisie, sought to free the thirteen colonies from British domination and to forge a new, independent nation.

The peasants of Québec, locked in their struggle

against the British landlords and merchants, expressed great sympathy for the revolution for democracy and freedom from colonial oppression that was unfolding to their south.[5]

The American revolutionaries worked hard to find allies among the people of Québec, pledging to defend the linguistic and cultural rights of the French-speaking majority and condemning Britain's perpetuation of the corvée system of forced labor. American revolutionary leader Benjamin Franklin traveled to Montréal in May 1776 to call for support to the anticolonial rebellion. The American independence fighters sent letters and manifestos explaining the goals of their democratic revolution to the people of Québec.

The Catholic church stepped up pressure to force the peasants of Québec to support the British crown. The landlords tried to enlist their tenants to confront American troops. But all these counterrevolutionary efforts were in vain. "The Canadian peasantry," pointed out the British governor of Québec during the American revolution, "not only deserted their duty but numbers of them have taken up arms against the crown." It is estimated that 500 Québécois joined the revolutionary Continental Army.

The American revolution gave rise to the first of numerous conscription crises in Québec. But it did not stop the British merchants from consolidating their domination.

The British rulers' fierce opposition to the American revolution also left its imprint on the development of agriculture in Upper Canada (present-day Ontario). To avoid the spread of republican ideas, the British authorities consciously tried to build up a colonial landed aristocracy by ceding immense amounts of land to a few big landholders. Large numbers of American Loyalists from the former thirteen colonies—the "contras" of that day—fled to Canada, and many were granted substantial plots of land in return for their loyalty to Britain.

In 1824, of the 16 million acres of land surveyed in Upper Canada, 11 million had been distributed, for the most part free, to wealthy landlords. The authorities also reserved one-seventh of all surveyed land for the crown and another seventh for the hierarchy of the Church of England, although most of the colonists belonged to other faiths.

Granting this land to a relative handful of better-off families and to the church, instead of distributing it to be cultivated by small farmers, slowed down the development of agriculture. Big landlords were often more interested in speculating on their land than in having it cultivated.

Land thus became the object of intense class struggles in both Upper Canada and Lower Canada (present-day Québec). Small farmers in both colonies fought against the monopoly in landed property and against the privileges of the clergy, who had been given more than 3 million acres of land.

1837–38 uprising

The struggle of rural producers for control of the land in both Upper and Lower Canada formed part of a series of democratic demands focused on the establishment of an elected government responsible to the people. Through these struggles in the first decades of the nineteenth century, farmers increasingly joined with other social layers—including a section of the rising Canadian bourgeoisie—in demanding independence from Britain.

In Lower Canada, the British not only maintained the seigneurial forms of class oppression of the peasantry;

they also added to it the relegation of the French language to second-class status and other forms of discrimination against the French-speaking inhabitants. In the context of the reactionary alliance established by the Québec Act, the peasants' struggle against the landlords took the form of a struggle against the British colonial power.

"They say that I am British," said the French-speaking Bishop Briand in speaking of the peasants' attacks on collaborators with the conquerors. "It's true, I am British. . . . They must all become British too," the bishop continued.[6]

The demands of the farmers of Lower Canada were summed up in February 1838 in the Declaration of Independence drawn up by Robert Nelson. The revolutionaries of Lower Canada demanded the liberation of Canada from "all allegiance to Great Britain"; establishment of a "republican form of government"; dissolution of "all union between church and state"; abolition of "feudal or seigneurial tenure of land . . . as completely as if such tenure had never existed in Canada"; and the use of "the French and English language . . . in all public affairs."[7]

The struggle of farmers against their exploiters helped fuel the armed revolutionary uprising of 1837–38 in both Upper and Lower Canada. This uprising marked the beginning of a bourgeois-democratic revolution against British colonial rule, which was cut short by the defeat of the rebel forces.

Farmers played a central role in this uprising. In Lower Canada, of the 108 court-martialed following the defeat of the rebellion, 66 were farmers. Of the 12 revolutionary leaders who were hanged, 5 were farmers. In Upper Canada, among the 885 democratic fighters listed as arrested or escaped following the 1837 uprising, 375 were farmers and 425 were wage workers or artisans.

Although the rebellion of 1837–38 took sharper forms in Québec than in Ontario, it revealed that the revolution's dynamic was to unite the democrats and working people in both colonies.

The English-speaking revolutionaries of Upper Canada gave their support to the French-speaking patriots of Lower Canada. "The Reformers of Upper Canada," said a resolution adopted in July 1837, "are called by every tie of feeling, interest, and duty, to make common cause with their fellow-citizens of Lower Canada, whose successful coercion would doubtless be in time visited upon us, and the redress of whose grievances would be the best guarantee for the redress of our own."[8]

THE DEFEAT OF THIS rebellion at the hands of the British authorities and their collaborators among the colonists, including the Catholic church hierarchy, made the farmers of Upper and Lower Canada the third victims of the struggle for land. It consolidated the domination of the big landholders and the big merchants and maintained British colonial rule.

The failure of the 1837–38 rebellion was also a defeat for the struggle to eliminate the legacy of the seigneurial system by revolutionary means that could have broken the power of the landlords in Québec and turned over the land to those who tilled it. If it had succeeded, such an agrarian revolution would have permitted a much more rapid development of agriculture in Québec. The defeat of this attempt had effects that are still visible.

At the time of the Second World War, for example, income from agriculture in Québec was still less than half that in Ontario, although the population engaged in agriculture was about the same in the two provinces

(254,000 in Québec in 1941, compared to 264,000 in Ontario). A third as many trucks were used on Québec farms, an eighth as many tractors, a fifth as many milking machines (although dairy farming was the most important agricultural sector in Québec), and half as much commercial fertilizer. Québec farmers used a third as much electricity and had a sixth as many silos.

Even these figures paint a picture that is still too rosy to reflect the true situation of the big majority of Québec farmers at the time of the Second World War, because it includes farmers in the Eastern Townships descended from the Loyalists who had never been subjected to seigneurial tenure.

Thus, the backwardness of Québec agriculture was both a product of and a contributing factor to the national oppression of the Québécois. Although this gap was substantially narrowed after the Second World War through rapid modernization of Québec's agriculture, it is still visible today. In 1981, the average valuation of Québec farms was half that of all farms in Canada. The total value of machines and equipment per farm was 50 percent higher in Canada as a whole than in Québec.

AFTER THE DEFEAT of the 1837–38 rebellion, the Canadian bourgeoisie that was emerging from the most well-off sectors of the colonists pursued a vast offensive aimed at dividing the farmers and other working people of Québec from those of English Canada.

In fact, one major consequence of the 1837–38 defeat was the halting of the process of unification of the working classes of Upper and Lower Canada that had begun during the course of the revolution.

The Canadian bourgeoisie undertook to institutionalize the national oppression of the Québécois. This goal was pursued on the instigation of and in direct collaboration with the British colonial authorities.

In an 1839 report to London, Lord Durham, who had been sent to Canada by the British government in the wake of the rebellion, proposed the ruthless suppression of the French language and national culture. The forcible imposition of the English language, Durham said, should aim to settle "at once and forever the national character of the province . . . the first object ought to be that of making it an English province . . . the ascendancy should never again be placed in any hands but those of an English population."[9]

The consolidation of the oppression of the Québec nation was ratified by Britain's adoption of the Union Act of 1840 and the British North American Act (BNAA) of 1867.

The Union Act, under which Upper and Lower Canada were joined in a single province, prohibited the use of French in parliament—a ban that was later reversed. This was the opening gun in an effort from that day to this to deny language rights to the French-speaking population in Québec and elsewhere in Canada. The Union Act gave Upper Canada, whose population was then only 60 percent of that of Lower Canada, an equal number of representatives in parliament. It transferred the weight of the enormous debt accumulated by Upper Canada to the shoulders of the Québécois peasantry.

Twenty-seven years later, the BNAA established a confederation of Britain's major colonies in North America. This act denied the distinct national character of Québec by reducing its status to that of one province among several others. This new constitution, under which Britain granted substantial autonomy to the developing Canadian state (while retaining control over military defense and foreign policy), severely limited the rights of the Québécois.

Using the backwardness of Québec agriculture as "proof" of the inferior intelligence and capacities of the Québécois, the bourgeoisie led a chauvinist anti-Québécois campaign among the workers and farmers of English Canada.

They used the conditions of impoverishment prevalent in the Québec countryside to exert a downward pressure on workers' wages, first of all in Québec but also in English Canada. If Québec farmers were capable of living on so little, all others would have to do the same.

Thus, the founding of the Canadian confederation in 1867 was the product of the defeat of the bourgeois-democratic revolution of 1837–38. In the wake of that defeat, the British colonial authorities teamed up with the major sectors of the emerging Canadian capitalist class to impose a bourgeois constitution that aimed at maintaining permanent division between English- and French-speaking working people by codifying the second-class status and national oppression of the Québécois.

For example, the constitution perpetuated the segregated, church-controlled school system in Québec, dividing the population along language and religious lines. A language- and religious-based school system remain in force to this day, ensuring inferior education for the Québécois. The Québécois' recent efforts to forge a single, unilingual French, and secular school system have been pushed back and declared unconstitutional by a series of court rulings since 1979.

The 1867 confederation registered the defeat of the Québec farmers' struggle for land and national independence from Britain, and the defeat of the steps that had been taken toward forging a common fighting front with the English-speaking democrats and working people in Upper Canada. The way had been blocked for a thoroughgoing bourgeois-democratic revolution that could have established a united, bilingual Canada of freeholding farmers and workers with equal rights regardless of language. Instead, the counterrevolutionary British and Canadian rulers constituted the Canadian state on the foundation of the oppression of the Québec nation, the Acadians, other francophones in Canada, and the Native peoples.

The servants of crown and capital, however, had not reckoned with the tenacity and fighting spirit of the farmers and other working people of Québec, who refused to bow before the efforts to obliterate their language and culture. If the capitalist rulers stand condemned for having forged an oppressed nation in the heart of Canada, it is the French-speaking producers who can take credit for forging the nationalist consciousness of the Québec people through almost 150 years of resistance and struggle against systematic discrimination and social inequality.

Suppression of the Métis

In the period that followed the establishment of the Canadian confederation in 1867, the center of gravity of the struggle for land shifted west, toward the prairies. The first official census in Canada showed that 3 percent of the population, a little less than 110,000 persons, lived west of Ontario in 1871. Among them were American Indians as well as a good number of Métis—a people of mixed Indian, English, and French origin. The Métis, most of whom spoke French and others English, were mainly engaged in agriculture, hunting, and trapping.

Following the adoption of the British North American

Act, the new Canadian federal government, which had obtained jurisdiction over Indian affairs, moved to take possession of the vast western empire of the Hudson's Bay Company. The company claimed title to this land under an English grant of 1670. Its presence there, however, was limited to a few fur-trading posts. Defined as all land draining into Hudson's Bay, the company's grant included almost all of the present Canadian prairies. The Canadian takeover was aimed at protecting the region from U.S. territorial expansion and establishing firm British dominion over the entire northern half of the continent.

The Métis waged a courageous struggle against this theft of their land. They took part in uprisings on two separate occasions—in 1869–70 and in 1885. Following the first of these uprisings, limited concessions were made to the Métis in the Manitoba Act of 1870, which constituted that territory as a province of Canada. Most important, the language rights of the French-speaking Métis were formally recognized, as well as Métis land rights.

Nonetheless, systematic persecution and land theft by speculators forced many Métis to move west to Saskatchewan, and it was there that the second rebellion erupted in the mid-1880s. The Canadian bourgeoisie crushed this uprising in blood. The leader of the Métis, Louis Riel, was hanged on November 16, 1885. The defeat of the revolt opened the way for a campaign of widespread terror and repression against the Métis. They were deprived of their most basic rights as a people. In 1890, a law was adopted declaring the province of Manitoba to be unilingual English, in flagrant violation of the terms of the Manitoba Act of 1870. In 1916 a further law barred all French-language school instruction. These laws were part of a largely successful attempt by the Canadian capitalist rulers to assimilate the French population of the Prairie provinces. French-speaking peoples, who were the majority in Manitoba at the time of Louis Riel, now make up only 5 percent of the population. They are still fighting to have their rights, codified in the Manitoba Act, recognized in practice.

Thus the Métis small farmers and hunters of western Canada became the fourth victims of the struggle to control the land.

The Métis revolt was the only mass rebellion against the BNAA in Canada, but it was part of much broader opposition among the oppressed and exploited masses to this reactionary constitution. A movement protesting the hanging of Louis Riel spread across Canada, especially in Québec. "He shall hang, though every dog in Québec bark in his favor," Prime Minister John A. MacDonald responded. Six days after Riel was hanged, 50,000 people demonstrated their indignation and anger in the streets of Montréal, in one of the biggest outpourings in Québec history to this day.

The question of land is today still at the heart of any attempt to resolve the national oppression of the indigenous peoples and the Métis. As for the Québécois and Acadian farmers, the relationship between their national oppression and their exploitation as independent producers is reflected today in the inferior conditions under which they work the land. The rise of the Québec national struggle in the post–World War II period has stimulated their present resistance against the effects of the farm crisis on their lives and against the threat of foreclosure and expropriation by the banks.

Farmers, labor, and political action

The Prairie provinces—Manitoba, Saskatchewan, and Alberta—are the heart of Canadian agriculture today.

About 80 percent of the land used for agriculture is located there.

The development of agriculture in the prairie region occurred much later in Canada than in the United States. In fact, agriculture in the Canadian prairies was able to develop extensively only after arable land began to run short in the United States. Its development accelerated considerably in the years that followed the defeat of the Métis in 1885. Several factors contributed to this.

In the first place there was the westward migration of workers in eastern Canada and a massive wave of new immigrants who aspired to own a piece of land and better their living conditions. A number of laws adopted in the years following Confederation enabled many working people to obtain free land in the west.

COLONIZING THE WEST corresponded to the class interests of the bourgeoisie, which aimed to develop Canada's national economy and state. The Canadian government also gave vast areas of land stolen from the Indians and Métis to the railroads. Canadian Pacific, for example, received from the Canadian government 44 million acres of land—that is, an area equivalent to New Brunswick plus twice the area of Nova Scotia. This giveaway contributed to making Canadian Pacific the largest and richest corporation in Canada.

Beginning in the 1880s, the Canadian bourgeoisie sought to stimulate agriculture in the west to form an economic base for their business interests.

In any event, development of agriculture in the prairies was rapid. From 1896 to 1913, the proportion of Canada's population living in the prairies increased from 7 percent to 20 percent. The area of settled land increased seven times, and wheat production multiplied ten times over.

Wheat producers for the most part, the farmers of the Prairie provinces were extremely vulnerable to the variations in yield and price that are quite frequent in this sector of agriculture. For example, in 1921 and again in 1930, production of wheat per acre fell to less than half the level of the year before. Income per acre from the sale of wheat in 1937 was one-tenth that in 1917. The price of wheat in 1932 was one-seventh what it had been in 1919. A host of similar examples could be cited.

These sharp fluctuations and farmers' resulting insecurity, combined with shameless profiteering at their expense by the transport and marketing companies and the banks, led to growing discontent among western farmers in the opening decades of this century. The Prairie provinces became the scene of repeated broad farmers' mobilizations. These mobilizations had effects visible today not only in the farmers' movement but also in the labor movement.

The farmers' movement and the trade union movement have been closely linked since the beginning. In Canada these two movements emerged at about the same time. Many of the farmers who settled in the west were former wage workers. A study carried out at the beginning of the 1930s showed that 37 percent of the farmers in Saskatchewan and Alberta had formerly been workers. Many of them were immigrants who had participated in the Socialist movement in Europe.

In the course of their mobilizations, Prairie farmers raised increasingly radical demands, including nationalization of the railroads, big monopolies, and banks. To counter monopoly pricing policies, farmers set up many cooperatives, particularly for wheat marketing.

Through their struggles and mobilizations, farmers

began little by little to undertake political action and to form farmers' parties in different provinces. These parties had great success at the polls in the years just after the First World War. The radicalization among farmers and other working people was fueled by the economic and social hardships of the war and immediate postwar period as well as by the impact of the 1917 Russian revolution. Many small farmers as well as wage workers became members or supporters of the revolutionary Communist Party, founded in 1921 by those who sought to emulate the Bolshevik Party that had led the workers' and peasants' revolution in Russia.

IN ONTARIO, the United Farmers carried the provincial elections in 1919. A farmers' party won the elections in Alberta in 1921. In both cases, the farmers' parties collaborated closely with or were supported by provincially organized labor parties. In the federal elections of 1921 the Progressives, another party that grew out of the farmers' mobilizations, won 65 of 245 seats, including 15 out of 16 from Saskatchewan. Once elected, however, the leaders of these parties revealed themselves as defenders of the capitalist order. The farmers' parties lost strength rapidly. They emerged in the specific conditions of the postwar period and were severely weakened by the onset of capitalist economic stabilization and political reaction in the early 1920s.

But in the late 1920s and the early 1930s, under the impact of the Great Depression and of a drought of historic severity, mobilizations by Prairie farmers grew significantly larger. The radicalization of these farmers converged with that of working people in the cities, leading in 1933 to the founding of the Co-operative

Commonwealth Federation.

From its origins, the CCF was an organizational expression of the links between the labor movement and the farmers' movement. In fact, the CCF had roots that went back not only to the post–World War I farmers' upsurge, but also to the big workers' struggles of 1919. That year saw general strikes in Winnipeg and Vancouver and many solidarity strikes across the country including in Toronto and Montréal. There was widespread support for these strikes from working farmers and their organizations. This was reflected in the 1920 Manitoba elections by the election of all of the seven labor candidates who ran in rural constituencies; four strike leaders were also elected in Winnipeg, Manitoba.

In 1929 the Independent Labour Party (ILP) of Manitoba—an organization of 500 members, most of them wage workers—initiated a conference of local labor parties from the four western provinces (British Columbia, Alberta, Saskatchewan, and Manitoba). They formed the Western Conference of Labor Political Parties with the goal of bringing about the "entire unification of the Labor and Socialist Movement throughout Western Canada." In 1932 the Saskatchewan ILP joined with the United Farmers of Canada (Saskatchewan) to form a new party, the Labor-Farmer Group.

These and similar developments elsewhere led to the launching later that year of the Co-operative Commonwealth Federation by delegates from labor, Social Democratic, and farmers' parties and organizations from the west and Ontario. The CCF's founding convention was held in Regina, Saskatchewan, in 1933.

This new organization was a farmer-labor party based on an alliance of exploited farmers and wage workers. It emerged from the struggles of working people and from their efforts to forge a political weapon to challenge the bosses' parties for governmental power. It was thus an expression of the thrust toward independent working-class political action.

The conservative leadership of the main pan-Canadian trade union organization of that period, the craft union based Trades and Labour Congress (TLC), stood aside from the formation of the CCF and opposed union support for it. The TLC leaders insisted that the unions should remain politically "neutral"—as if labor could be indifferent to the outcome of a political battle between a party based on working people and the parties run by and for the ruling rich. It was only with the rise of the North American-wide Congress of Industrial Organizations (CIO) and its affiliated Canadian Congress of Labour in the late 1930s and early 1940s, that this political alliance of the exploited producers began to be expressed through the affiliation of unions to the CCF.

Despite the obstacles placed in the way of the new party by the TLC bureaucracy, the CCF won significant support from the beginning from the ranks of the labor movement in British Columbia, the three Prairie provinces, and among the coal miners in Cape Breton, Nova Scotia, on the east coast. In the first provincial elections after the CCF's formation, it succeeded in winning mass support both in heavily working-class British Columbia, where it won over 31 percent of the vote in 1933, and in predominantly agricultural Saskatchewan, where it won 24 percent in 1934. Even in the latter province, which had a very small working class and labor movement at the time, the CCF, although largely composed of farmers at its base, bore the stamp of this alliance of farmers' organizations and the labor movement. There and elsewhere more than half of the CCF candidates in its first few years were farmers, workers, and union leaders. (Others were preachers, professionals, or small businessmen.) In 1944 the CCF was elected to head the provincial government in Saskatchewan.

In 1943 the newly established Canadian Congress of Labour endorsed the CCF. This step came in the context of a major strike wave demanding the end of wartime wage controls and the adoption of other measures to defend workers' living standards and their union rights. It also contributed to the first major growth of support for the CCF in Ontario. Among the thirty-four CCF candidates elected there in 1943, nineteen were trade unionists.

The CCF was thus able to develop across all of English Canada thanks to the experience of big mobilizations of workers and farmers during the first several decades of this century. In Québec the CCF gained a limited base with the rise of the industrial unions in the 1940s, electing a CIO organizer to the federal parliament from Rouyn-Noranda in 1944.

THE PROGRAM ADOPTED by the CCF at the time of its founding reflected the pressures and experiences of workers and exploited farmers, while remaining within the framework of capitalism. Its demands included the "socialization" of the biggest industrial monopolies and banks, a moratorium on farm foreclosures, nationalization of the land, and opposition to "imperialist wars." But the leadership of the CCF was class-collaborationist and Social Democratic in its political perspectives and strategy. Under its direction, nothing was heard of the more significant economic and social demands in the CCF's formal program.

Nonetheless, with the growth of the industrial unions during the late 1930s, and especially during the 1940s, more industrial workers turned toward the CCF. During the war, industrial unions began to affiliate to it in growing numbers.

While union affiliation and support for the CCF declined after the 1946–47 strike wave, in the late 1950s there was a new resurgence of union support for and interest in the building of a labor-based political party. In 1961 the CCF joined with the Canadian Labour Congress to launch the New Democratic Party. The NDP was based much more directly on the unions than had ever been the case with the CCF.

Today, many working farmers, like workers, tend to look toward the NDP for support when they go into struggle. And like trade unionists and other workers, many farmers have joined it. Some farmers have been candidates for the NDP including, in 1984, Canadian Farmers Survival Association leader Allen Wilford, the author of *Farm Gate Defense*.

Long march toward unity

Since the defeat of the revolution of 1837–38, political and ideological campaigns by the bourgeoisie and its spokespeople have succeeded in slowing down the process of uniting in action and organization the farmers of Québec and English Canada, just as they have sought to divide all working people in Canada along national and language lines.

For example, at the beginning of the 1920s the Catholic Church hierarchy promoted the formation of a Catholic farmers' organization to counter the influence of the United Farmers, which had begun to develop in Québec as well as Ontario. These efforts produced the Union of

Catholic Farmers (UCF), an organization much more conservative than the United Farmers. The UCF was the forerunner of the present-day Union of Agricultural Producers. The church did the same thing in the labor movement, promoting the formation of the Canadian and Catholic Confederation of Labour, the forerunner of the Confederation of National Trade Unions.

During the Second World War, the Canadian bourgeoisie succeeded in enlisting the top officialdom of English Canada's trade unions and farmers' organizations in their wartime offensive. This class-collaborationist, pro-war course went against the class interests of all workers in Canada, but it was especially unpopular among the great majority of Québécois workers and farmers. In the 1942 referendum on conscription into the wartime army, more than 80 percent of the Québécois voted against conscription while in English Canada more than 80 percent voted in favor. The pro-war policies of the top labor bureaucrats in English Canada, combined with their refusal to support language rights and self-determination for the oppressed Québec nation, reinforced divisions between the English-speaking and French-speaking working people in Canada.

In the course of their history of struggle, however, farmers have tried on several occasions to surmount these national divisions. (The same is true of the working class in Canada and Québec, of course, but the focus here is on the less well-known examples with regard to farmers.)

In the second half of the nineteenth century, the farmers of Québec and Ontario had several common organizations. Toward the end of the First World War, farmers from Québec and English Canada participated in a joint demonstration in Ottawa against conscription. This May 1918 action was probably the only antidraft demonstration ever held jointly by members of the two nations. The United Farmers of Ontario took the initiative in calling the action and Québec farmers elected delegates from their local organizations. About 1,500 Québécois delegates went to Ottawa.

Since then, farmers from English Canada and Québec have organized other joint demonstrations. But such actions have been rare. Since the Second World War, however, several factors have changed, improving conditions for united action by English Canadian and Québécois farmers today. One of the most important factors is the development of agriculture, particularly in Québec.

Although the productivity of Québec agriculture still lags behind that of the rest of Canada, it has grown significantly since the Second World War. Between 1976 and 1982, in fact, Québec was the province where farm production grew most rapidly. This modernization has made the conditions and concerns of Québécois and English Canadian farmers much more alike.

The development of agriculture, both in English Canada and Québec, has also broadened the horizons of all farmers. As they produce increasingly for the market and decreasingly for personal consumption, farmers have been pushed closer to the center of the country's economic and political life. This in turn has made the question of uniting the farmers' movement in the two nations more concrete.

The deepening of the class differentiation between capitalist and working farmers has also pushed the exploited farmers of each nation to turn for allies toward the workers and exploited farmers of the other nation. Especially since World War II, the conditions of rural producers and urban workers of both nations have become much more similar in terms of literacy, education, access to information, and mobility. Also to be noted in this regard is the development of pan-Canadian industrial unions. They remain today the only mass organizations that include exploited producers from both Québec and English Canada.

In recent years, new links have begun to be established between the pan-Canadian unions and the farmers' movement. The National Farmers Union (NFU), for example, supported the mobilization of the trade unions against the freeze on wages in the mid-1970s. The Canadian Labour Congress supported the demand of farmers to keep the Crow's Nest Pass rate, as did the NDP. The unions in Québec have supported the struggle of the farmers in Mirabel against the expropriation of 96,000 acres of choice farm land to build an airport that required only 16,000. The United Auto Workers has participated in militant actions against farm foreclosures by the banks.

This development of ties between farmers and the pan-Canadian labor movement enhances the possibility of closer links between the farmers of Québec and English Canada. Unlike the unionized workers of the two nations, however, the exploited farmers do not yet have any joint organizations fighting for their interests.

Farmers' organizations today

The organizations claiming to speak for the interests of farmers in Canada today vary enormously, including in their class character.

Some primarily represent the interests of the capitalist farmers. This is the case with the Canadian Federation of Agriculture, the Ontario Federation of Agriculture, and the Union of Agricultural Producers in Québec. While these are the biggest organizations numerically, their leaders are politically conservative.

The National Farmers Union, on the other hand, is an organization that to a great degree reflects the demands and aspirations of exploited farmers. It has about 6,000 members, all in English Canada. Even though officially it does not support any party, a significant proportion of its leaders and activists identify with the NDP, and many are active members of it.

Over the last several years smaller organizations, formed around specific struggles by farmers, have emerged. One example is the Canadian Farmers Survival Association in English Canada, which has led a series of struggles against farm foreclosures, on occasion with success. Another is the Québec Farmers Survival Movement. Groups of women farmers have also been formed in recent years. The emergence of these militant organizations reflects farmers' willingness to combat the attacks on their livelihoods, which have intensified since the early 1980s.

These organizations have helped reintroduce into the farmers' movement militant methods of struggle that have not been seen since the 1930s. Their mobilizations have, at times, forced banks to agree to reduce or extend debt payments of some farmers. The NFU has felt the influence of these mobilizations and is itself playing an increasingly larger role in such actions.

There have been initial steps by farm activists from English Canada and Québec to establish closer collaboration. In an August 1984 interview with the Canadian biweekly *Socialist Voice,* Allen Wilford underlined the problems faced by farmers in Québec and English Canada who want to know more about each others' struggles. "We're constantly fighting to get the news around, to give each other encouragement," Wilford said.

Two members of the Québec Farmers Survival Movement attended the December 1985 NFU convention, and its president, Jean-Claude Boucher, addressed the NFU delegates.

The farm crisis has led farmers to seek international allies, as well. The NFU is establishing links with farmers' organizations around the world. It has participated in work brigades in Nicaragua. Julio Ruiz, a representative of Nicaragua's National Union of Farmers and Ranchers (UNAG), attended the 1985 NFU convention. And two representatives of the NFU traveled to Managua in April 1986 to participate in UNAG's First Peasant Congress.

The NFU also helped sponsor and organize speaking tours in western Canada by representatives of the Peasant Movement of the Philippines in 1985 and 1986.

The NFU and the Canadian Farmers Survival Association have also joined the North American Farm Alliance. The latter is a coalition that includes several U.S. farmers' protest organizations. In September 1985 it organized a tour of North American farmers to Nicaragua, in which three Québec farmers took part.

Participation of women

From the beginning, women have played an important role in the Canadian farmers' movement. The militant farmers' organizations early in this century supported women's demand for the right to vote.

In recent years, particularly with the deepening of the economic crisis, there has been a considerable increase in the participation of women farmers in struggles. A number of organizations have been established by women farmers to defend their interests both as women and as farmers.

Women farmers have been hard hit by the effects of the capitalist economic crisis and government austerity offensive. They are the victims of drastic cuts in social services in the countryside. There are practically no day-care centers in the agricultural regions. A study conducted by Concerned Farm Women, a group of women farmers in Ontario, and published in *The Farmer Takes a Wife* by Gisele Ireland, showed that 53 percent of women farmers who have children under twelve years old have to take them along when they perform work on the farm. Women farmers have more difficulty than women in the cities in getting access to health centers or to battered women's shelters.

Women's participation in farm work has increased with the deepening of the farm crisis over the past decade. But their work still receives very little recognition. A study recently conducted by women farmers in Québec showed that 87 percent of farm women participate in farm work, with 36 percent of them taking responsibility for the farm's financial books. The Ontario study showed that more than 85 percent of farm women share farm-related financial decision making with their husbands. But these hours of labor that they expend in farm work receive little social recognition and go almost unacknowledged in official government statistics.

Women on the farm face discrimination at all levels. Women who own farms find it more difficult than other farmers to get loans and governmental subsidies. And women who operate farms jointly with their husbands have big difficulties in getting legal recognition as part owners. As a step toward overcoming some of these problems, the Québec Union of Agricultural Producers recommended that women list their occupation as "farmers" in the 1986 Canadian census, to gain acknowledgement of their contribution to farm production.

According to the Canadian Farmworkers Union, 70

percent of farm workers in British Columbia are women. They receive on the average $2 an hour, which is less than the legal minimum wage.

This participation by women in farm production, combined with the impact on them of broader struggles for women's rights, indicates that farm women will be a growing component of the activists and leaders of farmers' struggles in the years ahead, and that they will form a component of the movement for the liberation of women, as well.

III. THE CRISIS IN AGRICULTURE

THE FARMERS OF CANADA AND QUÉBEC are suffocating under a rising mountain of indebtedness. In 1984 the total debt of farmers in Canada reached almost $21 billion, nearly four times higher than ten years before. The most devastating effects of farm indebtedness fall on the exploited working farmers.

According to the official figures of the Farm Credit Corporation, 23 percent of the farmers in Canada were "under severe financial stress" in 1985, compared to 17 percent the year before. Many farmers are so deeply in debt that payments on interest and principle absorb their income; they now borrow even more to cover production costs for the year ahead and provide for their families' basic living expenses.

The rise in interest rates in the late 1970s and early 1980s also contributed to falling land prices, as did the fall in the prices of many farm commodities during these years. Between 1982 and 1984 the price of land declined by 20–25 percent in some parts of Canada, such as Ontario and Québec. In the St. Lawrence River valley in

Québec and in parts of the west, land prices dropped by as much as 50 percent.

A drop in the price of land creates grave problems for farmers who hold title to the land they work, since it reduces their collateral, which is demanded by the banks as a guarantee to obtain new loans. Moreover, such a decline leads the banks to demand more rapid repayment of existing loans.

THE COMBINED EFFECTS of increased indebtedness, falling crop prices, and plummeting land prices have produced a considerable decline in the farmers' net farm income (their total sales revenues minus total costs of production). Real net farm income in Canada in 1984 dropped to just over one-third of what it had been ten years earlier.

This decline in farm income has increased the number of bankruptcies to record levels: 488 in 1983, 551 in 1984. Québec has been hit particularly hard. With 15 percent of the farms in Canada, Québec had 35 percent of the bankruptcies in 1982, 26 percent in 1983, and 29 percent in 1984. Young farmers, just starting out, are often the most in debt and are thus the most vulnerable.

The reality is even grimmer than the number of bankruptcies would indicate. Faced with intensifying economic pressures, many farmers are abandoning farming before they go bankrupt. The NFU estimates that about seven times as many farmers lose their land through foreclosures and "voluntary" liquidations as through bankruptcy.

In defending the interests of the capitalist monopolies and the richest farmers, the federal and provincial governments have stepped up attacks on working farmers, aggravating the effects of the crisis. The harshest of these attacks in recent years has concerned the cost of transporting farm products.

In 1979 the Canadian government announced its intention to end the Crow's Nest Pass freight rate agreement, which was adopted in 1897 and revised in the 1920s. This agreement, a conquest of earlier farmers' struggles, was in effect a governmental subsidy to help Prairie farmers defray the costs of transporting grain east to the Great Lakes and Hudson's Bay and west to the Pacific.

In abolishing the Crow rate, the capitalist government in Ottawa had essentially two goals. First, it aimed to make the farmers pay a much larger portion of the costs of grain transportation. And second, it aimed to open the door to the overall deregulation of grain transport. This deregulation—already under way—will lead to increased attacks on the jobs and working conditions of rail workers and weaken their trade unions. It will permit the elimination of many spur lines and grain elevators. This will compel farmers to travel much farther to deliver their grain to grain elevators.

The Crow's Nest Pass rate was abolished in 1983. This led immediately to an increase in the farmers' transportation costs—54.8 percent in the first year. It is estimated that by 1991 farmers' transportation costs will increase more than five times over. The NFU demands that the Crow rate be reestablished. It also proposes that the Canadian Pacific railroad be nationalized and amalgamated with Canadian National, which is already government-run.

The battle over the Crow's Nest Pass rate showed the conflicting class interests that exist among farmers. Indeed, the farmers' organizations divided on this question into two groups with radically opposed positions. All the organizations representing the richest farmers supported abolition of the Crow rate in one way or another. The NFU is the only large farmers' organization that carried out a systematic and consistent struggle against its abolition.

The federal government is readying other attacks on farmers, such as drastic cuts in subsidies to farmers and in agricultural price supports. These moves would hit hard at farmers' incomes.

A crisis such as that experienced today by exploited farmers exacerbates deterioration of the soil. Farmers are compelled to extract the maximum from the soil at the least cost—especially when they are on the verge of bankruptcy. They cut back on the rotation of crops, and they reduce use of fertilizers. As a result, many square miles of fertile soil are transformed into a veritable wasteland. In addition, much land is now being left uncultivated because the banks and government agencies that have seized it through foreclosure cannot sell it for a price they consider adequate. All this shows to what degree capitalism is responsible for a vast waste of natural and human resources.

The agricultural crisis affects the entire rural community. Every layer that depends on agriculture is affected: farm machinery repairmen; truck drivers; workers who build boxcars; workers who maintain irrigation works; veterinarians; small merchants; salespersons of agricultural implements, cars, fertilizers; and so on. Social services are being cut in rural areas as part of the overall government austerity drive. The Québec government has not hesitated to close down entire villages in order to avoid having to supply road, water, and other services.

How is it that English Canadian and Québécois farmers, who produce enough food to end a good part of the world's hunger and who could produce much more if they did not constantly find sand thrown in their gears—how is it that these farmers themselves find it hard to live and that every year thousands of them go bankrupt or abandon their land, thus losing the main source of their livelihood? The answer to that question is found in the way that the capitalist system operates.

IV. FARMERS' STRUGGLES AND DEMANDS

CONFRONTED WITH the worst agricultural crisis since the thirties, farmers in Canada in recent years have greatly stepped up their protest actions, demonstrations, and rallies. Their struggles and demands have taken more militant forms.

Farmers today, as in past struggles, are making a very simple demand: that the prices they receive for their products from the state marketing boards and the big processing and distribution monopolies be high enough to enable them to cover their production costs and receive an adequate income for their families.

Modest as this demand may seem, it is fiercely resisted by the capitalist families who control the Canadian economy and state. When prices barely cover the real costs of production or even fall below them—as has been the case in recent years—then farmers are forced to take drastic cuts in their living standards, sink further into debt to meet costs, and resort to shortcuts in farming methods that often contribute to more rapid soil erosion and other negative consequences.

Rightly believing that what they produce is socially useful, farmers are demanding that the federal and provincial governments guarantee them an adequate income. Farmers' organizations have developed many kinds of formulas to define how this adequate income can be achieved.

Bill C-215, for example, twice proposed by NDP member of parliament Lorne Nystrom, aims to establish a formula to set the domestic prices of wheat, barley, oats, hogs, and beef when sold for human consumption. It aims to have the federal government establish what is referred to as "parity" between these products' prices and the prices of products from other sectors of the economy.

Claude Giroux, leader of a farmers' group in Essex County, Ontario, explained what many farmers mean by parity: "one sector of the economy can trade the product of one hour of labor for the product produced by another sector in one hour."[10]

Farmers in the United States have developed other parity formulas. But all of these aim at finding a mechanism so that farmers will receive a price that better corresponds to their real costs of production. Confronted by a market that they cannot control, farmers demand that the government guarantee them a decent income.

The struggle of farmers for an adequate income should be supported by the labor movement. This includes backing government-subsidized parity and farm price supports that aid working farmers.

Such programs need not raise the prices that working people pay for food and fiber. Instead, what is required are government subsidies to make up for the depressed prices that the processing and marketing monopolies pay for the commodities produced by farmers' labor. It is these same big capitalist companies that are responsible for the high prices that workers and farmers pay at the cash register. These monopolies reap superprofits from the difference between what they pay at one end and charge at the other. The National Farmers Union has estimated that for every dollar spent for food in Canada, 60 cents goes to the companies that process and distribute food; 31 cents to companies that supply farmers with machinery, seed, fertilizer, and other production inputs; and only 9 cents to the farmers themselves.

Escaping from the cost-price squeeze

Over the years farmers in Canada have proposed many measures to reduce their production costs or obtain better prices for their products. These measures can be classified in three broad categories: cooperatives, insurance programs, and marketing agencies.

The cooperatives experienced their greatest growth during the first two decades of this century. Many of them were established during the upsurge of farmers' struggles then under way.

By uniting in this way, farmers sought to protect themselves against the big corporations' worst excesses by eliminating intermediaries between producers and consumers and restricting competition among themselves.

In Canada, huge cooperatives were established, above all for the marketing of wheat (the Wheat Pools). Several cooperative companies were formed that functioned through mutual funds or shares. In Québec cooperative lumber yards were established. The cooperatives also played a key role in electrification, especially in Québec, where even in 1950 more than half the farms did not yet have electricity.

The cooperatives certainly brought small farmers some gains, but in general their effectiveness was undermined by the economic power of big capital. Many of them have disappeared. Others have themselves become capitalist corporations, operating solely to make profits. The big capitalist intermediaries that the farmers hoped to bypass by establishing their own marketing mechanisms have instead immeasurably strengthened their domination over agriculture during this century, and many of the cooperatives themselves participate alongside the private corporations in the exploitation of working farmers. A graphic example of this process is that all the Prairie wheat marketing cooperatives buckled under the government's attack on the Crow's Nest Pass rate, even where their membership conventions had taken explicit stands against its abolition.

There is no genuine cooperative movement today. The cooperatives continue to exist in the form just described, and the farmers utilize them. But the hopes that the cooperative movement inspired among farmers at the beginning of the century have been dashed by the power of big capital.

The second mechanism utilized by farmers in their efforts to limit the effects of the cost-price squeeze is insurance programs.

The existing government price and income stabilization programs are a special kind of insurance plan. These programs, to which farmers and the government make contributions, pay farmers when the prices of their products fall below a certain level. These programs aim to stabilize farm incomes and avoid too sharp a fall in prices. The most significant of these plans is the Western Grain Stabilization Program, by which the government contributes one dollar for each dollar contributed by farmers. This plan compensates farmers at a certain rate if grain prices fall below the average of the five preceding years.

Like all such programs instituted by capitalist governments, the price stabilization plans favor the rich farmers, even if exploited farmers also gain some benefits. Since payments are proportional to the quantity of the product that each farmer brings to market, those who have produced more, the richest farmers, receive more from the stabilization plan.

In addition, the compensation rates set by the government are often well below the working farmers' costs of production. For example, between 1976 and 1983, payments by the Western Grain Stabilization plan barely exceeded the amount paid into the program by the farmers themselves. While hundreds of farmers were going bankrupt, the government was content to let money accumulate in the fund without seeking to increase the compensation rate granted to farmers. In this way, more than a billion dollars accumulated in bank vaults.

Efforts to control the market

Finally, farmers also seek to utilize marketing boards. In Canada, the most significant such marketing scheme is the Canadian Wheat Board, which was established in 1935 after several decades of struggle by western farmers against the big grain companies. Since then marketing boards have also been set up for poultry, eggs, milk, and other products. One of the most important is the Canadian Milk Marketing Board, established in 1966. Altogether there are more than 100 such boards, accounting for half of Canada's total farm sales. A few are federal boards (wheat, barley, oats, dairy, and poultry), while most operate at the provincial level.

Many farmers and the National Farmers Union demand the establishment of such marketing boards for a range of other products, for example, potatoes and red meat. The boards demanded by the NFU would be named by the government, as are the existing marketing boards. They would have jurisdiction across all Canada, unlike most of the existing boards. They would be the only marketing agencies in Canada for each respective product. Farmers could sell their products only to these boards, which would establish a quota system to limit production and buoy up commodity prices. The boards would pay each farmer the same price. They would also limit imports of these products.

The goal that farmers seek to reach through these bodies is to regulate the market and achieve "orderly marketing," that is, stable prices for their products. The farmers recognize that the capitalist market works against them. They are hard hit by market instability and by big price swings, which can lead to mass bankruptcies in a bad year. And they feel powerless against the big processing and food distribution monopolies.

Farmers seek to use production quotas to compel all farmers to sell their products to a government marketing board and thus to regulate supply. In this way, farmers hope to hold in check the power of giant food processing and distribution corporations and achieve stable prices that are high enough to cover production costs and give them an adequate income.

But the marketing boards managed by capitalist governments cannot make the market work in the interests of small farmers. This is shown by the large number of farms abandoned even in sectors where markets are highly regulated.

The principal problem with these boards is that they favor the exploiting capitalist farmers at the expense of the exploited working farmers. At first glance, it can appear that the measures taken by these boards would lessen the competition and even out differences among farmers, since all are guaranteed that their crops will be purchased at a stable price and all receive the same price for their products. But a closer look shows that this equality is purely formal. Prices and production quotas are set at levels such that rich farmers can make substantial profits while working farmers who have tight budgets often benefit marginally or not at all.

THE EXAMPLE OF THE MILK industry shows very well the limited positive impact of marketing boards on small farmers.

Milk production is the most highly regulated and controlled agricultural sector in Canada. This has not prevented a large number of small dairy farmers from being forced out of farming, however.

In the second half of the 1960s, the Canadian Milk Marketing Board gave every dairy farmer a production quota. This quota, based on how much milk the farmer had produced in 1966–67, determined the amount of milk that farmer could produce in each subsequent year. From 1966 to 1971, the farmers were not allowed any rise in their quotas. This forced a number of smaller dairy farmers into bankruptcy, since the production levels allotted to them were insufficient to cover costs and leave a living income. In Québec, for example, the number of fresh milk producers fell between 1967 and 1971 by 16 percent.

In 1971, the provincial milk producers' associations began to take charge of the distribution of quotas among the farmers of each province. The quotas freed up by the disappearance of many small producers over the five previous years were put up for sale. The big producers bought most of them. This led to an increasing disparity among dairy farmers, with the richer producers allowed to raise their production while smaller producers were forced to maintain previous levels despite rising costs.

During the next ten years in which this system of "orderly marketing" functioned, the number of dairy farmers in Canada decreased by another 24 percent.

All the marketing boards are based on the apportioning of production quotas. The example of milk production shows that such quotas cannot serve the interests of exploited farmers. They are utilized to enrich the capitalist farmers. The allocation of production does not affect the companies that exploit the farmers. The big dairy processors and other food giants take advantage of reduced production to increase the prices paid by consumers and hold the farmers responsible, thus dividing the workers from the farmers.

Moreover, the notion that farmers should limit their production while billions of people in the world suffer from hunger makes sense only in a society that is completely dominated by the frenzied race for profits. This notion only makes sense in a society where those who have no money to buy food have no right to consume it.

Furthermore, marketing programs are almost always accompanied by protectionist measures. These measures aim to preserve the Canadian market for the farmers of Canada and to eliminate the import of commodities produced by farmers in other countries.

It is true that tariff barriers can permit some farmers in Canada to improve their situation temporarily. But the struggle for protectionist measures is not in the interest of either exploited farmers or workers.

A handful of the richest farmers, once buffered by tariffs against competition on the world market, can sometimes reorganize their business to produce more and gain higher profits. But these measures do not improve the market position of small farmers. They only strengthen the hand of capitalist farmers in Canada against working farmers in Canada. With or without protectionist measures, many small farmers will sooner or later be driven out of production unless they attack the source of their problems: the capitalists.

Protectionist measures divide the exploited farmers from their main allies in the struggle against the capitalists: other workers and farmers around the world. Protectionist measures also force consumer prices upwards, harming both workers and working farmers, who buy the big majority of their food at the grocery store. And they set the farmers of Canada against farmers of other countries, who in many cases are exploited by the same companies. They divide farmers in Canada from farmers of the oppressed countries of the colonial and semicolonial world.

Many working farmers have learned through bitter experience that marketing boards and price stabilization plans in their present form, regulated by capitalist governments, help enrich capitalist farmers and food processing giants. Many also understand the absurdity of cutting back production in a world where hunger still reigns and look forward to a more rational and humane system whereby farmers in Canada could put their productive farming methods to work to help feed the world.

SOCIALIST CUBA OFFERS an example of how these problems can be solved to the advantage of the producing majority instead of a tiny exploiting minority.

The workers' and farmers' government in Cuba guarantees farmers a market for their products and a price giving them a decent income. If more products than anticipated are marketed in a given year, farmers are not the victims. The government buys what they produce at the agreed price and resells it to consumers at a lower price. Farmers and consumers thus gain without having surpluses pile up in warehouses until they rot.

Unlike in Canada, the government in Cuba does not divert revenue to provide open or disguised subsidies to the capitalist owners of big corporations; the capitalist exploiters were expropriated more than a quarter of a century ago. On the contrary, government revenue serves to help those who produce the country's wealth—the farmers and the workers. Thus government aid serves directly to increase farm production and improve the conditions of small farmers.

"Orderly marketing," the goal of farmers in Canada, exists in Cuba. It works in the interests of the small farmers and of the entire Cuban people.

But these measures have been made possible only because Cuban workers and farmers built an alliance that enabled them to take power; expropriate the owners of the big corporations, the banks, and the capitalist plantations and farms; and reorganize the economy in their own interests along socialist lines.

For cheap credit

During recent years, farmers' struggles in both Canada and the United States have taken the form of militant mobilizations to block farm foreclosures by banks and government agencies.

One of the major demands of these mobilizations by farmers and their supporters in the unions and elsewhere has been for a moratorium on foreclosures on farms, agricultural equipment, and livestock, as well as a moratorium on debt payments.

Winning such a moratorium would give farmers a

badly needed respite. Moreover, it would encourage the struggle for a fundamental solution to the problems created for farmers by the whole rents and mortgages system.

Farmers have also demanded a system to make credit easily available at a low interest rate.

Through their struggles, farmers have achieved the establishment of lending agencies like the federal government's Farm Credit Corporation and the Farm Credit Office in Québec. These government bodies, however, actually exploit working farmers in much the same way as the private banks do, although the interest rates they charge are sometimes lower.

These agencies are entirely intertwined with the overall banking system.

They demand land as security for loans, thus participating alongside the private banks in one of the most onerous forms of the exploitation of farmers. They are part of the mechanism through which the farmers' land is torn out of their hands. What is the use to farmers of a government credit agency if it, too, exploits them?

Through the years farmers have also sometimes obtained laws enabling those in difficulty to renegotiate the terms of their debts. This was the case in the Prairies in the thirties, where the Farmers' Creditors Arrangement Act forced banks to reduce the debts of many farmers. In November 1985, about 1,000 farmers gathered in St. Thomas, Ontario, to call for such a law. The protest was organized by the NFU, Canadian Farmers Survival Association, Concerned Farm Women, and several other farm organizations.

The trade unions, the NDP, and other workers' organizations should unite in actively fighting for those demands of farmers that would give them a breathing spell, increase their income at the expense of the owners of the big corporations and capitalist farms, and reduce the effects of the cost-price squeeze and the constant threat of bankruptcy and being driven off the land. These demands include: price supports that guarantee farmers their production costs plus an adequate living income; reintroduction of the Crow's Nest Pass rate; a moratorium on farm foreclosures; and cheap credit programs and cancellation of the debts of exploited farmers.

Nationalization of the corporations and the banks

Strangled by the cost-price squeeze, crushed by the weight of the rents and mortgages system, farmers are kept in the dark about the financial operations of the big monopolies and the banks that exploit them.

The labor movement and farmers' organizations should demand that farmers be able to open the books of these corporations and banks. Opening the books would enable farmers to show that neither the prices paid to them for their commodities by these capitalist outfits nor the prices they charge consumers have any relation to the farmers' true costs of production. The capitalist "middlemen" pay farmers too little, charge consumers too much, and pocket the difference.

Farmers need to establish, jointly with the trade unions, committees that demand to see the corporations' books and that campaign to disclose their secret dealings, price gouging, stockpiles, tax loopholes, and their total disregard for human need. Such farmer-labor action would undercut the capitalists' efforts to pit urban and rural producers against each other by claiming that their demands for a living income are the source of rising prices of consumer goods.

Farmers' increasing struggles against their position as debt slaves will lead them to demand nationalization of the banks. This demand was raised by many workers' and farmers' organizations in the past, particularly in the 1930s, and it has been revived in recent years by sectors of the NDP and unions such as the Canadian division of the United Steelworkers of America. The banks directly control most farm credit, and nationalization of these institutions could advance the fight for cheap credit and for a halt to farm foreclosures and to all debt repayment by working farmers.

Nationalization of the banks and the establishment of a cheap credit system were among the first achievements of the Cuban and Nicaraguan governments after the triumph of the workers and peasants over the Batista and Somoza dictatorships. All debts were transferred to the central bank. That enabled the revolutionary governments to cancel the debts of a great many farmers. Foreclosures by banks to bolster their owners' profits were brought to a halt. In Nicaragua, the government has adopted laws canceling or drastically reducing the debts of cooperatives and individual producers and canceling those of all peasants who are fighting on the front lines against the U.S.-backed contra attacks.

Private property in land—a menace to farmers

As the cost-price squeeze cuts their income to the bone, more and more working farmers are being driven off the land or face the danger of foreclosure in the months and years ahead.

The possibility of being driven off the land is rooted in the very nature of landholding under the capitalist mode of production. Doing away with that ruinous prospect, which hangs over every working farmer, is bound up with ending farmers' exploitation under the capitalist rents and mortgages system.

This form of exploitation is part and parcel of the fact that land can be privately owned, bought and sold on the market, and rented out. Land to which a farmer holds title can be utilized as security for loans and can therefore serve as an instrument for capitalist accumulation and for exploitation of the farmer. Land can be expropriated by the bank or other capitalist lending institution if the debtor is forced to fall behind or default on interest payments.

During the past decade the rate of farm foreclosures in Canada has speeded up. A larger and larger number of farmers have found themselves unable to meet mortgage payments on the land they work and interest payments on loans to cover costs for machinery, seed, fuel, and fertilizer. It is therefore not surprising that farmers are beginning to debate alternatives to the rents and mortgages system.

An article in the November–December 1985 issue of *Union Farmer* by Bill Metke points to the existence of private property in land as the main cause of the threat weighing down on farmers of losing their farms. Metke raises a number of proposals that he believes would gradually end private ownership of land, guaranteeing farmers the use of their land and putting an end to mortgages and foreclosures.

METKE'S ARTICLE does not represent the first time that the need to abolish private ownership of the land has been raised and discussed by farmers and militant farmers' organizations in Canada.

At the end of the 1920s and the beginning of the 1930s,

the Great Depression and severe drought brought farmers in western Canada the worst crisis of their history. Between 1928 and 1931, farm income fell dramatically: the yield of wheat per acre in Saskatchewan went from 23.3 bushels to 8.8, while the price of wheat fell from $0.77 per bushel to $0.35.

Seymour Martin Lipset described this period of Prairie farm history in his book *Agrarian Socialism,* first published in 1950.

"The depression and drought of the 'thirties demonstrated to many farmers the comparative worthlessness of owning land if it would not produce income. As tens of thousands of farm families were forced to leave the province or to trek to the northern bush frontier to earn a living, fear spread throughout the province. It is impossible to overemphasize the farmer's continuing fear of losing his entire means of livelihood. He was unable to pay the accumulated interest on his debts and taxes. . . .

"Between 1928 and 1932 the interest owed on debts in rural Saskatchewan rose from one-tenth to nearly three-quarters of the net cash operating income of the farmers. The threat to the farmers' ownership of land seemed to come from the mortgage companies. Many Saskatchewan farmers literally had 'little to lose but their mortgages'."[11]

In 1931, a congress of the Saskatchewan section of the United Farmers of Canada (UFC) adopted a program demanding among other things that "use leases [on all farms] be instituted and that all land and resources now privately owned be nationalized as rapidly as opportunity will permit."[12] By "use leases," the resolution meant that farmers would be given titles to use the land for as long as they chose to work it, but could not sell, rent, or mortgage it.

"The proposal for land nationalization," according to Lipset, "came from the floor of the convention. It was introduced by delegates who had been influenced by the British Labour Party, which had a similar rural program. During the depression the lessening of the sense of security on the part of landholding farmers taught many of them that the ownership of property was not the crucial factor; rather, it was the use of that property. They proposed to let the Commonwealth hold title and modify the risks of fluctuating values, provided the farmers could farm the land and concentrate on their proper business as wheat growers."[13]

Thus a major organization of Prairie farmers at the beginning of the 1930s, after a substantial period of struggle and facing a crisis of historic magnitude, came to the conclusion that there was a contradiction between maintaining private property in land and guaranteeing farmers the right to continue cultivating it. These militant farmers recognized that, through the system of private land ownership, the banks had farmers by their throats.

In April 1932, the Independent Farmer Party of Manitoba also proposed nationalization of the land.

According to Lipset, in the months that followed the Saskatchewan UFC's 1931 congress, the escalating ruin of small farmers "provided further justification for the U.F.C. proposal that every farmer be given a use-lease title to his land instead of a private title that could be lost to a mortgage company."[14]

At the time of its formation in 1933, the Co-operative Commonwealth Federation also took up this demand for nationalization of the land. "The new party advocated socialization of all private industries in Canada. This applied to land as well," writes Lipset, "since the U.F.C. [which had become a section of the CCF], under the impact of the depression, advocated a form of land nationalization in which the state would hold title to the land and the farmers would be given a use-lease title. This appealed to many agrarians as a means of preventing foreclosures by banks and mortgages companies."[15]

"This proposal . . . was never suggested as a means of making farmers employees of the state or even members of cooperative farms. The CCF farmers accepted it as a means of guaranteeing permanent land tenure to working farmers."[16]

The exploiting farmers and other capitalists, however, responded to this proposal by raising a hue and cry about communism. Under this red-baiting pressure, the class-collaborationist leadership of the CCF began to retreat on this question. By 1944, the CCF had dropped its previous position altogether and limited itself to the demand "to reduce debts and mortgages to a figure at which they can reasonably be paid at prevailing prices for farm products."[17]

Land nationalization benefits working farmers

As many militant working farmers of the Prairies recognized some fifty years ago, the nationalization of the land, that is, the abolition of private property in soil, does not involve expropriation of farm families who work it. On the contrary, it is the only protection that working farmers have against the expropriation of their land by the capitalists. It is a guarantee that the exploited farmers will be able to use their land as long as they wish, free from the threat of foreclosure, ruin, and forced proletarianization. Nationalization of the land does not affect the farmers' ownership of their means of production—tools, machinery, livestock, and so forth—or of the products of their labor. Instead, it frees them to put their means of production to work producing food and fiber needed by people in Canada and around the world and to make a decent and secure living while doing so.

Land nationalization would put an end to the buying and selling of land. No longer would working farmers have to go deep into debt to get title to land and then put up that land as security on loans to finance other costs of production. The abolition of private property in land would also end the renting out of land by landlords under any form (tenant farming, sharecropping, or others). Never again would parasitic capitalist landlords and speculators grow wealthy off the labor of those who actually work the land. Once the land was nationalized, its use by working farmers who held a lease or title to it would be guaranteed. This land could change hands only through being returned to the state or passed on to an heir who wished to continue farming it.

The abolition of private property in land does away with the commodity character that comes to dominate the use and transfer of the land under the capitalist mode of production through the rental of land and its purchase and sale on the market. Nationalization of the land frees the exploited farmers from the burden of big land costs and the constant threat of bankruptcy or property foreclosure on land to which they hold title. It frees tenant farmers from the threat of ruinous rent increases and losing their leases.

It is for this reason that nationalization of the land is vigorously opposed today by the bankers, the big landowners, the speculators, the agribusinesses, and, generally, by the whole capitalist class. It goes right to the heart of the system of rents and mortgages, which is a fundamental mechanism for the exploitation of working farmers.

Nationalization of the land would liberate the farmers from the bankers and the landlords. It would free up funds for agriculture. It would promote the growth of production. The two billion dollars that the farmers of Canada put out in 1981 to repay their debts and the $630 million they paid in rents that year could be rechanneled into improving and expanding agriculture.

HOW CAN REVOLUTIONARY-MINDED workers and farmers who understand the necessity for nationalization of the land most effectively explain this demand to other exploited producers? The best way to approach this question is through a series of concrete measures addressed to solving the many problems created today for the exploited and oppressed by private ownership of land.

To begin with, the already nationalized lands in Canada can be used in the interests of the workers and farmers, instead of a handful of capitalist ruling families. About 90 percent of the land in Canada is already in the public domain. This represents a surface area as large as the United States. But the federal and provincial governments continually allow oil, mining, and forestry companies to remove the riches of the soil for their own profits.

The case of ITT-Rayonier—a subsidiary of the giant U.S.-based monopoly—is typical in this regard. In July 1972, the Liberal Party government in Québec gave this company the exclusive right to use a territory four times the size of Belgium. The government provided ITT-Rayonier with enormous subsidies to build a pulp and paper plant, while taking responsibility for building and maintaining access roads for the company. After laying waste to the most accessible part of the forest, ITT-Rayonier announced in September 1979 that it was shutting the plant down and laying off 1,300 workers. Nationalization of the land would put an end to such pillage.

Nationalization of the land would also result in the expropriation of the big capitalist landlords and farmers. Where land is being rented by working farmers, they would acquire title for its use. Where land is now worked by big capitalist farm-factories, state farms could be established. In many cases, however, these lands would be turned over to the agricultural workers who worked them, either to farm on an individual basis, as members of a cooperative, or in some combination of the two. Nationalization of the land would lay the basis for a genuine land reform to benefit not only landless farm laborers, but also farm families who currently do not hold leases or titles to a plot sufficiently large enough to produce efficiently and make a decent living.

Abolition of private property in land would also put an end to the orgy of land speculation and profiteering in the cities. It would thereby bring about an immediate drop in housing costs for workers. Land nationalization would mean a substantial rent reduction for tenants and a reduction of mortgage payments for working-class homeowners.

LAND NATIONALIZATION would create the preconditions for justice for the Native peoples, as well. In flagrant violation of many Indian treaties, the federal and provincial governments have stolen and continue to steal the lands belonging to the Native peoples in order to bolster the interests of the forestry, mining, and oil companies, and other capitalist interests. The abolition of private property in land can create the preconditions to restore once and for all the rights and improve the living conditions of the Native peoples.

To defend the interests of the exploited farmers, all the land must be nationalized, not just the land of the big capitalist landlords and farmers. As long as a substantial portion of the land can be legally bought and sold, neither land speculation nor the scourges of high rents, mortgages, and foreclosures will cease. The need to obtain loans to cover the purchase of new machinery and other production costs would force the exploited farmers to mortgage their land or even to sell a portion of it. Maintaining the commodity character of land would thus open the door to a new accumulation of land in the hands of the wealthy owners of the banks, real estate companies, and other capitalist outfits. More and more working farmers would be driven off their land or reduced to renters. Tenant farmers would still face onerous rental payments and the insecurity of losing their lease and the fruits of their past labor expended in improving the land.

Nationalization of the land is thus the only way to lay the basis for a permanent end to the exploitation of working farmers, whether they rent their land or hold title to it.

Opponents of nationalizing the land frequently argue that property-holding farmers are too attached to their ownership titles to be able to understand how they would benefit from the abolition of private property in land. The experience of farmers in the Canadian west is a powerful refutation of that argument. The demands raised by working farmers in the 1930s on the land question demonstrate that in the course of big struggles they can be won to the perspective of nationalizing the land.

Like the farmers of fifty years ago, many of those who

are fighting against debt slavery and foreclosures today can be convinced that abolition of private land ownership will not cause them to lose the right to cultivate their land and assure a living for their families, but is instead a precondition for maintaining that right.

To use Engels's expression from the 1890s, defense of private ownership "does not protect [the working farmer's] liberty but only the particular form of his servitude."[18]

As growing numbers of militant farmers come to recognize the truth expressed by Engels, they will once again place the fight for nationalization of the land at the center of their demands. The expanding work by socialists in Canada as participants in the struggles by working farmers will create greater interest in what we have to say about the need to abolish private land ownership and about the largely suppressed and forgotten record of the farmers' movement of half a century ago.

As farmers and farmers' organizations come to understand and champion nationalization of the land, they will learn through their struggles that the capitalist government cannot be relied on to carry it out. In fact, the government will fight hard to block this measure, which would deal a heavy blow to capitalist landowners, bankers, and other capitalist interests defended by the Canadian state.

Farmers' struggles, both those that have begun today and the bigger struggles to come, will converge with the battles by workers for decent living and working conditions in the face of the escalating austerity drive and antilabor assaults by the employers. This alliance of workers and farmers will more and more be pushed onto the road of political struggle, a road that points toward the need for a new kind of government—one that is based on the exploited producers and advances the interests of the vast majority, not a tiny minority of superrich capitalist families.

V. FOR A WORKERS' AND FARMERS' GOVERNMENT

THROUGH THE STRUGGLES that farmers are carrying out, they are developing greater confidence in their own strength. It is through class-struggle experiences such as these that growing numbers of working farmers will discover who their allies are and who their enemies are. They will learn to think socially and internationally, as part of the exploited producers not only of Canada but of the world. They will develop new forms of struggle, establish new organizations, forge a fighting alliance with the labor movement, and jointly with it chart a course toward the fight for power.

Thus, the prospects for constructing a powerful mass movement that can advance the interest of working farmers are intertwined with the struggle for the transformation of the trade unions into revolutionary instruments that fight uncompromisingly against the capitalists and their government for the interests of all the oppressed and exploited.

Seeking always to divide workers and farmers, the bourgeoisie portrays farmers as rich people who complain while seated on their moneybags. They say that the farmers themselves cause their own problems and if these "businessmen" go bankrupt, it is because they are incompetent managers. The truth is that it is the capitalists themselves and the workings of the capitalist profit system that drive the farmers to bankruptcy.

The most oppressed layers of the exploited producers in both the city and the countryside will play a leadership role in the struggle to unite the workers and the farmers and overcome the divisions promoted by the capitalists. It is these oppressed layers who have the greatest interest in strengthening the workers' movement and the movement of exploited farmers. By supporting the demands of women, Québécois, Native peoples, Blacks, immigrants, and youth, workers and farmers will strengthen their organizations, make them more militant, more determined, and more able to carry the struggle for power through to victory.

BOTH WORKERS AND exploited farmers have a stake in taking up the demands of farm workers and helping them to organize unions to fight for decent wages and working conditions. The presence of a large number of immigrants among farm workers makes these working people particularly attuned to political developments and struggles in Latin America, the Caribbean, Africa, and Asia and helps heighten the internationalist consciousness of the working population in Canada as a whole.

In British Columbia, some limited gains have been achieved through the formation of the Canadian Farmworkers Union. This union has waged struggles not only for decent wages and job conditions but also against racism and for immigrant rights. In 1983 it joined with the rest of the labor movement in British Columbia as part of the Operation Solidarity campaign against the Social Credit government's austerity and antilabor onslaught.

A workers' and farmers' alliance, led by a class-struggle leadership, would campaign to help farm workers unionize, obtain wages at union rates, and improve their working conditions. The exploited working farmers and farm workers have common interests. By defending the interests of farm workers, farmers and other working people strengthen their determination and their independence vis-à-vis their common exploiters.

The demands of exploited farmers cannot be won following the course of the class-collaborationist misleadership of the unions and of the NDP, which has gravely weakened these organizations and their capacity to defend the interests of workers and their allies. The industrial unions do in fact constitute the most powerful mass organizations of the working class in Canada, and that power could be brought to bear to advance the fight by all working people for their just demands. But the strength of the unions remains largely unused, since the existing officialdom retains a narrow, business-union orientation. This class-collaborationist course keeps the working class internally divided instead of uniting it against the employers and the employers' government. And it also keeps labor divided from its allies, such as exploited farmers.

Efforts by class-struggle-minded workers to involve labor in active support for farmers' struggles are a key factor in the fight to transform the unions.

As the effects of the capitalist system continue to worsen the conditions of both workers and farmers, larger numbers of fighters will discover that the problems confronting them and other exploited and oppressed working people cannot be resolved factory by factory, or farm by farm. Resistance to the deepening capitalist offensive will increasingly push workers and farmers toward independent political action in their own class interests against those of the bosses.

When developments in the class struggle moved in this direction earlier in this century, workers and farmers in Canada created common organizations. As explained earlier, that was how the CCF was born in the early 1930s. Following the formation of the CIO unions and subsequent labor struggles in the 1940s and early 1950s, that unity was a key factor in the founding of the NDP in 1961. Today the NDP is the mass party of the working class and the labor movement in English Canada. In addition, many exploited farmers in English Canada support the NDP and are members of it.

The CCF never had more than a minimal base of support in Québec, in large part as a result of its leadership's opposition to the fight for Québec's national rights and their support for military conscription during World War II. Nonetheless, the deep-going labor battles in Québec through the 1940s and 1950s led to a broad discussion in the Québec unions on the need for labor to build its own political party to fight the bosses and their governments—both the provincial government in Québec City and the federal government in Ottawa. This was one of the major factors that led to the participation of the pan-Canadian industrial unions in both English Canada and Québec in the broad-based movement that culminated in the formation of the NDP.

There were 167 Québec participants in the 1961 founding convention of the NDP. They fought for and won the almost unanimous support of the more than 1,800 delegates from across the country (more than a third of them from the unions) to recognize Québec as a distinct nation within Canada. That was something the CCF had always refused to do, and it was anathema to both the bourgeois parties, Liberal and Tory. Following the convention, however, it quickly became clear that the top party officialdom had no intention of breaking from the CCF's support for Canadian federalism, which is based on the continued subjugation of the Québécois. The NDP leadership's continued opposition to their just demands helped break the rising support within Québec unions for building a pan-Canadian labor party.

This default by the NDP officialdom permitted the union bureaucracy in Québec to divert the growing movement among working people for political change into support for the Liberal Party of Jean Lesage. While this was a party controlled lock, stock, and barrel by the bosses, it was able to use nationalist demagogy to win labor support in its victorious 1962 election campaign. This maneuver was made possible above all by the failure of the pan-Canadian labor leadership to defend Québec's national rights as part of a campaign to unify all working people in the fight against oppression and exploitation.

As a result of the upsurge of the Québec national struggle in the late 1960s, based on the mounting struggles of workers, farmers, and students, the reactionary character of the Liberals became increasingly clear to many. The Parti Québécois (PQ) was formed in 1968, a bourgeois nationalist party based on a split from the Liberals.

In this context, a new discussion on the need for building a labor party broke out in the unions in the late 1960s. While centered on the idea of building an independent labor party in Québec, this development was also reflected in the increased participation of Québécois within the NDP. But the rejection of support for Québec's right to self-determination by the NDP's 1971 federal convention—despite a sharp fight by rank-and-file delegates from both nations—led to the walkout of most of the NDP's Québécois members from the party.

As the NDP's support in Québec fell to a new low, the PQ won mass support from Québec's workers and farmers. Once again the NDP leadership's opposition to their national demands and struggles, combined with the support of the Québec union bureaucracy for a capitalist party, blocked the development of a promising movement toward a labor party.

As a result of the Parti Québécois's two terms in office between 1976 and 1985, growing numbers of working people became disillusioned with it. Not only had it shown itself unable to defend adequately Québec's national rights against federal government attacks, but it had also become a key weapon in the capitalist rulers' austerity drive leading to a series of major confrontations between the PQ regime and the unions. As a result, a discussion has broken out once again in the labor movement on the need for a political alternative to the PQ within Québec politics. In addition, growing numbers of working people are recognizing that their demands cannot be won without support from the rest of the pan-Canadian labor movement and without a political weapon to fight the bosses' parties and their government in Ottawa.

In this context, there is greater support for the NDP in Québec today than ever before—particularly at the federal level. It is not at all excluded that as the rulers' attacks are stepped up, the NDP could become a much more significant factor in politics and in the labor and farmers' movements in Québec. This in turn would sharply pose—as it has in the past—the need for a political fight within the NDP and the rest of the pan-Canadian labor movement to win it to champion the struggles and demands of the Québécois.

Whether the building of a labor party in Québec takes the form of a fight to transform the NDP into an effective weapon of class struggle or of the launching of an independent labor party within Québec, such a step would be a major advance for working people across Canada. It is the key next step for the exploited producers in English Canada and Québec to advance towards united political action against their common exploiters, the Canadian bourgeoisie.

The struggles of farmers and workers all lead to a single and same conclusion: no victory won by workers and farmers can be a durable solution so long as political power remains in the hands of the capitalists.

To end their exploitation and place themselves in a position to transform the entire society, workers and farmers in Canada must first take power and form their own government.

In Canada, taking into account the existing organizations of the working class and the fact that a genuinely pan-Canadian mass labor party does not yet exist, the struggle for a workers' and farmers' government in Ottawa is advanced most concretely today by the struggle for a government of the NDP and the Québec labor movement.*

---

* Since this article appeared in the French-language *Nouvelle Internationale* in the summer of 1986, growing numbers of Québécois workers and farmers have turned towards the NDP, despite the party's position on the national struggle. The party's electoral base has grown significantly in both Québec and English Canada, as evidenced by voting results and opinion polls. It has now become a serious governmental alternative to the bourgeois parties at the federal level for the first time in its history.

The NDP is becoming a significant political force in Québec with broad support among workers, farmers, and youth. A discussion has opened up among trade unionists active in the party's Québec wing on the need to wage a political fight in the province's three major labor federations against their leaderships' continued support for one or another bourgeois party and in favor of union backing for and involvement in the NDP.

At the same time, many of these workers and other party activists are seeking to transform the party into a weapon in the

The struggle for the establishment of a workers' and farmers' government is a perspective for uniting the broadest possible layers of the oppressed and exploited in English Canada and Québec and overcoming the divisions that the Canadian ruling class, with the help of the present labor officialdom, seeks to perpetuate and deepen. The existence in Canada of two distinct nations, speaking different languages, established on relatively well-defined and distinct territories, is a base the bour-

---

fight for Québec's national rights. As a result, the Québec NDP has become increasingly involved in the movement in defense of Québec's national and language rights after years of abstention or open opposition. In January 1987 it adopted a resolution that incorporated many of the key national demands of the Québécois and called on the federal NDP to adopt a similar policy at its March convention.

However, on the eve of the convention the leadership of the federal and Québec wings of the NDP reached a compromise in order to avoid a confrontation on this key question. The Québec NDP's resolution was replaced by one that, while making some minor concessions to Québec, did not break from the party leadership's support for the Canadian federal system. Nevertheless, despite the confusion that resulted from these maneuvers, the leadership was unable to prevent a major discussion from taking place at the convention on the Québec national question. The discussion reflected the growing openness that exists among working people in English Canada to the demands of the Québécois.

It didn't take long for the fragile compromise that was adopted at the March convention to begin to unravel. Now, only some two months later, the federal party leadership is backing a provisional agreement reached between Ottawa and Québec that proposes to codify the anti-Québec provisions of the existing constitution. On the other hand, the Québec NDP has joined all three major union federations in Québec and the major nationalist organizations in opposing the agreement.

geoisie uses to weaken the prospects for a fighting alliance of workers and exploited farmers. Thus, the struggle for a workers' and farmers' alliance to take power from the Canadian bourgeoisie can be carried out only on the basis of an unconditional defense of the national rights of the Québécois.

By taking political power in their own hands, the workers and farmers of Canada will establish the basis for taking the economy out of the hands of the capitalists. The land will be nationalized in order to free working farmers from the effects of the capitalist rents and mortgages system and to abolish the other destructive effects of private land ownership. The owners of the banks and the big corporations will be expropriated. The economy will be reorganized along planned, socialist lines to function not for the needs of the bosses, but for human needs.

As the crisis of Canadian capitalism deepens, this crucial discussion on how to unite all of the exploited and oppressed in the struggle for political power will shake up the pan-Canadian NDP and unions from top to bottom. A November 1986 meeting of the Revolutionary Workers League's leadership concluded that this new situation has led to an important shift in the perspectives for independent working-class political action in Canada. The RWL decided that its proposals for building a labor party in Québec should now be centered on the need to affiliate Québec's unions to the NDP and fight to transform the NDP into a genuinely pan-Canadian party that fights to defend the common class interests of workers in both English Canada and Québec.

The RWL will now advocate an NDP government in Ottawa as a concrete step pointing towards the establishment of a workers' and farmers' government in Ottawa and the building of the mass pan-Canadian revolutionary worker's party needed to achieve such a government—*Michel Dugré, May 1987.*

An anticapitalist revolution

The workers' and farmers' alliance has the central aim of overthrowing the state of the Canadian imperialist bourgeoisie. The mortal enemy of workers and farmers in Canada is found within Canada itself, not outside its borders. Despite the view expressed by the top labor officialdom and much of the Canadian left, Canada is not a nationally oppressed country. In fact, Canadian capitalism participates in an active way in imperialist military alliances such as NATO and in the exploitation of the oppressed peoples of the Caribbean, Latin America, and elsewhere in the colonial and semicolonial world.

What is on the agenda in Canada is an anticapitalist revolution, a socialist revolution, to organize the appropriation of the Canadian imperialist bourgeoisie. That will be the task of a victorious workers' and farmers' government in Canada, a task that goes hand in hand with the liberation of the oppressed Québec nation and other measures to begin the elimination of all forms of exploitation and oppression.

Capitalism has nothing to offer exploited farmers; it is the source of all the social evils that they suffer. The only solution for workers and exploited farmers is to expropriate their exploiters and to reorganize production along planned, socialist lines.

The pursuit of profit at the expense of human needs is no more in the interests of independent commodity producers than it is in the interests of wage workers. What the farmers of this country need, and what they demand, is not to live at the expense of other producers, but that they and other producers be able to live decently from the labor that they carry out.

A strategic alliance

The alliance that the working class must build with working farmers is a fundamental component of revolutionary proletarian strategy both before and after the conquest of power from the capitalist exploiters.

Constantly threatened with expropriation by the capitalist class, working farmers are impelled into struggle against the enemies of the working class. The forced proletarianization of family farmers has accelerated since the end of World War II, as shown by the sharp drop in the numbers of working farmers during those years. The working class has every interest in supporting the struggles undertaken by exploited farmers to combat foreclosure and preserve their right to continue working their land and to make a decent living.

The workers' movement foresees "the inevitable doom of the small peasant" at the hands of the capitalist farmers, landowners, bankers, and monopolies, Engels said in 1894. But, Engels added, "it is not our mission to hasten it. . . . The greater the number of peasants whom we can save from being actually hurled down into the proletariat, whom we can win to our side while they are still peasants, the more quickly and easily the social transformation will be accomplished."[19]

Exploited farmers who succeed with the help of the labor movement in staving off ruin will play a central role in the reorganization of agricultural production after the taking of power.

A workers' and farmers' government will guarantee to the small farmers that they can cultivate their lands as long as they want, and it will provide them assistance in doing so in the most efficient and scientific ways available. It will guarantee them a living income and social services such as free medical care, education, and a secure retirement, as it will to all the producers of city and countryside.

The revolutionary workers' movement is unalterably opposed to any kind of forcible collectivization of farmers. The historic line of march of the working class is not toward the rapid, involuntary transformation of working farmers into employees on state farms or large cooperatives under a workers' and farmers' government. As the Manifesto of the Communist Party underlines, "The distinguishing feature of Communism is not the abolition of property generally, but the abolition of bourgeois property. . . . Communism deprives no man of the power to appropriate the products of society; all that it does is to deprive him of the power to subjugate the labour of others by means of such appropriation."[20]

Where capitalist property has been expropriated by a workers' and farmers' government, the common source of the exploitation of workers and small farmers is abolished. The producers of city and countryside have a common interest in developing the most efficient, cooperative, scientific, and environmentally sound means of organizing the production of food and fiber to meet the needs of people here in Canada and worldwide. Proceeding in this way, workers and farmers will make use of the political power they have conquered to expand cooperation in the use of machinery and supplies, the application of scientific techniques, the cultivation of fields and harvesting of crops, and so on. It is along this road of voluntary cooperation that the communist goal of socialist production will be advanced in the countryside.

Socialist Cuba offers the best existing example of how a revolutionary working-class leadership has carried out such a policy. Following their victory over the U.S.-backed Batista dictatorship in 1959, the Cuban revolutionists carried out two radical land reforms in the early 1960s. They turned over titles to land to landless peasants and peasant families who had previously had too little land to make a decent living. To the extent of the Cuban government's resources and capacities, these producers were given financial and technical assistance to improve production. They benefited from the general social gains of the revolution in health, education, and housing, as well as from the government's restoration of devastated lands and forests. An organization of small farmers was launched to participate in the development and implementation of policies in agriculture.

At the same time, especially since 1977, the Cuban government has encouraged and devoted greater resources to the development of farm cooperatives, entirely on a voluntary basis. The big expansion in the cooperative sector has brought not only important gains in agricultural production but also further advances in living conditions for rural producers. The small farmers' organization has been the leading force in carrying forward these gains in agricultural cooperation in Cuba.

An internationalist alliance

Farmers' struggles in Canada are unfolding in the context of sharp struggles between the exploiters and the exploited producers in many other countries around the world. Driven by interimperialist competition for markets and sources of cheap labor and raw materials, the ruling classes in North America, Western Europe, Japan, Australia, and New Zealand are demanding more and more concessions from working people of countryside and city throughout the whole world. The debt crisis of the semicolonial and colonial countries is only one of the ways that the imperialist powers suck the wealth produced by the workers and peasants out of these countries and into the bank vaults of Toronto, New York, London, Paris, and Tokyo.

In pressing this offensive, however, the Canadian and other imperialist bourgeoisies meet resistance—in Nicaragua and other parts of Central America, in Haiti and across the Caribbean, in South Africa, in the Philippines, and elsewhere.

The struggles of farmers in Canada are part of this broad international movement. Farmers are increasingly looking for international allies. Many farmers in Canada admire the gains made by Nicaraguan peasants as a result of the workers' and peasants' government established there in 1979. These farmers, on their own or organized through the NFU and other organizations, are building solidarity with the Sandinista revolution and are opposed to Washington's war against the Nicaraguan people.

Struggles against imperialist wars like the U.S.-organized *contra* war in Central America are directly in the class interests of workers and farmers in Canada. In order to fight effectively against their own exploitation by Canada's capitalists, the workers and farmers must break with the imperialist foreign policy of the government of these exploiters. Canadian working people must combat chauvinism and Canadian nationalism. They must recognize that they share common interests with workers and peasants around the world.

A revolutionary movement of workers and farmers in Canada will reject the use of food as a weapon against those around the world struggling for their national liberation and social justice. It will reject protectionist measures such as those that Ottawa has taken against Nicaragua and against other countries oppressed by imperialism.

The mobilizations of recent years have also showed the importance of unity of the workers and farmers on both sides of the Canada-U.S. border. The high degree of economic integration of the United States and Canada requires close collaboration between the trade unions, farmers' organizations, and other organizations of the oppressed and exploited of these two countries.

This internationalist perspective is central to forging a worker-farmer alliance in Canada. It is central to the strategy for establishing a workers' and farmers' government that can advance the class interests of the exploited producers. Socialism in Canada will not be built against, apart from, or ahead of the oppressed and exploited peoples of the rest of the world, but together with them.

The workers and farmers of English Canada and Québec will use their government to come to the aid of all their brothers and sisters in other countries. Such a government will remove the capitalist-imposed shackles from the productive capacities of farmers in Canada.

The establishment of a government of the producers will mark the entry of the workers and farmers of Canada into the international struggle to overturn world imperialism—an essential condition for ending famine, poverty, illiteracy, war, racism, chauvinism of all kinds, environmental destruction, and the oppression of women.

August 1986

NOTES

1. A farm is defined here as an agricultural holding with annual sales of more than $250 Cdn.

2. Karl Marx, "The Class Struggles in France," in Karl Marx and Frederick Engels, *Collected Works* (New York: International

Publishers, 1978), vol. 10, p. 122.

3. Neither land nor labor has value. Value (or exchange value) is a social relation, not a natural or material product. Labor produces all value. Labor and land, on the other hand, are equally the source of use values, which are the material products that make up all the wealth of society. "Labour is the father of material wealth, the earth is its mother," Marx wrote in *Capital* (New York: Random House, 1977), vol. 1, p. 134.

For Marx's discussion of the relation between land (or nature) and labor in the production of value and wealth, see Marx, *Capital,* vol. 1, pp. 133–34, 176; Marx, "Value, Price, and Profit," in Marx and Frederick Engels, *Collected Works,* vol. 20, pp. 124–25; and Marx, "Marginal Notes to the Programme of the German Workers' Party" [Critique of the Gotha Program], in Marx and Engels, *Selected Works* (Moscow: Progress Publishers, 1977), vol. 3, p. 13.

4. Marx, *Capital,* vol. 3, p. 948.

5. In 1763, what had been the French colony of Canada along the St. Lawrence River was renamed by its new British rulers as the colony of Québec. In 1791, the sparsely settled western half of the colony was separated off and named Upper Canada; the eastern half was named Lower Canada. These two colonies were united in 1841 into the British province of Canada. In 1867 they were divided into two provinces within a broader Canadian confederation: the present-day Ontario and Québec.

6. Gilles Bourque, *Classes sociales et question nationale au Québec, 1760–1840* (Montréal: Editions Parti Pris, 1970), p. 88.

7. Stanley B. Ryerson, *Unequal Union: Roots of Crisis in the Canadas 1815–1873* (Toronto: Progress Books, 1975) pp. 77–78.

8. Ibid., p. 119.

9. Stanley B. Ryerson, *French Canada* (Toronto: Progress Books, 1980), p. 53.

10. *Windsor Star,* March 1985.

11. Seymour Martin Lipset, *Agrarian Socialism* (New York: Anchor Books, 1968), pp. 173–74.

12. Ibid., p. 109.
13. Ibid., pp. 109–10.
14. Ibid., p. 112.
15. Ibid., pp. 135–36.
16. Ibid., p. 175.
17. Ibid., p. 176.
18. Engels, "The Peasant Question in France and Germany," in Marx and Engels, *Selected Works*, vol. 3, p. 463.
19. Ibid., pp. 470–72.
20. Marx and Engels, *Collected Works*, vol. 6, pp. 498–500.

Also from Pathfinder

Capitalism's World Disorder

Working-Class Politics at the Millennium

JACK BARNES

The social devastation and financial panic, the coarsening of politics, the cop brutality and acts of imperialist aggression accelerating around us—all are the product not of something gone wrong with capitalism but of its lawful workings. Yet the future can be changed by the united struggle and selfless action of workers and farmers conscious of their power to transform the world. $25. Also in Spanish and French.

The Communist Manifesto

KARL MARX, FREDERICK ENGELS

Why communism is not a set of preconceived principles but the line of march of the working class toward power, "springing from an existing class struggle, a historical movement going on under our very eyes." The founding document of the modern revolutionary workers movement. $5. Also in Spanish, French, and Arabic.

Cosmetics, Fashions, and the Exploitation of Women

JOSEPH HANSEN, EVELYN REED, MARY-ALICE WATERS

Sixty years ago, an article published in the socialist weekly the *Militant* sparked a lively debate on how the cosmetics and "fashion" industries play on the economic and emotional insecurities of women and youth to rake in profits. Today that exchange, contained in this book, a Marxist classic, offers an introduction to the origin of women's oppression and the struggle for liberation. $15. Also in Spanish.

Teamster Rebellion

FARRELL DOBBS

The 1934 strikes that built the industrial union movement in Minneapolis and helped pave the way for the CIO, recounted by a central leader of that battle. The first of four volumes on the strikes and organizing drives that transformed the Teamsters union in the Midwest into a fighting social movement and pointed the road toward independent labor political action. $19. Also in Spanish, French, and Swedish.

We Are Heirs of the World's Revolutions

Speeches from the Burkina Faso revolution 1983–87

THOMAS SANKARA

"We wish to be the heirs of all the revolutions of the world, of all the liberation struggles of the peoples of the Third World. We draw the lessons of the American revolution. The French revolution taught us the rights of man. The great October revolution brought victory to the proletariat and made possible the realization of the Paris Commune's dreams of justice." Five speeches from *Thomas Sankara Speaks*. $10. Also in Spanish and French.

The Working Class and the Transformation of Learning

The Fraud of Education Reform under Capitalism

JACK BARNES

"Until society is reorganized so that education is a human activity from the time we are very young until the time we die, there will be no education worthy of working, creating humanity." $3. Also in Spanish, French, Swedish, Icelandic, Farsi, and Greek.

WASHINGTON'S FIFTY-YEAR DOMESTIC CONTRA OPERATION

by Larry Seigle

IN LATE 1972, AS THE Watergate scandal was bringing to light previously hidden facts about the FBI's covert domestic operations, the leadership of the Socialist Workers Party made a proposal to Leonard Boudin, the country's foremost constitutional attorney and general counsel for the National Emergency Civil Liberties Committee. The party suggested collaboration in a lawsuit against the FBI and other federal police agencies that would seek to establish that the SWP and the Young Socialist Alliance are entitled to engage in political activity without being spied on and infiltrated by agents provocateurs, having their phones tapped and their offices broken into, and being blacklisted and victimized in countless other ways by the political police. The case would be at the center of a fight to establish that FBI operations against the SWP violate the First Amendment to the U.S. Constitution, which guarantees freedom of speech and association, and the Fourth Amendment, which protects the privacy of individuals and organizations against arbitrary searches by government agents.

Such a case had never been brought before, Boudin

was quick to point out. Defendants in criminal cases had often won acquittals based on government violations of their constitutional rights in arresting or prosecuting them. But there was precious little precedent for taking the offensive to counter FBI spying and disruption. In particular, no court had ever restricted the FBI's use of informers.

Nonetheless, Boudin agreed that the time was ripe for such an attempt. If sufficient public support could be mobilized, and the funds raised to finance such a massive undertaking, there was reason to believe that important gains for democratic rights could be won. And he stressed that rights won for the SWP and YSA—two communist groups—would strengthen the rights of everyone in this country and open a broader space for politics by working people seeking to defend themselves and advance their interests. This made the undertaking doubly worthwhile.

Boudin immediately began working to put the case together. The SWP started contacting other defenders of civil liberties to join in establishing the Political Rights Defense Fund, which would organize public support and raise funds for the battle in court. In July 1973 the case was filed in federal district court in Manhattan and assigned to Judge Thomas Griesa, a Republican appointed to the bench by President Richard Nixon.

Thirteen years later, in August 1986, Griesa handed down his opinion. The decision affirms the right of the Socialist Workers Party and Young Socialist Alliance to publicize their views and engage in political activity free from government interference. Griesa ruled—the first such ruling by a federal judge—that the FBI's use of undercover informers against the SWP violated the constitutional rights of the party and its members and supporters to privacy, an essential part of freedom of association.

He also ruled that the FBI's covert break-ins of SWP offices and its disruption operations ("Cointelpros") were unconstitutional.

On that basis, Griesa ruled that the SWP is entitled to collect damages for the violations of these constitutional rights, totaling $264,000. And he ruled that the SWP will be granted an injunction making it illegal for federal agencies to make use of files containing information that was obtained by the FBI through means that the judge has ruled to be illegal.

Following the issuance of the injunction, Griesa will consider a motion by the SWP to require the Justice Department to pay several million dollars in attorneys' fees for the time put in by Boudin and the other lawyers who have worked on the suit. The issue of the attorneys' fees will itself be an important one: lawyers who vigorously defend the rights of communists have in the past often wound up themselves doing time for contempt of court or victimized in other ways. Collecting fees from the government for the work done on the SWP suit will be another substantial victory for democratic rights.

Lawyers for the Justice Department, headed by Attorney General Edwin Meese, are preparing the ground for their appeal of Griesa's decision, which seems certain to wind up in the United States Supreme Court. Supporters of the Political Rights Defense Fund are now undertaking a new round of activity to publicize the victory and its meaning and to rally support for the fight to defend the decision in the higher courts.

IT IS, THEREFORE, an appropriate time to step back and look at the interconnections between this case and the broader fight by the unions and the Black movement in the United States to defend the right to organize and to expand the room for political activities free from government interference.

We will look at the origins and continuity of the FBI's covert war against the Socialist Workers Party. We will also attempt to answer some questions that this case has raised in the minds of many of its supporters. Why has the United States government organized such a massive assault on a small communist vanguard organization? Why has it been the Socialist Workers Party that took the lead in this initiative and has worked with others to carry it successfully to this point? Why not the Social Democrats, who have substantially greater resources and a larger following than the SWP? Why not the Communist Party, which has suffered more than the SWP from the FBI's illegal campaigns of spying, harassment, and disruption?

In tackling these questions, we will come up against some important problems of strategic perspectives for the working-class vanguard in the United States and for the broader international communist movement.

I. Origins of the FBI assault on the Socialist Workers Party

In the predawn hours of a Saturday in September 1939, FBI agents in Iowa and Nebraska simultaneously descended on the homes of union leaders in Omaha, Des Moines, and Sioux City. Teamsters union officials in the three cities were rousted from bed and placed under arrest. They were held on newly filed charges that accused them of burning a bakery truck during a strike in Sioux City more than a year earlier.

Acting under the direction of the U.S. attorney general, the Justice Department in Washington, D.C., coordinated the FBI raids. The arrests occurred at a turning point in the U.S. class struggle—a turning point whose significance became fully clear only much later. The arrest of the Teamster leaders by the federal police marked the opening of the government's systematic use of the FBI as a weapon against class-conscious workers and farmers and against determined fighters against racist discrimination and national oppression in the United States. The response to the raids and arrests also marked the opening of the fight by the working-class vanguard to mobilize all defenders of democratic rights to oppose the FBI's subversion of the Bill of Rights. That fight would soon deepen. In 1941 the FBI and Department of Justice—in the first use of the newly adopted thought-control legislation, the Smith Act—would move directly against the Teamster organization in Minneapolis, a stronghold of Teamster union power and union democracy in the Midwest. The Minneapolis Teamster leaders were effective advocates of political independence of workers and farmers from the capitalist parties.

What was the background to the September 1939 arrests? A year earlier, bakery truck drivers in Sioux City, organized in Teamsters Local 383, had struck the city's bakeries. They demanded higher wages and improvements in working conditions. The bosses charged that during the strike one of their trucks driven by a scab had been stopped and burned on a highway near the Iowa-Minnesota state line. The union denied any involvement. If in fact a truck had been damaged, the union pointed out, the employers probably did it themselves to undermine growing public support for the strike. The alleged incident was a brief sensation in local newspapers but was soon forgotten. Or so it seemed.

The bakery strike was won. The victory had a positive

impact on the union movement throughout the Midwest. It came at a time when the Teamster-led effort to organize over-the-road drivers throughout the upper Mississippi Valley was making important strides. Several months after the strike victory, the International Brotherhood of Teamsters signed a one-year contract with the majority of freight operators in a dozen Midwest states, covering 200,000 drivers and helpers.

The Teamster local officers charged with burning the bakery truck were leaders of the strongest locals in this organizing drive. Only Local 383 in Sioux City had been involved in the bakery strike. But Local 90 in Des Moines and Local 554 in Omaha were also decisive links in the multistate formation through which the over-the-road drive was being organized. That's why their leaders were included in the FBI's charges.

The nature of the frame-up became clear as soon as the trial opened in federal court in Sioux City. The case hinged on a procedural question: did the federal government have jurisdiction to try the union leaders, or were only state laws involved?

Justice Department lawyers offered testimony from FBI agents based on elaborate road surveys. The driver had been heading south from Minnesota to Iowa on a highway that made a ninety degree turn to the left near the state border, continued east for a few miles, and then made another right-angle turn south into Iowa. According to the FBI, by strange coincidence the truck just happened to have been halted at a place where the state line ran precisely down the middle of the road. The perpetrators stopped the truck on the Minnesota side of the road, the FBI witnesses testified, but then made the fatal mistake of moving the truck a few feet across the highway. As a result, it seems, they had transported a stolen vehicle across state lines—a federal crime. Accepting this ploy, the judge upheld the indictments.

"Their argument was as crooked as the road," wrote Farrell Dobbs in *Teamster Politics,* which tells the story of this frame-up trial and its importance in the developing antilabor offensive.[1] Nonetheless, an obliging judge and a biased jury bought the FBI testimony and Justice Department arguments. The seven defendants were convicted. Earl Carpenter, Jack Maloney, Francis Quinn, and Walter K. Stulz were sent to federal prison at Sandstone, Minnesota. Howard Fouts and Ralph Johnson were imprisoned in Terre Haute, Indiana. Louis Miller was assigned to Leavenworth, Kansas. All were given two-year terms.

The Teamsters organized a defense effort. In an appeal circulated to the labor movement and its supporters, Thomas Smith, secretary treasurer of Local 554 in Omaha, urged unionists and defenders of democratic rights to draw the lessons:

> In the interests of the union movement of the United States, we submit the record of FBI operations against the drivers' movement in the Middle West, with the hope that trade unionists everywhere will give these facts serious thought; and with the further hope that even now the weight of public opinion will cause the FBI to withdraw from its present road, a road which is surely leading to the development on American soil of the same sort of anti-labor political police which is the instrument of the ferocious dictatorships in Europe and Asia.

ENDNOTES BEGIN ON PAGE 325

Smith's account of the facts and his appeal for support were published in the *Northwest Organizer,* voice of the Minneapolis Teamsters' local. The paper stressed that the Sioux City trial, together with other recent federal frame-ups of union activists, made it clear "that the FBI is systematically persecuting the labor movement as part of the Roosevelt government's preparations for dragging America into the war. Roosevelt wants first to crush the labor movement, especially its most successful and progressive sections."

Thomas Smith's warnings in the *Northwest Organizer* were right on the mark. The Sioux City frame-up signaled an important new development.

For several years after the First World War, the FBI had functioned as a political police force, carrying out the arrest or deportation of some 3,000 unionists and political activists in 1920 (the infamous "Palmer Raids"). But following widespread protests over these and other FBI actions, and with the decline of the postwar labor radicalization, the capitalist rulers decided against a federal secret police agency. They relied instead on city and state cops with well-established "bomb squads" and "radical units" and on state national guard units in cases of extreme necessity. These local and state agencies had intimate connections with antilabor "citizens" organizations organized by the employers and with hated private detective agencies, such as the Pinkertons, with long experience in union busting.

By the mid-1930s, however, a vast social movement was on the rise, with the Congress of Industrial Organizations (CIO) at the forefront. The relationship of forces was shifting in favor of working-class organizations. The bosses' old methods could no longer always be counted on. Communist perspectives did not come close to commanding majority support among working people, and in fact remained the views of a small minority, but the bosses were nonetheless concerned that progressive anti-capitalist and anti-imperialist political positions advanced by class-struggle-minded union leaders were winning a hearing among a substantial section of the ranks of labor. Especially in times of crisis, such as war, minority points of view defended by established and respected working-class fighters could rapidly gain support.

With this in mind, the administration of President Franklin Roosevelt expanded and centralized federal police power.

During and after the Watergate scandals of the mid-1970s, the immense scope of FBI disruption, spying, and provocations against the people of the United States came to light in an unprecedented way. But the origins of these operations are not—as most commentators place them—in the spread of McCarthyism in the 1950s or in Washington's attempts to disrupt the anti–Vietnam War movement and social protests of the 1960s.

THE FACT IS THAT these FBI operations began on the eve of the Second World War. They were central to preparations by the U.S. capitalist rulers to lead the nation into another carnage to promote their interests against their imperialist rivals and against the peoples of Asia, Africa, and Latin America struggling for liberation from colonial domination. These operations were directed against the leadership—and potential leadership—of the two major social forces in the United States that threatened to interfere with the ability of the U.S. ruling families to accomplish their objectives: the labor unions and the Black movement. The government's aim was to isolate class-struggle leaders who could provide guidance to a broader movement that might develop.

World War II had begun in Europe in September 1939—just a few weeks before the arrests of the Teamster leaders in Iowa and Nebraska. On September 1 Germany's armed forces invaded Poland. Two days later the British and French governments declared war on Germany. Washington proclaimed neutrality and would maintain this as its stated policy until Japanese naval air forces attacked Pearl Harbor in December 1941. But official neutrality was a cover allowing the Roosevelt administration and Congress to take concrete steps toward entry into the war, while avoiding the nationwide public discussion that would have been set off by a Senate debate over a proposed declaration of war.

The drive toward war necessitated an assault on working people at home and against democratic rights in general. Roosevelt gave FBI chief J. Edgar Hoover free rein to use the FBI against the labor movement and Black organizations. The White House and Justice Department secretly authorized many of the illegal methods used by the FBI and turned a blind eye toward others.

This authorization for the FBI to assume the functions of a political police force was done without legislation, which would have had to be proposed and debated in Congress. It was accomplished instead by "executive order," a device that was rapidly assuming a major place in the operations of the government and would increasingly become a major mode of governing in the decades to come.

On September 6, 1939, Roosevelt issued an executive order directing the FBI "to take charge of investigative work" in matters relating to "espionage, counterespionage, sabotage, subversive activities and violations of the neutrality laws." The key phrase was "subversive activities," and the most important decision was to include this slippery concept in the list of responsibilities given the FBI. While there were federal laws against espionage, sabotage, and violation of U.S. "neutrality," no law explained what "subversive activity" might consist of.

TWO DAYS LATER Roosevelt—again by executive decree—made a "finding" of the existence of a "national emergency." This allowed an increase in military spending without having to ask Congress for additional appropriations, thereby avoiding a sharpening public debate over the U.S. government's march toward war. Simultaneously, the president ordered an expansion of the FBI's forces. His objective, Roosevelt told a news conference, was to avoid a repetition of "some of the things that happened" during World War I:

> There was sabotage; there was a great deal of propaganda by both belligerents, and a good many definite plans laid in this country by foreign governments to try to sway American public opinion. . . . It is to guard against that, and against the spread by any foreign nation of propaganda in this country which would tend to be subversive—I believe that is the word—of our form of government.

Forty years later, in a Foley Square courtroom in New York City, top Justice Department officials would cite Roosevelt's words as providing legal authority—derived from the president's "inherent powers" under the U.S. Constitution—for the FBI's campaign of spying, disruption, and provocation against the Black movement, unions, and antiwar and women's liberation fighters and against communist organizations such as the Socialist Workers Party and Young Socialist Alliance.

As the trial of the SWP lawsuit unfolded during the spring of 1981 in Judge Griesa's courtroom, it became increasingly clear that the case revolved around issues far deeper than particular FBI abuses. The historical evolution of the FBI is part of a broader phenomenon in the United States. Underlying the threat today to the rights of privacy and freedom of association is the arbitrary rule by an expanding federal executive power. This power carries out policies at home and abroad that it is less and less able to openly proclaim or mobilize majority support for. It relies increasingly on covert methods to accomplish hidden or half-hidden objectives.

AMONG THE GOVERNMENT'S chief witnesses at the trial in the SWP case was Robert Keuch, deputy assistant attorney general. At the time, Keuch was the third-ranking official in the Justice Department—one of those in the government who remain in place while other, more public, officials come and go with changes in administrations or other political shifts. When he spoke it was not with the voice of a particular administration but on behalf of a part of the state power itself.

Keuch's task on the witness stand was to make the case that the FBI's operations against the party, which span the decades since the SWP's founding convention in 1938, were constitutional because they had been authorized by the president. According to Keuch, the president of the United States has the "inherent power" under the Constitution "to protect our government against those who would seek to change it by unlawful means." This executive power is the source of the legal authority for "intelligence investigations" such as the one against the SWP. The purpose of such "investigations," Keuch testified, is to enable government officials "to take steps to protect ourselves[!] and protect our form of government. . . ."

According to Keuch, in 1939 President Roosevelt authorized the FBI to go after the SWP and other "subversives" because Roosevelt "wanted to know what were the activities and the aims and intentions of groups who potentially could be acting inimically to our form of government. . . ." When asked to define what "acting inimically" meant and how it differed from committing crimes, Keuch replied:

> Well, of course there can be many actions taken to attempt to influence the policies of the United States, its actions, et cetera, that do not necessarily involve or constitute a violation of law. It could be an attempt, for example, to do away with the classification program [for secret government documents]. There could be agitation to do away with security programs totally. An intent to weaken the defenses of the United States. . . .
>
> *There are simply ways that individuals and groups can act that may not necessarily constitute violations of the criminal statutes.* (Emphasis added.)

In other words, advocating ideas and taking actions that are not illegal—even as defined by reactionary legislation—but are nonetheless considered inimical to the interests of those in power can make you the target of the political police.

When asked what Roosevelt had in mind when he used the term "subversive," Keuch responded that the president had been referring first and foremost to those "who were trying to influence public opinion to keep the United States out of war, to keep us neutral." Roosevelt was targeting those who were exercising their constitutional right of free speech to oppose government policies.

There is a term for this concept of the authority to use police power to suppress political dissent and debate within the population: *totalitarianism.* It is exactly what Thomas Smith, the Omaha Teamster official, was warning against in 1939 when he sounded the alarm about the need to combat the emergence in the United States of "the same sort of anti-labor political police" used by repressive regimes in other countries.

Shining a spotlight on this genuinely totalitarian expansion of arbitrary rule by executive power, and laying bare its deep roots, has been one of the major accomplishments of the SWP case.

II. Target: Black fight for equal rights

The employing class and its government set a high priority on isolating those who opposed the use of U.S. military forces to defend capitalist interests overseas. The U.S. rulers foresaw a war in which their vast empire would emerge dominant over its imperialist rivals, and after which they would rule unchallenged over peoples of color in the expanded parts of the globe staked out for U.S. capital. Undisputed power in the "American Century" that they anticipated was beginning would allow them to rule without difficulty at home: holding the working class down and keeping "the colored" under control. At the same time, they hoped that the war launched by imperialist Germany against the Soviet Union would sufficiently weaken the workers' state to make possible its future overthrow and once again open that vast territory to capitalism.

As Washington prepared to enter the war under the banner of fighting the white-supremacist Nazi regime and its allies, Blacks in the United States were battling racist oppression. This struggle centered on the fight to overturn segregation, which existed not just in the South but in every federal government institution throughout the land and to a large extent in private industry and many aspects of social life.

During the decade of the Great Depression, Black working people had suffered even more than their white counterparts. Unemployment among workers who were Black was much higher than among workers who were white. Black farmers lost their land at an even higher rate than did white farmers. Education, health care, and other social services were qualitatively worse for Blacks.

In many parts of the country, particularly in the South, Blacks were systematically denied the right to vote. Segregation laws were backed up with extralegal terror to intimidate those who tried to organize to change these conditions. Lynchings were frequent in the Jim Crow South. The membership of racist terror outfits such as the Ku Klux Klan was intertwined with the cops, courts, and government officials. Throughout the country, police violence and frame-ups of Black defendants were widespread. Even the labor movement was segregated in much of the country. Many craft unions in the American Federation of Labor (AFL) organized to exclude Blacks from membership, and many AFL unions maintained separate locals for Blacks and whites in southern states.

The rise of the industrial union movement in the mid-1930s marked a big step forward in the struggle against segregation. The new industrial unions opened more doors for Black workers, often actively soliciting their participation in the unionization of basic industry. Militant

Black workers had an opportunity to demonstrate their leadership capacities in many labor battles. But race barriers still existed, including within the labor movement itself.

On the eve of the war, the percentage of Black workers in basic industry was still quite low. Most plants engaged in war-related production still refused to hire workers who were Black. Federally funded job-training programs would not enroll Blacks on the grounds that war plants would not hire them anyway.

The U.S. armed forces were segregated from top to bottom. Blacks were assigned to all-Black units under white officers or were relegated to be cooks, porters, laborers, or servants for the white officer corps. The idea of large numbers of Black soldiers in combat, let alone Black officers with the right to command on an equal basis with their white counterparts, was still unthinkable to the military brass and their superiors in Washington.

A measure of the degree of racism that Blacks faced in the military, and in society as a whole, was an order issued at an army camp in Pennsylvania at the beginning of the war. The camp commander proclaimed that "any association between the colored soldiers and white women, whether voluntary or not, would be considered rape." Under pressure from the NAACP, the War Department was forced in January 1942 to cancel the order.

More and more Black people decided that the time had come to step up the fight against this kind of racist oppression. If the United States had entered the war in the name of democracy and against Nazi doctrines of white race superiority, then the fight for changes at home could no longer be postponed. Moreover, as the war unfolded overseas, the rise of national liberation struggles, particularly in Asia and the Pacific, inspired confidence and greater militancy in the fight against racial oppression at home. While the imperialist powers fought each other over redivision of the planet, many colonial peoples seized the opportunity to advance the fight to take control of their own destinies. Inside the United States, peoples of color likewise saw an opportunity to step up the fight for their rights.

THE U.S. RULERS, however, portrayed the fight for equal rights for Blacks as "disruption of the war effort." Supporters of the government in the labor movement and in Black organizations argued that the battle against racism at home, while a worthy one, should nonetheless be kept in check until after a U.S. victory in the war. The fight against racist discrimination, they argued, must not be allowed to go so far as to interfere with the "national unity" needed to win the war. This position was advanced by liberals, by the social democratic Socialist Party, and by the Stalinized Communist Party.

A growing number of Blacks, especially the youth, refused to accept this excuse for inaction. A young worker at an aircraft plant in Wichita, Kansas, captured the sentiment of this growing militancy in a letter published in January 1942 by one of the major newspapers aimed at Black people, the *Pittsburgh Courier:*

> Most of our leaders are suggesting that we sacrifice every other ambition to the paramount one, victory. With this I agree; but I also wonder if another victory could not be achieved at the same time. . . .
>
> Being an American of dark complexion . . . these questions flash through my mind: "Should I

> sacrifice my life to live half American?" "Will things be better for the next generation in the peace to follow?" "Would it be demanding too much to demand full citizenship rights in exchange for the sacrificing of my life?" "Is the kind of America I know worth defending?" . . .
>
> I suggest that while we keep defense and victory in the forefront that we don't lose sight of our fight for true democracy at home.
>
> The V for victory sign is being displayed prominently in all so-called democratic countries which are fighting for victory over aggression, slavery and tyranny. If this V sign means that to those now engaged in this great conflict, then let we colored Americans adopt the double VV for a double victory. The first V for victory over our enemies from without, the second V for victory over our enemies from within. For surely those who perpetuate these ugly prejudices here are seeking to destroy our democratic form of government just as surely as the Axis forces.

The *Pittsburgh Courier* picked up this suggestion and launched what it called the "Double V" campaign. This campaign reverberated throughout the country, drawing its power from its expression of the determination among many Blacks not to accept continued postponement of their demands for full citizenship rights.

The FBI was working overtime to counter this growing civil rights fight. The facts about the FBI's crusade against the Black movement in this period unfortunately remain largely unknown and only sketchily documented publicly. What is known, however, makes it abundantly clear that the FBI's campaign of slander, frame-up, blackmail, and assassination against Malcolm X, Martin Luther King, the Black Panther Party, and other fighters for Black rights in the 1960s was not an aberration. It was the continuation of a course that began the day that the Roosevelt administration called on the FBI to go after "subversives."

IN FACT, FROM THE STANDPOINT of the Justice Department and FBI, the Black population as a whole was, if not subversive, at least suspect. The FBI prepared a secret wartime "Survey of Racial Conditions in the United States" for the benefit of the Roosevelt administration. In this 714-page report, the FBI explored the question—deeply troubling to them—of "why particular Negroes or groups of Negroes or Negro organizations have evidenced sentiments for other 'dark races' (mainly Japanese), or by what forces they were influenced to adopt in certain instances un-American ideologies."

The FBI survey concluded that while it might be going too far to say that "Negroes as a whole or the Negro people in a particular area are subversive or are influenced by anti-American forces . . . it must be pointed out that a number of Negroes and Negro groups have been the subjects of concentrated investigation made on the basis that they have repeatedly acted or have exhibited sentiments in a manner inimical to the Nation's war effort."

The FBI focused particular attention on newspapers such as the *Pittsburgh Courier,* whose nationwide circulation had skyrocketed with its Double V campaign. The report decried the fact that "the Negro press is a strong provocator of discontent among Negroes." (Like all cops, the FBI insists that "discontent" is created not by injustice and oppression but by instigators and agitators.) The secret FBI report went on to complain that the "general tone" of the Black press "is not at all, in many instances, informative or helpful to its own race. . . . More space is devoted to alleged instances of discrimination or mistreatment of Negroes than there is to matters which are educational or helpful."

TO DRIVE THIS POINT home to editors and writers for Black newspapers who insisted on saying things that were not "helpful," FBI agents began systematically visiting them. FBI agents also began calling on members of groups such as the NAACP, who were often enthusiastic supporters of the Double V campaign. The NAACP in particular, which was growing rapidly in size and activity, was targeted for infiltration by FBI stool pigeons and provocateurs. When fifteen Black sailors assigned as waiters for white officers in Washington, D.C., protested racial discrimination, the navy's response was to ask the FBI to investigate the protesters. The FBI obliged by opening a full-fledged, nationwide "investigation," including the massive use of informers, against the NAACP.

"FBI investigation of the NAACP [during the war] . . . produced massive information in Bureau files about the organization, its members, their legitimate activities to oppose racial discrimination, and internal disputes within some of the chapters," a U.S. Senate committee concluded in 1975. But these "reports and their summaries contained little if any information about specific activities or planned activities in violation of federal law."

In mid-1942 Attorney General Francis Biddle summoned several editors of Black weeklies to Justice Department headquarters in Washington, D.C. Biddle arrogantly told the editors that their coverage of clashes between white and Black soldiers at army bases was a disservice to the war effort. Biddle did not challenge the accuracy of the reports but nonetheless insisted that the information should not have been printed. The attorney general, a liberal and staunch Roosevelt supporter, told the editors that if they did not change the tone of their papers, he was "going to shut them all up" on charges of sedition.

Then, according to one account of the meeting, Biddle picked up a copy of the *Chicago Defender* and

> complained about an article on nine black soldiers being transported through Alabama and having to wait twenty-two hours to eat because white restaurants in railroad stations would not feed them. Biddle said it would have been better if such an article had not appeared. In addition, he said, a number of the paper's other articles "came very close to sedition," and the Justice Department was watching it closely "for seditious matter."[2]

Biddle's threats of prosecution for sedition did not come out of the blue. The editors he was threatening knew that leaders of the Teamster union and the Socialist Workers Party had been convicted in Minneapolis in 1941 for violation of the Smith Act, which outlawed advocacy of revolutionary ideas. In addition, sedition indictments had been brought in September 1942 against sixty-three members of the Temple of Islam (the Black Muslims), including its leader Elijah Muhammad. The Muslims were accused of sedition because they refused to accept the racist, anti-Japanese stereotypes that were a major part of U.S. war propaganda and expressed solidarity with the Japanese as a people of color. Although the Justice Department could not make the sedition charge stick, it did succeed in convicting Elijah Muhammad and the other defendants on draft-evasion charges.

The government blocked shipment to troops overseas of Black newspapers that continued to publish condemnations of racism and other "unhelpful" facts and opinions. These papers were also often confiscated on military bases in the United States.

Early in 1943, at Biddle's urging, the U.S. Post Office began proceedings to suspend the second-class mailing rights of several newspapers with uncompromising stands against race discrimination. These included the *Militant,* whose contributors and editors included members of the Socialist Workers Party. The Postmaster General banned the *Militant* from the mails on the grounds, among others, that its articles included "stimulation of race issues." All fighters for Black rights were supposed to get the point. The *Militant* won restoration of its mailing rights after a year-long battle that included the mobilization of protests from leaders of Black groups, trade unions, and civil liberties organizations.[3]

THE RACE DISCRIMINATION that Blacks fought against during the war had its counterpart in the treatment of other peoples of color at the hands of the government. While Mexican-American soldiers were not segregated into separate units, they nonetheless faced racist discrimination and abuse inside the U.S. armed forces. In 1943 hundreds of Chicanos in Los Angeles were beaten up by cops and white vigilantes during several consecutive nights of a rampage through Mexican-American neighborhoods. Many of the racist gangs were made up of off-duty navy sailors or marines, but U.S. military officials did nothing to stop the nightly attacks or punish those involved. Although none of the vigilantes were arrested, some seventy of their Chicano victims were picked up by the cops.

Exploitation of immigrant workers intensified during the war. In 1942 Washington began the so-called Bracero Program, which provided capitalist growers with a steady flow of superexploited immigrant farm labor from Mexico. The U.S. government underwrote $120 million in costs to organize the teams that went to Mexico to recruit laborers and transport them into the United States during harvest seasons. These workers had no rights, were legally barred from joining unions, and were subject to deportation at their employers' whim.

The Bracero Program was in part designed to offset the upward pressure on agricultural wages caused by the internment of many Japanese-American farm laborers in the months just after U.S. entry into the war. These workers were among the more than 100,000 Japanese-Americans interned during World War II.

This infamous action was carried out under the authority of an executive order issued by Roosevelt in February 1942. Roosevelt authorized military commanders to designate "military" areas "from which any or all persons may be excluded. . . ." This power was immediately used to declare California, Oregon, and Washington "strategic" areas. Every Japanese-American living in those states was ordered into concentration camps. Compelled to settle their affairs in a matter of only days or a couple of weeks, they were forced to sell their farms, businesses, and homes at far below their market value. They were locked up in camps unfit for human habitation—not on the basis of anything they had done but on the grounds of their Japanese ancestry. Not only interned, they were thus expropriated to the benefit of the propertied classes.

In the U.S. colony of Puerto Rico, many working people were unwilling to postpone their fight for national independence and against miserable living and working conditions in the name of a "wartime emergency." Sugar workers in the island's fields and mills waged strike battles for higher wages and decent working conditions. Puerto Rican independence fighters were a special target of the FBI during the war. Several years earlier, in 1936, Pedro Albizu Campos, the central leader of the Puerto Rican Nationalist Party, had been railroaded to a federal prison in Atlanta on charges of conspiracy to overthrow the government and "inciting rebellion" against the United States. When Washington entered the war, the U.S. government offered to free Albizu Campos and some sixty other imprisoned Nationalists if they would agree to suspend all proindependence activity during the war. The Puerto Rican patriots unanimously refused. The Nationalist Party voted to reject conscription into the U.S. Army, since "the United States holds Puerto Rico under a military, illegal government." Washington prosecuted a number of Nationalist Party members for draft evasion, including its former secretary-general, Julio Pinto Gandía. In a June 1945 interview with the *Militant*, Gandía explained:

> I do not evade anything. I simply refuse to fight as a slave of an imperialist power. I will fight as much as is needed, but only for the freedom and independence of my people. I know there are many young men from Puerto Rico in the U.S. army. . . . They think they are fighting for freedom and democracy. But they will learn . . . that kind of fight begins at home.

In Canada, Washington's imperialist partner to the north, opposition to the war and conscription ran deep among the people of another oppressed nation denied its right to independence—the Québécois. In a 1942 Canadian government referendum on instituting a draft, 80 percent of the Québécois voted no. Refusal to register or serve in the armed forces occurred on a massive scale in Quebec. The Canadian government, too, interned and expropriated its west coast Japanese population. Political organizations that opposed Canadian entry into the war, such as the Socialist Workers League, predecessor to today's Revolutionary Workers League, were banned.

III. Target: labor movement

The crusade to root out "subversives" in the name of the war for democracy reached far into the working-class movement. The Democratic and Republican parties mouthed support for constitutional freedoms. But the capitalist parties and their government appointees approved the steady expansion of the power of the executive branch to act—publicly when possible, covertly when necessary—to restrict the ground covered by the Bill of Rights.

At the end of the 1930s, war preparations were increasingly being used as a justification to restrict democracy and labor rights. The overriding question facing the labor movement became what attitude to take toward the militarization drive of the ruling class.

There was significant sentiment among working people against another imperialist war, and antiwar forces in the labor movement won a sympathetic hearing from many unionists. There was also widespread sympathy for revolutionary struggles in the colonial countries for independence and self-determination. The coming to power of fascism in Germany and the crushing of the German workers' movement reinforced the determination of millions of workers in the United States to strengthen their class organizations, the unions, as weapons in defense of the working class and its allies.

The attitude of class-struggle forces in the unions was well put in a resolution adopted in 1937 by the Minneapolis Central Labor Union. The adoption of this position was the result of an antiwar campaign spearheaded by Teamster Local 544 in Minneapolis, which had prepared the expansion of Teamster power in the Midwest with its victory over the employers in 1934, opening the door to transforming Minneapolis into a union stronghold. The leadership of Local 544 included leaders of the communist forces who in 1938 initiated the formation of the Socialist Workers Party.

"Be it resolved," said the Minneapolis labor body:

> 1. That the Central Labor Union of Minneapolis, voicing the determination of fifty thousand trade unionists, declares its unalterable opposition to all war preparations and military budgets, and any and all bills in which they are embodied, and stigmatizes the war being prepared as a war of imperialist conquest, and declares its firm opposition to any war launched by the Government;
>
> 2. That we demand that all war funds now proposed for the military budget and naval expansion be transferred immediately to the relief of the unemployed;
>
> 3. That we demand the immediate withdrawal of any and all armed forces of the United States from the Far East, since it is only Big Business and not Labor that has any interests there to protect;
>
> 4. That we assert militant Labor's determination to support . . . the brave Chinese people in their

> fight for independence against the Japanese invaders and all other foreign exploiters; and
>
> 5. That we shall join with all other forces in the labor movement who share our views for the purpose of consolidating the strongest possible movement of resistance to war and to the war-mongers.

As Roosevelt's New Deal was revealed to be also a war deal, the labor movement as a whole began a political retreat. By the latter half of 1937, the momentum of the CIO's rise was largely spent. There were still important strikes, including in auto, coal, and steel, but these were largely rearguard actions. Bureaucratic control of the unions was becoming tightened in both the CIO and the AFL. With the entry of the U.S. government into the war, top union officials—with the notable exception of a grouping around John L. Lewis of the United Mine Workers union—were accepting Roosevelt's insistence that the interests of union members had to be subordinated to "national unity." The result was a further weakening of the unions, though one that remained largely hidden from the awareness of most union members, given the economic upturn brought about by expanding production for war.

At the same time, the labor movement continued to retreat from its position in the front ranks of the fight for political rights and democratic liberties. During the rise of the CIO, the new union movement had fought to expand labor's right to organize and as a result had widened the latitude for political activity of everyone in this country. But as the union officialdom lined up behind the bipartisan war policies of the ruling class, they were increasingly willing to turn their backs on defense of the Bill of Rights, even when the rights of the unions were directly involved. The capitalists consequently were largely free to use government power—including the FBI and the courts—to try to isolate, if not silence, those in the labor movement who refused to get in step with the war policies of the Roosevelt administration.

During the 1940 presidential campaign, Roosevelt personally ordered a wiretap on the phone of John L. Lewis, at that time head of the CIO and the miners' union. The president viewed Lewis as a special threat—and a potential troublemaker—because of his decision to break ranks and refuse to support Roosevelt for re-election. The following year, Harry Bridges, leader of the West Coast Longshore union, discovered an FBI tap on his phone. Bridges, who was fighting government moves to deport him on political grounds, made the wiretap public.

Attorney General Biddle later recounted the White House meeting that took place following public protests against the violation of Bridges's constitutional rights. "When all this came out in the newspapers," Biddle wrote, "I could not resist suggesting to [FBI director J. Edgar] Hoover that he tell the story of the unfortunate tap directly to the President. We went over to the White House together. F.D.R. was delighted; and with one of his great grins, intent on every word, slapped Hoover on the back when he had finished. 'By God, Edgar, that's the first time you've been caught with your pants down!' The two men liked and understood each other."[4] The snapshot is revealing. The liberal president, the equally liberal attorney general, and the director of the FBI share a hearty laugh over the subversion of the Bill of Rights.

Nor was this an isolated incident. In 1937, the U.S. Supreme Court had ruled that a federal law prohibiting wiretaps applied to the FBI. In 1940, however, Roosevelt secretly instructed the Justice Department to ignore the court's ruling:

> I am convinced that the Supreme Court never intended any dictum in the particular case which it decided to apply to grave matters involving the defense of the nation. . . . You are, therefore, authorized and directed in such cases as you may approve, after investigation of the need in each case, to authorize the necessary investigating agents that they are at liberty to secure information by listening devices directed to the conversation or other communications of *persons suspected of subversive activities* against the Government of the United States, including suspected spies. (Emphasis added.)

Around the same time, the FBI expanded its army of informers and provocateurs in the labor and Black movements. FBI field offices were instructed to recruit or place informers in every plant engaged in war production—most of the large factories in the country. By the end of 1942, there were nearly 24,000 FBI stool pigeons rcporting on union and political activitics in almost 4,000 factories, mines, and mills.

IV. Frame-up in Minneapolis

In 1941 the Roosevelt administration, working in concert with the top International officials of the Teamsters, moved against the class-struggle leadership of the Minneapolis Teamsters. This leadership had refused to retreat from its position that labor must organize itself and set its priorities independent of the needs and prerogatives of the capitalist government and political parties. It continued to argue for the formation of a labor party based on the unions. It defended the colonial freedom struggle and championed the fight for the rights of oppressed nationalities in the United States. And it fought every move to sap the power of the labor movement by bringing unions under the control of government agencies.

The legal centerpiece of the Roosevelt administration's antilabor offensive was the use for the first time of the Smith Act, which had been adopted in 1940. For the first time in the United States since the Alien and Sedition Acts of 1798, this gag law made the *expression of ideas* a crime.

In June 1941, FBI agents and U.S. marshals raided the branch offices of the Socialist Workers Party in St. Paul and Minneapolis. They hauled away cartons of communist literature from the bookstores and libraries on the premises.

In Washington, D.C., Attorney General Biddle himself announced the plans for prosecution. "The principal Socialist Workers Party leaders against whom prosecution is being brought are also leaders of Local 544-CIO in Minneapolis," he told the press. "The prosecution is brought under the criminal code of the United States against persons who have been engaged in criminal seditious activities, and who are leaders of the Socialist Workers Party and have gained control of a legitimate labor union to use it for illegitimate purposes." Biddle's harangues against editors of Black papers provide a pretty good idea of the broad scope the attorney general gave to the term "seditious activities." From the standpoint of the government, any union activity dissenting from the drive toward entry into the war was illegitimate.

The government had three objectives in the crackdown on the Teamster local and the SWP.

First, it aimed to purge the labor movement of those who would not go along with imperialist war goals and militarization of the country and to intimidate into silence others, inside and outside the unions.

Second, the government wanted to erase the stronghold of union power and democracy represented by the Minneapolis Teamsters. The leadership of that union was inspiring emulation of class-struggle methods throughout the Midwest and educating workers in the need for socially conscious labor action and political independence from the capitalist parties. Although these leaders represented a minority point of view in the labor movement, that could change. The fight they were waging could become a rallying point to draw together significant forces in the unions, among the unemployed and unorganized, among Blacks, and among working farmers.

Third, the government sought to push the SWP in the direction of going underground. It wanted to force the party to give up some of its public activities and to concede that it must function at least in part illegally. The rulers' goal was to restrict the space for working-class politics.

THE RELATIONSHIP OF CLASS FORCES imposed by the labor movement's retreat allowed the capitalist government a good measure of success in its first and second objectives. But it totally failed in driving the SWP underground. One of the party's first responses to the indictments was to nominate James P. Cannon, its national secretary and one of those facing trial, for mayor of New York City. The SWP launched a vigorous petition campaign to win Cannon a spot on the ballot. The party also initiated a nationwide defense effort that continued until the last of the defendants was released from prison. Throughout this fight, the SWP forcefully asserted its constitutional right to carry out political activity. It published and distributed Marxist literature. It participated in and helped to advance the activities of the unions, the NAACP, and other organizations. SWP members explained communist ideas to fellow GIs, fought together with them against race discrimination in the armed forces and other abuses of citizen-soldiers, and took advantage of every opportunity to present the views of the party.

A CENTRAL ISSUE IN the Minneapolis trial was the SWP's opposition to any policy of subordinating the interests of unionists, Blacks, GIs, farmers, or other working people to the profits and power of the exploiters, who called for "national unity" in wartime to silence opposition to their policies. In time of war, the SWP explained, the struggle for the independence of the trade unions from the capitalist state and the fight for trade union democracy become even more critical.

SWP leaders turned the courtroom into a platform from which to explain the party's views on the war. They explained that the Second World War was really three wars in one.

First, it was a war to defend the Soviet Union, the first—and at that time the only—workers' state, against imperialist efforts spearheaded by Germany's rulers to overturn it and restore capitalist rule. In this conflict the workers' movement throughout the world stood with the Soviet workers' state.

Second, it was a war for national liberation, especially in Asia. The Chinese, Indian, Vietnamese, and other colonial peoples were waging massive struggles against imperialist occupation and domination, taking advantage of the conflict between the world imperialist powers to push for their own freedom. In this war all of progressive humanity stood with the colonial peoples against their imperialist overlords.

Third, it was a war among imperialist rivals for domination of the world. In this conflict, the capitalist rulers of the United States and those of its allies sought to enlist the political support of working people by presenting their goals as the defeat of fascism and defense of democracy. But, as SWP leader James P. Cannon explained from the witness stand, U.S. working people could combat fascism only by strengthening their own organizations not by subordinating their struggle to support for the imperialist government, in wartime or not. Cannon was asked:

> What is the party's position on the claim that the war against Hitler is a war of democracy against fascism?
>
> Answer: We say that it is a subterfuge, that the conflict between American imperialism and German imperialism is for the domination of the world. It is absolutely true that Hitler wants to dominate the world, but we think it is equally true that the ruling group of American capitalists has the same idea, and we are not in favor of either of them.
>
> We do not think that the Sixty Families who own America want to wage this war for some sacred principle of democracy. We think they are the greatest enemies of democracy here at home. We think they would only use the opportunity of a war to eliminate all civil liberties at home, to get the best imitation of fascism they can possibly get.[5]

The government's case at the trial consisted largely of testimony from FBI stool pigeons and other opponents of the elected leadership of Teamster Local 544, together with evidence such as copies of the *Communist Manifesto* and other books and pamphlets by Marx, Engels, Lenin, and Trotsky that had been seized from bookstore shelves.

A jury returned convictions against eighteen of the twenty-eight defendants on one count of the indictment, finding them guilty of a conspiracy to "advise and teach the duty, necessity, desirability and propriety of overthrowing and destroying the Government of the United States by force and violence. . . ." Sentencing took place on December 8, 1941, the day after the Japanese forces attacked the main naval base in the U.S. colony of Hawaii, and the day Congress voted a formal declaration of war. Twelve of the defendants received sentences of sixteen months in federal prison, and six were sentenced to one year.

Opponents of this political persecution joined together to organize the Civil Rights Defense Committee (CRDC). The guilty verdict brought forth a round of protests from union locals and central labor bodies speaking for more than a million union members. Union bodies contributed money to the CRDC to pay for legal appeals and help spread the word about the case. Support came from NAACP chapters around the country. W.E.B. DuBois, the historian and Black rights leader, declared his solidarity with the Smith Act defendants. Adam Clayton Powell, then a member of the New York City Council and a prominent figure in the Black community, declared: "Whenever the civil liberties of any American or any American group are threatened, then the civil liberties of all are in danger, and this is the issue in Minneapolis." The American Civil Liberties Union announced its support for the appeal, warning that the Smith Act is a "dangerous weapon against civil rights of labor and radicals of all varieties."

Support for the defense effort was not universal in the working-class movement, however. Most AFL and CIO officials remained silent; some even publicly supported the prosecution.

A TREACHEROUS STAND was taken by the Stalinized Communist Party, which gave political support to the Roosevelt administration and its appeals for "national unity." In the union movement, the CP was among the most fervent backers of the no-strike pledge agreed to by most of the top labor officialdom for the duration of the war. When the United Mine Workers went on strike in 1943, the CP's *Daily Worker* openly opposed it and called for the "[John L.] Lewis line" of defying the no-strike pledge to be "utterly defeated." In the Black movement, the CP opposed the Double V campaign on the grounds that too much emphasis on the fight against race discrimination in the army and in the war plants would disrupt "national unity." The CP also supported the internment of Japanese-Americans, suspended from the party its Japanese-American members, and urged these former members not to resist their own internment.[6]

Consistent with these positions, the Communist Party actively supported the prosecution of the Minneapolis defendants. The *Daily Worker* branded those who supported the Civil Rights Defense Committee as "tools" being used by "Hitler agents."

When the guilty verdicts were returned, the *Daily Worker* published a major article on December 19 by Carl Winter headlined "Minneapolis Trial Shows Labor Wary of Trotzkyites." Winter argued that no support should be given to the Minneapolis defendants because they were not a legitimate part of the labor movement. If the federal prosecutors deserve criticism, Winter said, it was for falsely portraying the SWP leaders as revolutionary communists rather than agents of Hitler. He went on:

> Their fifth column service to Hitlerism through spreading disunity in labor's ranks, trying to undermine and weaken the all-out defense effort, and viciously inciting against the Soviet Union received little attention. Instead, the "radical" mask under which all this was carried on was taken at face value by the prosecution and the Trotzkyite pretense of being a militant working-class organization was used to obtain the first conviction under the reactionary Smith Act.
>
> While the trial has aroused a vigilance in Minnesota labor and progressive circles against the danger of misuse of this precedent, there has been a general refusal to accept the evaluation of the Trotzkyites as "radicals," as painted by the prosecution, instead of their known worth as servants of reaction. Significantly, there have been no local unions to date with the possible exception of those under their control to come forward in joining the Trotzkyites in their appeal in this case. . . .
>
> If the federal prosecution of the Trotzkyites failed to fully reveal their fifth column character, current events and the growing alertness of the American people will soon contribute to pulling the fangs of these copperheads in labor's ranks.

It is easy to see how damaging this position was to the working-class movement and to the fight against imperialism. But it is not as simple to understand why so many CP leaders and members believed it to be the right position, just as they deeply believed that a ban on strikes during the war was essential, and that the fight for civil rights for Blacks had to be put on the back burner.

THE RECENT OUTPOURING of books and articles examining the history of the U.S. Communist Party, both by academic historians and by former CP members, sheds little light on this question. Anticommunist liberal and social democratic writers argue that CP leaders simply took orders from Moscow and that the membership was either duped or corrupted into going along with positions that they did not understand or believe in. Those more sympathetic to the CP of the past try to make an often sentimental case that the party's positions on world political developments were largely irrelevant to the day-to-day political work of the rank-and-file. For its part, the Communist Party today disavows some of the most extreme formulations from the World War II period, dismissing them as excesses for which a single individual, CP general secretary Earl Browder, was responsible. (Browder was dumped without ceremony from the CP leadership in July 1945 on instructions from the Soviet party leadership.)

All these explanations are false. None explains why tens of thousands of working people who considered themselves dedicated communist fighters argued for and believed in the party's political positions. They were not fools, and they were not cowards. Nor, by and large, were they simply careerists or opportunists.

Revolutionary-minded working-class fighters who joined the CP understood that the Soviet workers' state had to be defended against imperialism by the working-class movement everywhere. They recognized in the Soviet Union an historic conquest of the world working class. But they were taught in the CP that this meant that the conjunctural needs of the Soviet government, as defined by the Stalin regime, coincided with how best to advance the interests of the working class in the United States and worldwide. Thus, all other considerations had to be subordinated to the Soviet government's current policies. The main positions of the CP in the United States, as elsewhere, were dictated in accordance with the frequently shifting requirements of Stalin's diplomacy. The members of the Communist Party believed this was in the interests of the U.S. and international working class and believed it deeply. Those who did not share this perspective did not stay in the party very long.

Following the Seventh Congress of the Communist International in August 1935, the U.S. Communist Party turned toward increasingly open political support for the Roosevelt administration and the New Deal. This was in accord with Stalin's new Popular Front line, which put forward—as the only road to defeat German fascism and its growing military threat to the Soviet Union—the subordination of independent working-class politics to an alliance with bourgeois governments and liberal capitalist parties in the imperialist countries. In the CIO, the CP actively opposed motion toward a labor party based on the unions that would challenge *both* capitalist parties. The CP's 1936 presidential campaign was waged around the slogan of defeating Roosevelt's Republican Party challenger "at all costs."

When Stalin signed a nonaggression pact with Hitler in August 1939, however, Communist Party members immediately became opponents of both Roosevelt and his militarization policy. Then, after Hitler tore up the nonaggression pact and invaded the Soviet Union in June 1941, CP members immediately once again became ardent supporters of Roosevelt and campaigners for war by the United States against Germany and Japan. They did not have to be "ordered" by Moscow to reverse their line over night. They *believed* it was correct to do so, because it served the Soviet Union's needs, as Stalin defined them and CP members understood them.

NOWHERE WAS THIS more striking than in the position of the CP on the colonial revolution. With the wartime military alliance between the United States, Britain, and the Soviet Union, the struggles for independence in the colonies and semicolonies of the Allied imperialist powers became, in the CP's view, an obstacle to the fight against fascism. The toilers of Latin America were told to unite with U.S. imperialism and its local henchmen.

In Cuba, formally an independent republic but in reality a U.S. semicolony, the Stalinists proclaimed themselves "the most tenacious defenders of the unity of our country with the United States." The leadership of the Communist Party posed the question directly: "Why isn't the struggle against imperialism put first?" And it answered: "the principal task of all peoples of the world today is to defeat Nazism; every other interest must be subordinated to this task." Blas Roca, then central leader of the party, went so far as to quote with approval the assertion of Sumner Welles, U.S. ambassador to Cuba, that the "imperialist era has ended."

The Cuban Stalinists likewise sought to deepen class collaboration with the Cuban capitalists and landlords. (In line with this, the party dropped the name "Communist" in 1944 and became the Popular Socialist Party.) In 1945 Blas Roca, in a speech to union officials on "The Collaboration Between Workers and Employers," criticized workers who "do not understand the new conditions [and] still cling to the concepts which, while formerly correct, are now unrealistic. . . ." He added, "Whereas, previously collaboration was an attempt to save capitalism, now we want to defeat Hitlerism, guarantee peace, gain national liberation." The PSP campaigned against strikes, for universal conscription, and for sending Cuban troops to fight in the imperialist war.

With the Popular Front turn of the Communist International, the Cuban party had resolved in 1938 to change its attitude toward the proimperialist dictator Col. Fulgencio Batista, since "he has ceased to be the center of reaction and now professes democracy." During the war, the party strengthened its backing for Batista, and he appointed two PSP leaders to his cabinet in 1943–44.

THROUGHOUT LATIN AMERICA, Communist parties followed similar lines. In a recent interview, Tomás Borge, a leader of the Sandinista National Liberation Front and Nicaragua's Minister of the Interior, reviewed the obstacles created by this policy to the development of the working-class movement in that country and elsewhere:

> The workers' movement of Nicaragua emerged as a political organization May 1, 1944, in the midst of the World War and at a time when "Browderism" was making deep inroads in this continent. Earl Browder, general secretary of the Communist Party of the United States, held the view that the antagonistic contradiction between the bourgeoisie

> and the working class had disappeared. This concept was developed by a party that came onto the scene prior to the Nicaraguan Socialist Party, the Peoples Vanguard Party of Costa Rica.
>
> Thus, a notion that held great influence was the idea that any government that had declared war on fascism had to be supported to the utmost. The workers' movement in Nicaragua emerged with the deviation, one shared by other politically organized workers' movements in Latin America, that local dictators should be supported.
>
> The Nicaraguan Socialist Party emerged on the scene supporting the Somoza dictatorship. That's why Marxism in Nicaragua has no history.
>
> The history of Marxism in Nicaragua began in 1944 and it is a sad history; in other words, properly speaking, it is not even the history of Marxism. Marxism, which is a revolutionary theory, cannot be tarnished by sadness.
>
> In the concrete case of Nicaragua, those who in those days called themselves Marxists were mired in a policy of class collaboration, of support to the bourgeoisie and to U.S. imperialism, which, as we know, was at that time at war with fascism. I don't want to go back over who was historically responsible for this; I don't want to point to those who were guilty. This was, objectively, the history, regardless of the sins and the sinners.[7]

To those who did not understand the Stalinist political framework in which members of the Communist parties had been educated, the sudden switches by these parties seemed irrational. But to those trained in the school of Stalinism, any other course would have been unthinkable. Loyal CP members followed, without a great deal of difficulty, the reversals of line required by Moscow's shifting relations with various imperialist powers. What mattered to them was the defense of the Soviet Union as they understood it.

Those who broke from this position had no reason to stay in the Communist Party, and they did not. This explains why thousands, perhaps tens of thousands, of members and supporters of the U.S. Communist Party who stuck through the twists and turns of its policies in the 1930s and 1940s, and through the worst days of the McCarthyite reaction in the 1950s, broke definitively from the CP when Khrushchev's speech at the twentieth congress of the Soviet Communist Party in 1956 revealed some of Stalin's crimes against the Soviet workers' state and its vanguard. The basis of their whole world outlook appeared to have shattered overnight.

Over time, this Stalinist course corroded all communist principles. The CP was no longer guided by how the working class and its allies in the United States and worldwide could best advance along their historic line of march in the struggle against imperialist exploitation and oppression. Instead of recognizing the Soviet Union as a bastion to aid the world revolution, the Stalinists subordinated the struggles of workers and farmers to the perceived diplomatic needs of the Soviet government.

Communist Party members themselves rationalized this course based on their belief that, whatever the political price, the course of the Stalin regime did serve the long-term interests of the world revolution. But many other working people could not be easily convinced. So the real reasons for positions taken by the CP on a strike, a fight for Black rights, or a presidential election campaign were often no longer identical to the "good" reasons given to the workers and their allies.

Along with this came the introduction of the idea, which became widespread in the Popular Front era, that it was necessary and desirable to have members of the party who were not known as Communists even to their fellow workers and political collaborators. That way it was easier to help the liberals, without running the risk of embarrassing them. It became acceptable to lie to the working class about political positions—in the name of defending the Soviet Union.

A necessary by-product of this Stalinist course was the superfactionalism introduced by the CP into the workers' movement. The tradition of working-class solidarity in the face of government attack despite political differences was consciously broken by the CP. Those who disagreed with Communist Party positions were branded enemies of the Soviet Union, then tools or conscious agents of Hitler. Communists who proposed an alternative to Stalin's course in the Soviet Union, including Leon Trotsky and other opposition forces in the Soviet CP and the Communist International, were slandered and killed by Stalin's murder machine.

It was in line with this overall course that the U.S. Communist Party gave backing to the government's jailing of SWP leaders under the Smith Act. No other course was possible for the CP even to consider.

V. McCarthy-era witch-hunt

With the defeat of Germany and Japan and the new rise of revolutionary struggles set in motion by the world war, Washington quickly moved to end the wartime alliance with Moscow. It was soon replaced by the cold war. The U.S. government and its British and French allies intensified their efforts to stop the advance of colonial revolts in Asia and Africa and the establishment of workers' and farmers' regimes in countries occupied by the Red Army following its smashing of the Third Reich. With the victory of the Chinese revolution in 1949 and the outbreak of the Korean War the following year, the confrontation sharpened between the imperialist powers on the one hand and the colonial revolution and the workers' states on the other.

IN THE UNITED STATES the economic boom (which had begun during World War II, brought about by massive war spending) was the new framework in which the struggle between labor and capital was taking place. In the unions, the bureaucracy further consolidated its hold. The strength of the labor movement continued to erode, although this was difficult for many union members to recognize since labor was still wresting wage gains despite the class-collaborationist methods and policies of the officialdom. The labor bureaucracy and its supporters focused attention on the steady, if slow, improvement in real wages for those sections of the work force already organized in the strongest unions. At the same time, they went along with policies that eroded union control over pace and conditions of work and sapped union power by further entangling the labor movement in red tape and restrictive government regulations.

As part of this retreat, the union officialdom refused to wage any battle against the spread of the witch-hunt that had begun before World War II. In relation to democratic rights, this postwar period, which came to be known as the McCarthy era, is often presented as a sharp break from the political direction of the Roosevelt administration. Far from a reversal, however, the McCarthy period was an extension of the assault on constitutional liberties that had begun at the end of the 1930s in the name of vigilance against subversives. To their horror and genuine surprise, many who had been willing to keep their mouths shut or even support the government when the FBI went after the Black Muslims or John L. Lewis or the Socialist Workers Party now found themselves targets of the thought-control police.

Within the working-class movement, the strategic orientations of both the Social Democrats and Stalinists were obstacles to an effective fight for democratic rights.

The Socialist Party leaders rejected the perspective of revolutionary struggle by workers and farmers against U.S. capitalism as part of a worldwide fight. Instead they sought to persuade working people to team up with enlightened elements of the U.S. ruling class in defense of "democracy" and against the creation of new workers' and farmers' governments, which would only spread what they condemned as "communist totalitarianism." When SP leaders said "we," they didn't mean the working people of the world but an alliance with a section of the capitalist class. The "they" to be fought against were not the capitalist exploiters but revolutionary democratic struggles in China, Korea, and elsewhere in the colonial and semicolonial world, as well as communists everywhere. With the advent of the cold war, the Social Democrats' course coincided more and more with that of U.S. imperialism, earning them the name "State Department socialists."

While some individual Socialist Party members and leaders took principled stands in defense of victims of the witch-hunt, the party's political course undermined the political fight against it. The tradition of the militant working-class movement in this country had been to defend all victims of government repression as a matter of principle. Evidence of "guilt" produced by the government was irrelevant to this class standpoint. During the McCarthy years, the Social Democrats followed an opposite course: arguing that the witch-hunt must not victimize the "innocent" and should target only real spies, real communists, real "subversives." Those who could not *prove their innocence* to the satisfaction of these guardians of democracy did not get any support.

The fight against the witch-hunt was also hampered by the course of the Communist Party, whose members and supporters bore the brunt of government victimization and harassment. The Stalinist party was by far the largest organization speaking in the name of Marxism in the United States. The CP had already declined some in size because of the political conservatization of the working class resulting from relative postwar prosperity. And it had lost the goodwill of many class-conscious workers due to its extreme factionalism and support for the no-strike pledge and government union-busting during the war. But the CP still commanded the political allegiance of hundreds of thousands of workers and could appeal to many more for active collaboration in defense of civil liberties despite political disagreements.

The Communist Party was incapable of mobilizing an effective fight against government repression, however. During the Popular Front period, the CP had oriented toward and loyally served liberal capitalist forces and those in the unions and Black movement who looked to the liberals. With the onset of the cold war, these capitalist forces turned on the CP, as did their lieutenants in the labor movement. Many CP members, as a result, felt they had nowhere to turn in order to counter this new anticommunist offensive by the ruling class. For too long their eyes had been not on the ranks of the labor movement and labor's allies, but on the very forces that were now spearheading the attack on democratic rights.

IN 1948 TWELVE MEMBERS of the Central Committee of the Communist Party were indicted under the Smith Act. They were charged with conspiring to "teach and advocate the overthrow and destruction of the government of the United States by force and violence"—the very charges used against the Minneapolis defendants seven years earlier. The indictment asserted that this alleged conspiracy had been advanced in three ways: (1) by organizing the Communist Party; (2) by arranging to "publish and circulate, and cause to be circulated, books, articles, magazines, and newspapers advocating the principles of Marxism-Leninism"; and (3) by organizing "schools and classes for the study of the principles of Marxism-Leninism. . . ."

The trial lasted nine months in the federal courthouse at Foley Square in New York City. It concluded with a verdict of guilty against eleven CP leaders. The case against the twelfth, William Z. Foster, had been severed owing to ill health. Ten defendants got the maximum sentence of five years; one received a three-year term. In addition, all the defense attorneys were sentenced to prison terms for "contempt of court" during the trial.

While the Smith Act convictions were on appeal, the legal and political situation worsened. In 1950 Congress adopted the McCarran Act, which required the CP and its members to register with the government. The new law, enacted with bipartisan support, also provided for the setting up of concentration camps where opponents of government policy could be imprisoned without trial during a "national emergency."

In March 1951 Ethel and Julius Rosenberg and Morton Sobell were tried and convicted on frame-up charges and concocted evidence of stealing the "secret" of the atom bomb and giving it to the Soviet Union. On April 5 the Rosenbergs were sentenced to death by electrocution; Sobell was given thirty years. A few months later the U.S. Supreme Court upheld the constitutionality of the Smith Act, rejecting the appeals of the eleven CP defendants.

THE INTENSIFICATION of the witch-hunt since the end of the 1940s had sparked a debate in the Communist Party leadership over what to do next. A sharp dispute erupted in the leadership over whether the Smith Act defendants, who had been out on bail while their appeals were pending, should turn themselves in or should go into hiding or exile if the Supreme Court ruled against them. Those who favored the latter course argued that fascism was spreading across the country and that the outlawing of the CP was inevitable.

In the end the leadership was unable to reach a decision one way or the other. The upshot was that those defendants who favored going into hiding or exile did so; the others turned themselves in. Whether this was an agreed-upon compromise or the result of a failure to resolve the conflict was not clear to those who were not involved. In any event, when the time came to surrender to federal marshals, four of the eleven defendants did not appear. A fifth, Eugene Dennis, the party's general secretary, had intended to go into hiding but ended up turning himself in when the arrangements got messed up. Of the four who did not appear, Gus Hall was arrested a few weeks later in Mexico. Robert Thompson was taken into custody a year afterward in a cabin in the Sierras. Two others, Gil Green and Henry Winston, stayed in hiding for five years and eventually turned themselves in voluntarily to serve their sentences.

The course followed by the CP leadership was costly. It made no political sense to follow such a split policy. Many members concluded that the outcome reflected paralysis, even panic, in the party leadership. Many CP activists read the decision as a signal that pulling back from public political activity was necessary. A substantial number of secondary leaders dropped out of public view, even though they were not facing any charges. Many cadres severed connections to the party. Some who still considered themselves communists went to the extremes of burning their Marxist books or sealing them in crates and burying them in backyards or hiding them in basements.

An indication of the CP leadership's panicky retreat was its response to the arrest and trial of the Rosenbergs and Sobell, who were charged with having been Communist Party members who spied for the Soviet Union. The case against them was cooked up by the FBI and the Justice Department. The prosecution included secret—and illegal—collaboration between the judge and government lawyers. The frame-up artists in the Justice Department drew on deep prejudices, including anti-Semitism, to make their slanders stick.

Although the Rosenbergs were known to many of their comrades as having been members of the CP, the party leadership decided not to acknowledge this fact publicly. It was not until the mid-1970s, after the Rosenbergs' two sons published a book proudly defending their parents' Communist Party affiliation,[8] that many CP members would publicly acknowledge that the two victims of McCarthyite reaction had been party members.

Julius and Ethel Rosenberg were arrested in the summer of 1950 and tried and convicted in March 1951. Throughout this time, no defense committee was organized to expose the frame-up and mobilize opposition to the charges. Neither the Communist Party nor the defendants took any initiative in this direction. The CP leadership apparently hoped in this way to insulate the party against government accusations that some in its ranks had engaged in espionage for the Soviet Union. This dissociation from the defendants was carried so far that the *Daily Worker* did not even report on the trial, publishing only a short three-sentence news item on a back page when the guilty verdict was returned.

It was only after the death sentence was pronounced on April 5, 1951, that the *Daily Worker* condemned the frame-up and barbaric penalty. But even then, no defense committee was initiated. Finally, several months later, the *National Guardian* (now the *Guardian*), a New York radical weekly, launched a campaign to expose the frame-up and to seek to block the executions. This led in November 1951 to the formation of the National Committee to Secure Justice in the Rosenberg Case. Many CP members joined in activities organized by the committee, as did many other individuals and some organizations, including the Socialist Workers Party.

THE MCCARTHY ERA is sometimes referred to as a period during which the CP functioned in a partially underground way. But this is not true in any meaningful sense. The CP had no underground party press and no political activity of any kind organized in clandestinity. When CP leaders went "underground," they removed themselves from public political activity—though rarely from FBI surveillance. The "underground" organizers stayed in touch with party structures, such as they were, participated in leadership discussions through articles in the party's discussion bulletins and attendance at committee meetings, and waited for the political situation to change.

In fact, any real underground functioning would have been ludicrous, since the CP was never legally proscribed throughout this entire period, despite government attempts in that direction. The repression hit hard at CP members and former members. A total of 160 people in the United States and Puerto Rico were arrested on charges under the Smith Act; forty-one eventually served prison terms. Many individuals, CP members and others, were victimized through blacklisting, FBI harassment, blackmail, and deportation or threat of deportation. Others were imprisoned for refusing to inform on their comrades when called before witch-hunting bodies such as the House Un-American Activities Committee.

But the government's attempts to outlaw the CP failed. Repeated efforts to force it to register members' names with the Justice Department were stymied in the courts and finally defeated. The party's publications, including the *Daily Worker,* continued to be printed legally and sent through the mails without restriction.

Most members of the Communist Party did not identify themselves as communists, even to their fellow workers and others they collaborated with in political activity. But this policy did not begin with the witch-hunt; it began and became generalized during the Popular Front period. Far from an aid to the Communist Party in combating attacks on the democratic rights of its members and supporters, this policy made CP members especially vulnerable to the witch-hunters. Congressional committees and right-wingers specialized in "naming names" of Communist Party members and those accused of being members. Members of the CP who had concealed their affiliation from co-workers and those with whom they collaborated in political activity faced self-imposed obstacles in organizing support for their democratic rights as members of the CP. Those who were more widely known as CP members were less easily victimized by the McCarthyite "investigators."

Much of the ground lost for public functioning by the CP was not terrain given up inch by inch in determined battle for democratic rights, but was forfeited as a result of the party's crisis of perspective. In the labor movement, large numbers of workers were ready to extend a generous helping hand of working-class solidarity to all victims of right-wing reaction and government repression. Others, especially in the Black community, recognized the need for united action to defend the rights of minority viewpoints and democratic rights in general. But the Stalinist leaders, exaggerating the fascist threat, kept their backs turned to the ranks of labor and its allies. Their course increased the damage inflicted by the witch-hunt on the Communist Party and on the working-class movement as a whole.

VI. FBI's domestic contra operation

With the end of the Korean War in 1953 and the repudiation of Sen. Joseph McCarthy by the dominant sections of the ruling class the following year, the witch-hunt began to wane. The political situation in the country shifted. In 1954, the Black-led fight for civil rights, which had continued without letup since World War II, won an historic victory when the U.S. Supreme Court ruled that school segregation violated the Constitution. This in turn spurred further fights against Jim Crow segregation. Public opposition to further prosecutions under the Smith

Act also grew. Those who fought back against violations of constitutional rights—encouraged by groups such as the newly formed Emergency Civil Liberties Committee (ECLC)—were able to score victories, including some favorable rulings in the federal courts.

In 1956 the National Security Council convened a special meeting in the White House to hear a report and consider proposals from FBI Director Hoover on how to counter the stiffening popular resistance to government moves against the Bill of Rights. The facts about this meeting were first revealed in 1981 during the trial of the SWP lawsuit, when Justice Department officials introduced into evidence a report on the meeting previously classified top secret. The document was submitted in an effort—ultimately unsuccessful—to show that the FBI's covert "Counter-Intelligence Program" (Cointelpro) was lawful on the grounds that it had been set in motion at this NSC meeting, where it received presidential approval.

To explain the document's significance, the government lawyers called to the witness stand Herbert Brownell, who had served as attorney general in President Dwight Eisenhower's cabinet. Brownell testified that those present at the 1956 NSC meeting included Eisenhower, Vice-president Richard Nixon, CIA chief Allen Dulles, FBI Director Hoover, and other government officials. At the meeting, Hoover outlined the situation. The government's efforts to disrupt the operations of the Communist Party, the Socialist Workers Party, and other groups were running into greater public opposition, he said. This was being reflected in the growing reluctance by federal judges to sustain prosecutions under the Smith Act, to uphold denials of passports to "subversives," and to approve other witch-hunting measures such as driving communists out of the merchant marine by lifting their seaman's papers.

"To illustrate," Hoover told the National Security Council, "42 prominent persons, including Mrs. Franklin D. Roosevelt, Norman Thomas, Henry Steele Commager, and many others who should know better, recently signed a petition calling for amnesty for persons now serving prison terms for Smith Act convictions and a cessation of further prosecution." Hoover went on to complain bitterly about court rulings "such as the Judge Youngdahl decision in the passport case of Leonard Boudin on November 22, 1953, and the actions of the Circuit Court of Appeals for the Ninth circuit, San Francisco, California, ruling out the Coast Guard screening program [for the merchant marine] on October 26, 1955. . . ."

FORTUNATELY, HOOVER emphasized, the power of the government's executive branch to act was not restricted to what the people of the country would support and the federal courts would accept. What could not be accomplished openly could be achieved covertly. The FBI possessed the weapon of "counterintelligence." Hoover proudly reported, "We have sought to infiltrate, penetrate, disorganize, and disrupt the [Communist] party. . . . Informants have been the key to penetration of the party. . . . We currently have 921 active informants operating in the security field, providing hourly intelligence reflecting the innermost plans and policies of the Communist Party."

On the witness stand in 1981, Brownell stressed that Hoover's report covered not just the Communist Party itself, but also "those who were aiding it in various ways. For example there were some splinter groups which sent representatives to international communist meetings, secret meetings, things of that sort. They were included in what we call the subversive groups who were operating secretly in conjunction with foreign powers." This included the Socialist Workers Party, the former attorney general added.

Brownell was asked to identify "the source of the authority for the FBI to conduct the countermeasures as set forth in this page against the Communist Party and other subversive groups." "Presidential directive," he shot back. "I think the legal situation was that the President did not give any restriction to the methods that were to be used to accomplish the ends that he sought." The techniques approved by the National Security Council included disruption operations by informers, break-ins, wiretaps, and microphone bugs installed without warrants, as well as opening the mail and sorting through discarded trash of "subversive" targets. Six months later, the FBI formally inaugurated its Cointelpro operations, first against the CP, then against the SWP, Black organizations fighting for civil rights, and others.

If the majority of U.S. people could no longer be mobilized to support the openly proclaimed goal of breaking up communist groups by government prosecution and blacklisting, the National Security Council had decided, then the FBI would wage a secret operation against the "subversives"—what we would today call a domestic *contra* operation.

The expansion of the FBI's covert operations against critics of government policy took place at a time when the right to organize political activity was being extended. This advance was a by-product of the revival of working-class political action represented by the growth of the civil rights struggle, particularly in the segregated South. Despite continuation of the trade union movement's political retreat, the new rise in the struggle waged by Black people was registering important conquests. In the course of the battle to bring the Jim Crow structures crashing down, the civil rights movement was expanding the room for individuals and groups to organize to fight for their interests without government interference.

The most far-reaching conquest in this area was extension of the First Amendment guarantee of freedom of association to include the right of organizations to privacy from government cops and regulation. This victory was codified in a string of civil rights cases. One of the first and most important of these was won by the NAACP against the Alabama state government. This battle grew out of the NAACP's support for the Montgomery, Alabama, bus boycott, which began in December 1955 and ended with the desegregation of that city's buses. In retaliation for activities such as this, Alabama officials tried to force the NAACP to register the names and addresses of its members and contributors with the state. The NAACP refused, arguing that its list of members and supporters was no business of the government, and that if the names were turned over this would result in victimization of individuals.

In 1958, the U.S. Supreme Court ruled in favor of the NAACP, affirming that there is a "vital relationship between freedom to associate and privacy in one's associations." The court held that "Inviolability of privacy in group associations may in many circumstances be indispensable to preservation of freedom of association, particularly where a group espouses dissident beliefs." (This constitutional right to privacy was extended still further in 1973, when the Supreme Court ruled that a "right of personal privacy . . . does exist under the Constitution" and that it "is broad enough to encompass a woman's decision on whether or not to terminate her pregnancy.")

From the standpoint of the executive branch of the government, however, these court rulings did not affect covert FBI operations in the United States. These operations, the Justice Department maintained, derived their justification from the "inherent powers of the president," and were beyond the reach of court rulings and laws passed by Congress. So long as these operations remained hidden, or largely hidden, from public view, this position was not put to the test. But when the covert operations began to be exposed in the early 1970s, the issue was joined. The result has been the posing of the most fundamental questions of constitutional rights, many of which have been presented directly as a result of the SWP's legal initiative against the attorney general and the FBI.

VII. Forcing the covert operations to light

The SWP lawsuit was filed in July 1973 as the Watergate scandal was breaking. Watergate was the first governmental crisis resulting from the growing contradiction in the latter part of the twentieth century between what the U.S. ruling class is compelled to do against its class enemies at home and abroad, and what it can openly proclaim as its goals and methods.

In the Second World War, the country's rulers were able to mobilize the country behind their war aims. Those who opposed this course were in a small minority; some were imprisoned for their minority views without a major national outcry. By the time of the Korean War, however, there was little enthusiasm among working people for the war, and a good deal of opposition was openly expressed. A measure of this shift was the decision by the government not to seek a declaration of war by Congress as required under the Constitution. The Korean War was also the first war the United States failed to win.

When the U.S. government escalated its intervention in

Vietnam in the mid-1960s, conditions existed, for the first time in the history of the country, for the emergence of a massive antiwar movement in the middle of a shooting war. Antiwar sentiment was accompanied by deepening popular suspicion and distrust of the secrecy and lies of Washington about its war aims and its methods. As in the Korean War, there was no declaration of war proposed to Congress. The government acted throughout on the basis of "executive power."

As the Watergate revelations developed, it became clear to a growing number of people that the lies and covert operations that were used by the government to further its aims in Vietnam were the very methods it used at home. The "inherent powers" that the president used to wage a murderous war against the peoples of Indochina were also being used against fighters for Black rights, against Puerto Rican and Mexican-American activists, against the women's liberation movement, against antiwar organizations, and against communists. As more of the truth about Cointelpro and other covert FBI operations began to emerge, it further became clear that these methods had been used *at home first.* Washington's wars against its class enemies overseas are an extension of the capitalist government's war against its domestic class enemies.

Today the U.S. government is in the midst of a second crisis, triggered by the exposure of the secret Iran arms deal and the covert funding of the *contras* trying to overthrow the government of Nicaragua. Like Watergate, the current crisis has its roots in the inability of U.S. imperialism to stop the march of history. The U.S. rulers must increasingly turn to covert operations to carry out policies and employ methods that they cannot openly proclaim or defend, and at least some of these covert operations are inevitably exposed publicly.

The SWP suit against the government has attracted new attention and broader support as the current government crisis has developed, since the issues at the heart of the case are the very questions posed by the contragate scandal: Can the rule of law be suspended in the name of "national security"? Are the president, the attorney general, the CIA, the FBI, and the National Security Council above the law?

THE DEPTH OF WHAT IS at stake was revealed in a dramatic confrontation that occurred during the pretrial battles in the SWP case. From the outset, the most important issue in the case was whether or not the FBI has a legal right to use covert informers to spy on and disrupt the SWP and YSA. To help prove that this government practice violated constitutional rights, the SWP's lawyers asked that Judge Griesa order the FBI to turn over the files on its informers. The judge ordered that a sample consisting of files on eighteen informers be produced. The Justice Department immediately appealed that order, first to the Court of Appeals and then to the United States Supreme Court. Turning over *any* informer files, government lawyers argued, would breach the absolute rule that the identity of undercover informers can never be disclosed without their agreement. To allow this principle to be violated would have "a devastating impact on the overall investigative effectiveness of the FBI," Justice Department lawyers contended. The higher courts nonetheless declined to reverse Griesa's order.

The government then took an unprecedented step: Attorney General Griffin Bell (a member of President James Carter's cabinet) informed Judge Griesa that he was refusing to obey the order. It was one of the moments in the case when the routine legal maneuvering between lawyers was suspended. The attorney general was acting not as a political appointee but as the direct spokesperson for the police power of the government, of the state power itself. Griesa responded by finding the attorney general in contempt of court, the first such ruling in U.S. history. "The Attorney General has no 'right' to defy a court order," declared Griesa. "The Court possesses and must possess under our system of law, the authority to enforce an order for the production of evidence. . . ."

THE JUSTICE DEPARTMENT immediately appealed the contempt ruling. The Court of Appeals, which had earlier refused to overturn Griesa's order, now ruled that a contempt finding was too drastic a sanction for Bell's defiance of a court order and reversed the ruling. The contents of the files were eventually summarized by a special appointee of the court and this summary was made part of the trial record.

In a television interview show in 1977, former President Richard Nixon was asked whether he believed that a president could authorize illegal acts such as burglaries against opponents of the Vietnam War. He answered:

> When the President does it, that means that it is not illegal.
>
> Question: By definition?
>
> Answer: Exactly. Exactly. If the President, for example, approves something because of the national security . . . then the President's decision in that instance is one that enables those who carry it out, to carry it out without violating a law.

The same position was argued at great length by Justice Department officials in the trial of the SWP lawsuit. The former attorney general, Herbert Brownell, testified about a document he had written in 1954 in response to a Supreme Court decision that the cops had violated the Fourth Amendment by breaking into a private home and planting a microphone in the bedroom of a man accused of gambling violations. Brownell directed the FBI to ignore the ruling when going after "subversives." Brownell wrote:

> Obviously the installation of a microphone in a bedroom or some comparably intimate location should be avoided wherever possible. It may appear, however, that important intelligence or evidence relating to matters connected with the national security can only be obtained by the installation of a microphone in such a location. It is my opinion that under such circumstances the installation is proper and is not prohibited by the Supreme Court decision. . . .

On the witness stand, Brownell argued that when it came to "intelligence" or "national security" investigations—that is, when the target is political, rather than criminal, activity—the executive branch of government has the authority to ignore the Bill of Rights. Under cross-examination the former attorney general became visibly irritated that anyone could question this doctrine. When the judge himself asked some pointed questions, Brownell's voice hardened. Finally, he was asked whether it was "your view as the Attorney General that the Fourth Amendment was applicable to intelligence investigations?" Brownell responded:

> We didn't have any guidance from the Supreme Court on that. I think the matter is still open as far as the Supreme Court is concerned. On the one hand you have the express powers of the president to conduct foreign affairs and to be the Commander in Chief. On the other hand you have the Fourth Amendment.

Brownell then paused, glared directly at Griesa, and said, "So far there has been no court decision which prohibited such activities in the field of intelligence."

The message was unambiguous: this has been going on for a long time and no federal judge has ever tried to stop us, so don't make trouble for yourself. Griesa reserved response until his ruling, which explicitly rejected the claim by Brownell and the Justice Department that the executive branch has the power to trample on the Bill of Rights.

VIII. Why the SWP?

Why was it the SWP that was able to take the initiative in this fight for democratic rights? Why didn't the Communist Party, which has been hit harder than the SWP by government harassment, spying, and disruption, take such a step once the opportunity presented itself? Why wasn't such a move made by a social democratic organization such as the Democratic Socialists of America, which could call on legal and financial resources far greater than those available to the SWP case?

The answers to these questions shed important light on the results of the differing perspectives of the major currents in the working-class movement today. A look at some of the ways the Justice Department attempted to derail and defeat the SWP case helps to clarify the fundamental questions involved.

One of the government's tactics was repeated attempts from 1976 through 1980 to persuade the SWP to settle the case out of court. The proposed terms of the settlement were as follows: the FBI would pledge to obey the law, but make no specific mention of barring such methods as informers, burglaries, and disruption operations. In return for the SWP's acceptance of this promise and dropping its suit, the Justice Department would agree to a substantial financial payment to the party.

The government did reach such settlements in a number of other lawsuits against the FBI. Many of these cases had been inspired by the early successes of the SWP suit in forcing into the open previously secret FBI operations. Some of these cases were settled when the individuals or groups who brought them were unable to sustain the burden of an expensive and time-consuming court fight against the vast resources of the federal government. Other lawsuits, however, were settled because the plaintiffs were politically persuaded that FBI "guidelines" announced by the Justice Department in 1976 essentially accomplished what they had set out to achieve and there was no reason to press further.[9] Those who agreed to settlements on this basis refused to challenge the U.S. government's claim that it must have a political police force to defend "us" against "them"—whether "they" are subversives, terrorists, or the world communist movement. Those whose goal was to try to get the FBI and other federal police agencies to operate in a more enlightened and democratic way were paralyzed when it came to forcing the real questions of democratic liberties into the forefront.

The SWP took a different course. As the SWP case headed toward trial, the Justice Department stepped up efforts to achieve an out-of-court settlement. Sporadic probes by government lawyers had been made for several years, as other cases were settled. Boudin and the SWP did not rule out a possible settlement and explored every proposal. But each turned out to offer no concrete conquests for democratic rights. In the spring and summer of 1980, Justice Department lawyers renewed their efforts, significantly raising the amount of money offered. (It was estimated that the final payment could go as high as a million dollars, including payments for attorneys' fees.) But there was no substantive change in the content of the agreement proposed by Washington.

IN SEPTEMBER 1980 the Attorney General's office submitted a "final" offer for settlement. It followed the basic pattern of other settlements reached in suits brought by victims of FBI operations. In response, Leonard Boudin sent a detailed letter to the Justice Department spelling out the reasons for rejecting the proposal. He wrote:

> It is inconceivable to me that *SWP v. Attorney General* could or should be settled without addressing the violations of the Bill of Rights by the defendants, and affirming the rights of the plaintiffs to be free of government harassment, victimization, blacklisting, and "investigation," whether of the Cointelpro type, or the more routine varieties. It is my view that Judge Griesa, who has spent seven years supervising discovery in this action, will not approve any settlement of this case that fails to face these issues squarely.
>
> The Attorney General's office has been evading the constitutional issues posed by FBI, CIA, and

> other defendant agencies' wrongdoing ever since the major public revelations of the mid-1970s focused public opinion on these "intelligence" agencies. Congress, despite many hearings and much discussion of a charter for the FBI, has not come to grips with these questions. Settlements like the one reached in [Jane] *Fonda* [*v. the FBI* and] *Alliance to End Repression v. Chicago*, likewise skirt the issues that, from the standpoint of constitutional rights, are paramount. . . .
>
> The extraordinary record that has been developed in this case over seven years establishes that plaintiffs have engaged solely in activities that are protected by the First Amendment. Plaintiffs have a right to pursue these activities free from investigation, disruption, and penalization of any kind by the government. The entire purpose of this litigation is to vindicate that First Amendment right.

One provision of the Justice Department's "final" offer was especially troubling to Boudin and the SWP. The government draft settlement stated that the SWP's "activities and advocacy of ideas shown in the record in this case do not constitute a sufficient basis for initiating a domestic security investigation of plaintiffs under current law and guidelines. . . ." But elsewhere the document stated that the court record "does not consist of all the information available to the FBI."

The maneuver was transparent. The government wanted to be able to continue to claim that there was evidence of crimes by the SWP that had not been submitted to the court in order to protect supersecret sources and methods of obtaining information. "If there is any such evidence," Boudin responded, "it should be produced. If there isn't, it should be stated that none exists."

This issue emerged as a central one at the trial, which opened in April 1981. Early in the proceedings, the government lawyers announced that the FBI had compiled evidence of illegal activities by the SWP. This evidence, they said, provided legal justification for all the FBI's actions against the SWP. The sources and methods by which this information was obtained were so sensitive, however, that revealing the evidence to the SWP would bring grave consequences for "national security."

THE GOVERNMENT'S strategy was more dangerous than might appear at first glance. Under court rules of evidence, material withheld from one side cannot be considered because there is no opportunity to rebut the evidence or question witnesses about it. Judges normally refuse to consider such "secret evidence." And that was Griesa's initial ruling: if the Justice Department did not want to disclose the contents of the secret material, then he would not consider it in reaching his decision in the case.

But this course posed a danger. Even if Griesa refused to consider the secret material as evidence, the material could nonetheless become part of the record in the case in an appeal to a higher court. Thus, an appeals court could not only read the secret material but even base a ruling on it. Although extremely rare, it was not unheard-of for courts to consider such secret materials.

For this reason, the SWP took an unusual—in fact unprecedented—step. The party asked Griesa to consider and weigh the secret material. Although the party's lawyers would not be able to rebut the documents directly since they would remain in the dark about the allegations contained in them, the judge could evaluate the charges in light of the totality of facts that would be presented in the trial. On that basis, the judge could decide for himself whether the accusations in the secret material were credible.

This move surprised the judge and caught the government lawyers off guard. Griesa listened carefully as attorney Margaret Winter, who headed the SWP legal team at the trial, argued that only if the judge examined the secret files could the party hope to remove what could become a major, even fatal, obstacle to a ruling favorable to the SWP in the Court of Appeals or Supreme Court. Griesa understood and agreed with the point. There followed a series of private meetings between the judge and government attorneys, in which Griesa evidently put considerable pressure on the Justice Department either to voluntarily withdraw the secret material or disclose its contents so the SWP could read it.

Finally, Griesa announced a ruling on the issue that, he stated, represented "in part, an agreement by the Government." The judge would give "no evidentiary consideration whatever" to the secret materials and the Justice Department "has agreed that it will not rely on these matters as evidence in this court or in any Appellate Court." The government lawyers had been forced to agree to forego relying on the secret file in any appeal in the lawsuit.

The episode highlighted a fundamental fact about the Socialist Workers Party. To this day, one can only guess at the contents of the secret file. Yet the SWP had no hesitation in urging the judge to read and consider it. A similar question had arisen earlier in the case when the Justice Department was objecting to turning over secret FBI informer files. Leonard Boudin then recommended to the SWP leadership that it agree to let Griesa read the files himself since Griesa was not yet prepared to overrule the FBI claims of "informer privilege."

Looking back on that decision later, Boudin viewed it as a turning point in the case. "I will never forget when Judge Griesa walked into the courtroom after reviewing those FBI informer reports," he said. "Of course he was barred from revealing anything about the content of the files. But he turned to me and said, 'Mr. Boudin, you would never believe what is in those files.' He was shocked by the kind of information on legal political activity and details of personal lives that the FBI was compiling."

It was not a difficult decision for the Socialist Workers Party to agree to the judge reading the informer files and then the secret file, even though the party was denied the right to see the materials itself. The SWP was confident that nothing in the secret files would show policies or actions of the party that would contradict what the SWP said publicly. (Of course, no one could be sure that the FBI did not concoct such evidence—indeed it was assumed they had. But any such manufactured material would be contradicted by the massive factual record based on decades of activity in the working-class movement.) This confidence was based on a fundamental political fact. The Socialist Workers Party, like all genuinely communist organizations, *has no special goals of its own as a party.* It analyzes the stage of development of the worldwide struggle of the working class and its allies. The party offers proposals for how best to advance along the lines indicated by that struggle that will lead to the conquest of power by the workers and farmers. Because the SWP has no special goals of its own, separate from the historic course along which the working class is marching, it can have no program or policies kept secret from the working class. Moreover, any organizational practices or structures not consistent with this would cut across the party's political perspectives.

This principle was established with the founding of the modern communist movement 140 years ago. Marx and Engels fought in 1847 to free the newly formed Communist League from the conspiratorial traditions and organizational methods that had up until then dominated the league's forerunners and the revolutionary workers' movement in general. Secret structures, a secret program, even a secret language—all had to give way to a movement that consciously rejected conspiracy as a mode of functioning, Marx and Engels insisted.

AS THE OPENING LINES of the *Communist Manifesto* itself put it, "It is high time that Communists should openly, in the face of the whole world, publish their views, their aims, their tendencies and meet this nursery tale of the Spectre of Communism with a Manifesto of the party itself."

This approach flowed from the rejection of any idea that a real revolution can be carried out by a small group acting on behalf of the working class. A "true revolution is the exact opposite of the ideas of a *mouchard* [cop], who . . . sees in every revolution the work of a small coterie," Marx explained.

At the SWP trial, the *mouchards* kept trying to prove that the party said one thing in public and something different in its closed meetings. They tried to establish that the party maintained dual structures, one for public purposes and the other hidden from view. In every case, the facts showed the opposite. While a workers' party has the right, in fact the responsibility, to protect the privacy of its members and supporters from the bosses and the police, it has no right to keep its ideas, methods, and organizational concepts hidden from working people. If the SWP had, at any time in its history, adopted any other course or engaged in specific activities that contradicted this policy, the SWP lawsuit against the FBI would have been precluded. The party would have been paralyzed by concern that a trial might well expose a duplicitous history.

As the trial demonstrated, the FBI's accusation of conspiracy and hidden goals were *pure projection.* It turned out to be the White House and FBI, not the SWP, that conceal their true aims and methods. It turned out to be the White House and FBI, not the SWP, that maintain a covert structure to carry out what they cannot openly proclaim. It turned out to be the White House and FBI, not the SWP, that rely on conspiratorial modes of operation to achieve their goals behind the backs of the people of the United States.

Social democratic forces in the United States were incapable of taking an initiative like that of the SWP in defense of democratic rights because their starting point is to convince the exploited that they share common interests with "democratic" elements among the U.S. rulers. Their framework is to bring these more enlightened forces into positions of power and administration of the capitalist state, including its political police apparatus. These socialists do not rule out the day when they will share administrative duties in a capitalist government, including in running the police—as their counterparts have done in many countries in the world. In this position, they would be loyal defenders of the capitalist state.

The Communist Party, for equally important political reasons, could not take an initiative like the one taken by the SWP. The CP long ago departed from the communist starting point of seeking to advance the struggle of the working class of the United States, as part of the world working class, along its historically necessary line of march. This had been replaced by the starting point of the diplomatic interests of the Soviet regime. Once the Stalinists set out along this road, they abandoned the principle of telling the truth to the working class about their political aims and organizational forms. As a result, they became vulnerable to government frame-ups and witch-hunting smear campaigns, which they were handicapped in combating.

The consequences of this course blocked the CP from leading the fight to expose capitalist frame-ups such as the one against the Rosenbergs and made it impossible for the CP to take a political and legal offensive against the FBI such as the campaign set in motion by the SWP, which has had such positive results for the democratic rights of the people of the United States.

IX. Expansion of political rights

Judge Griesa handed down his opinion in the SWP case in August 1986. The ruling is a victory for political rights, codifying in a court opinion for the first time many rights and liberties that have been fought for over many years. By vindicating these rights, the decision further strengthens them, giving an important new weapon that can be used by others in future battles for prosecution against secret police spying, disruption, and harassment.

Griesa's 210-page ruling affirms the constitutional freedoms claimed by the SWP and YSA. The court found that the FBI disruption program, the "black bag job" break-ins at SWP and YSA offices, and the use of undercover informers constituted "violations of the constitutional rights of the SWP and lacked legislative or regulatory authority."

Leonard Boudin said of the consequences of this ruling: "The impact of this decision goes far beyond the SWP and YSA. It is a contribution to constitutional law, extending important new protections to the rights of all politically active individuals and organizations." The ruling expands the space for political activity and individual privacy for everyone in this country. It strengthens constitutional protection against government meddling in people's private affairs and in the affairs of groups to which they belong.

The court ruling includes the following points:

• The constitutional right of privacy includes protection against the use of government informers to infiltrate a political organization. The decision is unambiguous: "The FBI's use of informants clearly constituted invasion of privacy." Drawing on past precedents such as the victory of the NAACP against the state of Alabama, the court reaffirmed that in addition to the rights of individuals "an association has a right of privacy" under the Constitution.

• FBI break-ins in the name of "national security" were violations of the SWP's rights under the Fourth Amendment to the Constitution, which bars arbitrary searches by government agents. These burglaries, Griesa wrote, "were invasions of privacy of the most aggravated form. The FBI's own nomenclature—'bag jobs' and 'black bag jobs'—indicates something of the nature of these stealthy invasions of private premises for the purpose of obtaining private information."

• The FBI's Cointelpro operations "were patently unconstitutional and violated the SWP's First Amendment rights of free speech and assembly. Moreover, there was no statutory or regulatory authority for the FBI to disrupt the SWP's lawful political activities."

• Victims of such FBI operations are entitled to collect

money damages from the government in compensation. Griesa awarded the SWP and YSA $125,000 for invasion of privacy by informers, $96,500 for invasion of privacy by FBI burglaries, and $42,500 for specific Cointelpro operations.

In reaching these specific conclusions, Griesa dealt with even more far-reaching questions of constitutional law. He rejected the claim that the Constitution gives the president the "inherent power" to ignore constitutional rights in the name of "national security." The Justice Department had argued that the SWP could not claim damages for the FBI operations because of a provision in federal law making the government immune to lawsuits for actions that fall within the government's "discretion," even when "the discretion involved is abused." But the government "cannot have discretion to behave unconstitutionally," Griesa ruled.

These findings were strengthened further by the judge's decision that the SWP is entitled to an injunction that will prevent the FBI or any other government agency from using files containing information that was obtained illegally by the FBI. (As of this writing, the judge has not issued an order spelling out the details of this injunction.) This illegally obtained information is being used to victimize people who are or have been members of the YSA or the SWP in the past or who have expressed support for or interest in these organizations. The dossiers are used to discriminate against noncitizens who apply for citizenship papers, permanent residence, or visas to visit the country. They are used to justify denials of security clearances for workers in factories with military contracts, leading to harassment, denials of promotions, or even firings. They are used to single out government workers for special interrogation or as the basis for denying jobs at the post office or in other federal agencies.

How many files are there? The FBI alone admits to maintaining *ten million pages* on the SWP and YSA and individuals associated with these organizations.

Once Judge Griesa decides on the extent of the injunction on the files, his ruling on the case as a whole will be entered, and the stage of appeals will begin. During the legal arguments regarding the terms of the proposed injunction, the Justice Department gave a preview of the arguments it will use to try to get Griesa's entire opinion overturned. In court papers, Justice Department officials argued that barring the use of the files on the SWP and YSA will place at risk "the Nation's vital interests of self-preservation." Attorney General Edwin Meese's lawyers invoked the decision of the U.S. Supreme Court in 1951 upholding the Smith Act convictions of the Communist Party leaders: "The Supreme Court has noted that self-preservation is the 'ultimate value of any society.'" The need to protect this "ultimate value" overrides constitutional protections of the rights of groups and individuals, they argue. Moreover, the Justice Department insists, the fact that the FBI could come up with no evidence of SWP lawbreaking after decades of investigation did not of itself make the investigation or the techniques used in it illegal—"the FBI was *and is* authorized to conduct such investigations." (Emphasis added.)

In the nearly five decades since the U.S. government unleashed the FBI in a war against political rights and democratic liberties, the vanguard of the working-class movement has learned invaluable lessons about the importance of the fight for democratic rights. The consequences of not defending the rights of those one may have political disagreements with have been painfully evident.

The negative results of policies that require sacrificing the fight for democratic rights in the name of some seemingly more important objective have been seen. The importance of the conquests won by the Black movement and labor for the right to organize and for privacy of association has become better appreciated by politically conscious workers and farmers in the United States.

In the course of its lawsuit against the government, the SWP itself has acquired a far richer and more complete understanding of its own fight for the codification in a court ruling of its rights and the rights of its members and supporters—a ruling that also will be used by others. The decision that has been won is a genuine acquisition for the democratic rights of the people of the United States. Defending that conquest against efforts to weaken it or overturn it in the higher courts is a battle that should be joined by everyone—in the United States and around the world—who understands that a blow to the U.S. secret police and a victory for democratic rights in the United States will be a gain for working people everywhere.

NOTES

1. Farrell Dobbs, *Teamster Politics* (New York: Anchor Foundation, 1975), p. 21.

2. Recounted in Charles Washburn, *A Question of Sedition* (New York: Oxford University Press, 1986), p. 90. This is one of the most substantial existing resources documenting government harassment of the Black press during World War II.

3. An important part of the story of the fight against racism and political repression during World War II is told in the Pathfinder book *Fighting Racism in World War II*, a collection of articles from the *Militant*.

4. Francis Biddle, *In Brief Authority* (Garden City, NY: Doubleday & Co., 1962). Biddle was not bashful about defending wiretapping. Testifying about the Bridges wiretap before the Senate Judiciary Committee in September 1941, he said, "It is a dirty business of course, but . . . we have abandoned civil rights before in time of war."

5. The complete transcript of Cannon's courtroom testimony is contained in James P. Cannon, *Socialism on Trial* (New York: Pathfinder Press, 1973).

6. Patti Iiyama, "American Concentration Camps," *International Socialist Review* (April 1973), p. 28.

7. An English translation of the interview with Borge was published in the *Militant*, November 14, 1986. The interview first appeared in the May 1986 issue of *Crisis* published in Buenos Aires.

8. Michael and Robert Meeropol, *We Are Your Sons* (Boston: Houghton Mifflin, 1975).

9. In March 1976, the Justice Department announced new "guidelines" for FBI "counterintelligence" operations. With this cosmetic reform, the government sought to create the impression that it was curbing FBI abuses of democratic rights such as those exposed in the SWP lawsuit and other post-Watergate revelations, without restricting FBI powers in any meaningful way.

World War II and the failure of the 'American Century'

The Socialist Workers Party in World War II

Writings and Speeches, 1940–1943

JAMES P. CANNON

Preparing the communist workers movement in the United States to campaign against wartime censorship, repression, and antiunion assaults. $25

Fighting Racism in World War II

FROM THE PAGES OF THE *MILITANT*

An account from 1939 to 1945 of struggles against racism and lynch-mob terror in face of patriotic appeals to postpone resistance until after US "victory" in World War II. These struggles—of a piece with anti-imperialist battles the world over—helped lay the basis for the mass Black rights movement in the 1950s and '60s. $25

The Struggle for Socialism in the 'American Century'

Writings and Speeches, 1945–1947

JAMES P. CANNON

The challenges posed by the post–World War II labor upsurge, the rapid expansion of openings for the communist movement, and the subsequent ebb in face of the stabilization of US capitalism and the employers' antilabor offensive and witch-hunt. $25

Speeches to the Party

The Revolutionary Perspective and the Revolutionary Party

JAMES P. CANNON

Writing in the early 1950s, Cannon discusses how class-conscious workers, in face of the conservatizing pressures of the emerging capitalist expansion and anticommunist witch-hunt, carried out effective union work and political activity to build a communist workers party. He discusses Washington's failure to achieve its goals in the Korean War and why the rulers reined in McCarthyism. $24

WWW.PATHFINDERPRESS.COM

The working class and the defense of political rights

SOCIALISM ON TRIAL

Testimony at Minneapolis Sedition Trial
James P. Cannon

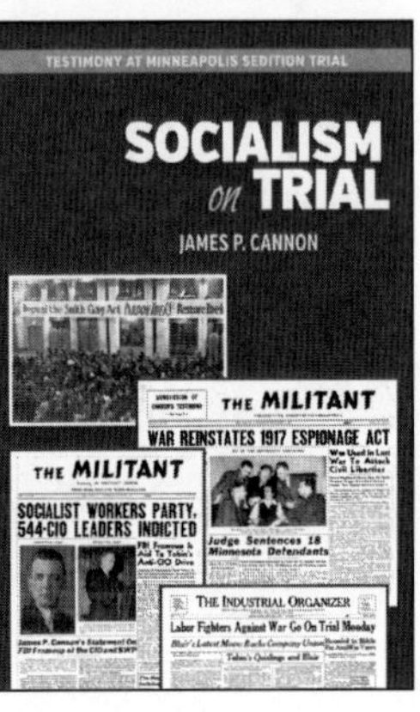

The revolutionary program of the working class, as presented during the 1941 trial—on the eve of US entry into World War II—of leaders of the Minneapolis labor movement and the Socialist Workers Party on frame-up charges of "seditious conspiracy." Includes Cannon's answer to ultraleft critics of his testimony, drawing lessons from Marx and Engels to the October 1917 revolution in Russia and beyond. $16. Also in Spanish.

New

50 YEARS OF COVERT OPERATIONS IN THE US

Washington's political police and the American working class
Larry Seigle, Farrell Dobbs, Steve Clark

The 15-year political campaign of the Socialist Workers Party to expose decades of spying and disruption by the FBI and other federal cop agencies targeting working-class organizations and other opponents of government policies. Traces the origins of bipartisan efforts to expand presidential powers and build the "national security" state essential to maintaining capitalist rule. Includes "Imperialist War and the Working Class" by Farrell Dobbs. $12. Also in Spanish.

www.pathfinderpress.com

The Militant

Socialist newsweekly published in the interests of working people

THE MILITANT

A SOCIALIST NEWSWEEKLY PUBLISHED IN THE INTERESTS OF WORKING PEOPLE

INSIDE
Harlem meeting: Fight to free Cuban 5 is 'near and dear to us'

'Militant' welcomes new readers

BY EMMA JOHNSON

SOCIALIST WORKERS BUILD ACTIVE WORKERS CONFERENCE

—See page 2

Separatists' 'takeover' in east Ukraine unravels

BY JOHN STUDER

Turkish gov't contempt for miners fuels protests

More than 300 killed by bosses' profit drive

BY SETH GALINSKY

- Covers labor battles from garment workers in Bangladesh and Cambodia to miners in Ukraine and South Africa, from textile workers in Egypt and health-care and factory workers in Israel to farmworkers, longshore workers, and truck drivers in the US and Canada.
- Reports on fights against cop brutality and frame-ups, against attacks on women's right to choose abortion, and against deportation of workers who are foreign-born.
- Explains the roots of the worldwide capitalist economic crisis and defends oppressed nations, from Ukraine to the US colony Puerto Rico.
- Champions the fight to free the Cuban Five — framed up and jailed by the US government — and defends the socialist revolution in Cuba against Washington's unremitting hostility.
- Explains the road of the working class to take political power out of the hands of the capitalist class.

The Militant • 306 West 37th Street, 13th floor • New York, NY 10018

Subscribe today!

New readers 12 weeks for $5

6 months $20   1 year $35   2 years $65

WWW.THEMILITANT.COM

CUBA: A HISTORIC MOMENT

by Mary-Alice Waters

THE TWO SPEECHES BY Fidel Castro published below reflect a turning point in the Cuban revolution. The developments unfolding in Cuba today have been virtually ignored by the press around the world. Inside Cuba, however, the last year and a half has been a period of intense public debate and action, led by the Cuban Communist Party and involving every sector and level of society. Both speeches in this issue were broadcast and telecast live and then replayed so that Cubans working any shift could hear them.

The aim of the current rectification process, as it is called in Cuba, is to carry through a historic correction in the course of the revolution itself. In his speech to the deferred session of the third party congress in December 1986 published here under the title "Important Problems for the Whole of International Revolutionary Thought," Castro explains that the questions now being confronted and dealt with are not new. Problems had been developing for more than a decade. But the evidence was mounting, Castro says, that the mistaken course of the revolution was leading Cuba not toward socialism and communism but "to a system worse than capitalism."

Had the mistakes remained unacknowledged and uncorrected the consequences would ultimately have proved "irreversible," Castro adds. Discouragement, depoliticization, and demoralization would have eventually developed to the point where the revolutionary consciousness and internationalist commitment of the masses of Cuban working people would have been destroyed—all under the banner of building socialism.

The process that the Cuban Communist Party is leading can be described as a genuine political revolution. It is a battle to eradicate the mistaken idea that there is some mechanism—whether it is the Economic Planning and Management System or People's Power—whose automatic functioning provides the motor power of the advance toward socialism. It is a battle to once again place at the center of the revolutionary process the only force that can drive forward the transition from capitalism to socialism—the working people themselves, mobilized to take increasing control over the administration and leadership of their own state and to chart the path of the Cuban economy.

WHERE THE CUBAN leadership was going off course, Castro explains, was in thinking and acting as if "the construction of socialism is basically a question of mechanisms." That was the heart of the errors, Castro insists, because "the construction of socialism and communism is essentially a political task and a revolutionary task, it must be fundamentally the fruit of the development of an awareness and educating people for socialism and communism." Even an Economic Planning and Management System or a People's Power structure, reformed and improved, can serve only as an auxiliary instrument, however important, to be *used*, not turned into fetishes.

Only revolutionary men and women, communists, who have conquered a new political and social consciousness, can lead humanity to build a better world. That will be a world in which free, voluntary social labor assumes a larger and larger place, as the mechanisms and separate administrative apparatuses wither away and the field of operation of blind laws increasingly gives way to the conscious decisions of humanity.

The Cuban socialist revolution is advancing, qualitatively deepening its proletarian and internationalist roots, and mobilizing Cuba's working people to take new steps in conquering the leadership of their revolution. In this framework, the question of leadership is dealt with directly in Castro's speech "Renewal or Death."

Castro explains the criteria that guided the election of the new Central Committee and Political Bureau at the third party congress in February 1986. Previous attempts to renew the leadership were only partial and incomplete, he notes. "The most revolutionary thing" about the second congress, Castro told a public rally in December 1980, "was the composition of our Central Committee. The leadership of our Party was given a strong dose of worker cadres, a strong dose of women, and a strong dose of internationalist fighters." Moreover, he noted, "the number of workers in our Party has almost tripled, which means that our Party has become more proletarian and, therefore, more Marxist-Leninist and more revolutionary."

The 1986 party congress, however, went far beyond the important initial steps of 1980. It carried out a deep-going renewal and the beginning of a historic transition in leadership to a new generation. Forty percent of the members of the new Central Committee and 50 percent of the new Political Bureau had not served on the outgoing committees. Moreover, the congress recognized, the process of renewal and transition could be carried forward only by advancing the working-class composition of the leadership. That meant consciously confronting the legacy of race and sex divisions and stratifications within the working class inherited from imperialism, because the consequences of these divisions are not eliminated overnight. The new, more proletarian, leadership included a strong infusion of youth, of women, and of blacks and mestizos.

Since the February 1986 congress, the example it set on leadership selection has been extended, and similar measures implemented in the trade unions, the Union of Young Communists, and other organizations.

A WEIGHTY FACTOR in the ability of the Cuban Communists to advance the battle to deepen the revolution in Cuba is the hundreds of thousands of Cubans who have volunteered to work as internationalists overseas. They have dedicated their energies and skills as teachers, doctors, engineers, and construction workers in countries such as Ethiopia, Kampuchea, Nicaragua, and Grenada and in return acquired a deeper revolutionary consciousness about the fight against imperialism and Cuba's place in the world. Of decisive importance have been the experiences of the Cuban soldiers who have volunteered, beginning in 1975, to fight to defend Angolan independence and sovereignty against the South African army and the U.S.-backed mercenary forces. These experiences have educated, politicized, and mobilized the best and most conscious of the young generation of Cuban communists "to pay our debt to humanity," as they often put it.

A new, more profound understanding is now being forged, a realization that there can be no separation between proletarian internationalism and communist class consciousness at home. Moreover, it is only fresh victories against imperialism by workers and farmers elsewhere in the world that will bring forward new revolutionary leadership and make possible the continued deepening of the Cuban revolution. Without the advances for the world revolution in Angola, Nicaragua, and Grenada over the past decade, Cuba, too, would have been pushed back.

This is true above all because the rectification process is not primarily a struggle over ideas. As Castro explains, the Economic Planning and Management System, left to function "blindly" without the counterweight of leadership and control by communist workers, has bred a social layer of administrators and functionaries, some of whom began to act like capitalists, dress like capitalists, and develop the tastes of capitalists. They sought support within the better-off layers of the working class who became accustomed to and corrupted by unearned bonuses and privileges, and those small farmers who raked in windfall profits on the sale of scarce food items and other consumer products. These social layers benefited under the economic system of the last decade. Many of them are opposed to the steps being taken to deepen the politicization and revolutionary mobilization of the working class to take command and to make conscious choices to advance the broadest social interests of all working people in Cuba and abroad.

The most telling fact about the seriousness of the challenge facing the Cuban leadership was the recognition that the corrupting influence and weight of these social layers had begun to be felt within the Communist Party as well. The party itself, Castro commented, "was starting to go to pot."

The heaviest counterweight to these negative pressures in Cuba over the last decade have been the advances of the world revolution. Proletarian internationalism and the direct revolutionary experience of hundreds of thousands of internationalist volunteers have been powerful politicizing factors. They have become a material force. With the aid of the workers and peasants of Africa, Central America, and the Caribbean, the workers and farmers of Cuba were able to begin their correction process in time, to change course before depoliticization, demoralization, and corruption could become irreversible.

THE RECTIFICATION PROCESS now under way is not the first time in recent years that the Cuban leadership has taken up this fight. In 1979 Raúl Castro made several powerful speeches in which he addressed these issues. In 1980 millions of Cubans poured into the streets three times in one month, responding to growing U.S. military threats and provocations and the Mariel exodus with the Marches of the Fighting People. Later in 1980 the voluntary Territorial Troop Militias were formed, rapidly mobilizing over a million and a half Cubans and revolutionizing Cuba's defense system. In 1982 at the Communist youth congress and the congress of small farmers Fidel Castro spoke out sharply against numerous manifestations of corruption and bureaucratism. All these resulted from growing consciousness about the problems Cuba was confronting and were steps to mobilize working people to combat them.

The conclusions reached by the third party congress, however, and the course that has now been charted mark a definitive turning point and the opening of a new stage of the Cuban revolution. Leadership renewal is no longer partial or symbolic. The necessary political mechanisms and economic planning systems, no matter how reformed, are being assigned their proper place as instruments, forms to be used and altered in practice by a politicized, communist working class. The course that has been charted is not a short-term campaign against isolated examples of corruption. It is a course of mobilizing working people to take command of their own present and future, advancing humanity towards a future that is far better—not worse—than capitalism.

"The road to communism is completely new to humanity," Castro explains. There are no blueprints; there can be none. Ever higher levels of social understanding and class consciousness are needed to keep correcting the course and moving forward. All these factors indicate the centrality of the revolutionary political developments in Cuba today to working people the world over. As Castro says, they are important to "the whole of international revolutionary thought."

IMPORTANT PROBLEMS FOR THE WHOLE OF INTERNATIONAL REVOLUTIONARY THOUGHT

by Fidel Castro

COMRADES ALL: the congress approved the program of the Communist Party of Cuba, our first program, and resolved that it be proclaimed today to coincide with the thirtieth anniversary of the Granma landing.[1] I therefore declare the program of the Communist Party of Cuba approved. (*Prolonged applause*)

The unorthodox idea of holding a deferred session of the third congress turned out to be a practical and wise one. This allowed all our party members and our entire people to analyze and discuss the draft program and also to improve it.

This speech was given by President Fidel Castro, first secretary of the Central Committee of the Communist Party of Cuba at the close of the Deferred Session of the Third Congress of the Communist Party of Cuba on December 2, 1986. The text was translated by the Cuban Council of State and is reprinted from Granma Weekly Review. *It has been checked against the Spanish-language version published in* Granma, *December 5, 1986. Minor corrections and stylistic revisions have been made and the annotation supplied by* New International.

ENDNOTES BEGIN ON PAGE 384

Its drafting for the third congress didn't allow for the time needed for its mass discussion before the congress was held.

The analysis made by our people and our party members resulted in many proposed amendments, and many new ideas were introduced, which were carefully examined by a commission and, lastly, by the congress commission.

A large number of the thousands of ideas and suggestions submitted were approved—perhaps not thousands but certainly hundreds of them—and even then we had no illusions that our program was perfect; there may be concepts that could be made clearer, more precise, more perfect; yet we were quite certain that the essential ideas were embodied in our program and that it was a good program.

The approval of our first program is a historic event. It is also, of course, a far-reaching event in the life of our revolution and our party. It expresses our hopes projected toward the future. But we might draft the best program in the world and yet fail to fulfill it.

I am fully convinced that if we fail to rectify our errors and negative trends, neither this program nor anything else worthy of that name could ever be implemented.

We have already fulfilled some programs since our revolutionary ideas emerged, since we started our struggle against the [Batista] dictatorship. The Moncada Program was not only fulfilled—the Moncada Program was fulfilled in a relatively short time during the first years of the revolution—it was amply overfulfilled;[2] what the revolution has done in the past twenty-five years is much more than what we dreamed of back in those times.

And so it would be nothing new for us to approve a program and fulfill it, yet we must be aware of the requirements of carrying out a program.

Fulfilling the Moncada Program demanded a lot of struggle, effort, and sacrifice; yet the requirements were met to carry out that program, to implement it, and overfulfill it. That's why it is necessary that we be fully aware of the premises for implementing this program, which explains why we have dedicated nearly all the time of our deferred session to the process of rectification of errors and the struggle against negative trends. This program has the added advantage of having been approved now instead of during the first session of the congress—it now contains many of our ideas concerning these problems, this rectification process, and the struggle we are waging; and so our program was brought up to date, and correctly so, in that regard.

Although the essence of a series of problems had already been set forth in the congress and the main report, they weren't as broadly outlined as they were later on, during the months after the congress. And even as we looked into all those questions, we discovered many things, many elements and factors that weren't completely clear during the first session of the congress.

THROUGHOUT THESE PAST months, during the period between the first and this session of the congress, our awareness grew about all these problems, and we saw them more clearly. It was realized that, logically, that had to be the main topic of the deferred session. There was nothing else we could best work on.

These final sessions of the congress already showed, as did the first session, the efforts made for months, because it took months to work out the contents of the early session of the third congress at the meetings held throughout the island, and it took months for the party to work out the contents of these final sessions of the congress.

The party and the country have gone through a process of discussion. This has been a year of countless meetings in many different spheres; many plenary meetings dealing with this, plenary meetings of the party at the grass roots and in the provinces, meetings with all the country's enterprises, meetings with all the country's agricultural cooperatives, countless work meetings at the grass-roots level. And over the past few weeks plenary meetings were held in all the municipalities to discuss these questions, and then plenary meetings were held in the provinces to make serious, well thought-out, profound analyses. All of this gradually paved the way for these final sessions.

It is the unanimous opinion of the participants here that this final part of the congress was not good, it was excellent—some of you were frightened when I said that. (*Laughter*) It was not just good but magnificent. It has possibly been one of the best political meetings we have ever held in the history of the revolution. (*Applause*) We've held good meetings and very good Central Committee plenary meetings, and yet I believe that at no time have we reached greater democratic spirit, greater freedom of expression, greater sincerity, greater conviction, openness, clear thinking, and, above all, penetrating analysis. Dozens of comrades participated, and no doubt hundreds more perhaps were left with the wish to say something. Yet I believe that the fundamental things were, in essence, discussed.

The questions related to the implementation of the Economic Planning and Management System, work organization and salaries, labor discipline, utilization of resources, work style, demanding attitude, and verification were discussed by the party and the Union of Young

Communists, by the mass organizations, and by management—problems relating to cadre policies, ideological problems, social problems, the youths' problems, the peasants' problems. In short, all the subjects pertaining to this policy of rectification and struggle against negative trends were discussed. They involve extremely broad contents that range from diverting resources—which so irritates the population, brings so much corruption, so much disorganization, which is so demoralizing, so harmful to the revolutionary process—all the way to the questions related to the chaotic situation regarding salaries linked to amount produced, work norms, fulfillment and overfulfillment of work norms. Then there was the method of using money to solve all problems, the policy of corruption, and even deceiving people. How could anyone pay out easy money which is not really backed by production, by the creation of material values or services! It's simply deceit.

That's why all this is so broad, because it encompasses the whole activity of the revolution and the need for rectification wherever we have made mistakes or wherever negative trends have developed in our revolutionary process.

OUR FINAL SESSIONS spent a lot of time on the problem of work organization and salaries and the problems of work discipline, making the most of the workday, the temporarily laid-off workers, and all those far-reaching questions for the life of our country and the revolution. A lot of time was also spent on one question of fundamental and decisive importance for our future, namely, a demanding, efficient educational system, and also considerable time was given to the discussions on the method and style of party work.

I wouldn't say, of course, that all our problems were discussed; I'd say that the essential problems were, but not all our problems. That's why we must include, as part of our policy, the conclusions and analyses that were previously made throughout the country, in all the municipalities and all the provinces.

That's why we shouldn't just consider the party program, we shouldn't just bear that in mind. We must also take into account the summarized versions sent to you of the discussions in the municipalities and the provinces, for it seems to me they are documents of great value. All the problems are analyzed there in greater detail: the problems of land leasing in the countryside, in every municipality, how many of these farms turned up, how many illegal land holdings—which were, in short, the problems being faced by the peasantry; the problems with the youth relating to those who aren't studying or working in some of the activities where we needed manpower, above all, in agriculture or construction, reforestation, etc. We have the data on those who accepted and those who didn't.[3]

In those summaries are all the problems systematically discussed throughout the country, and I believe they are documents worthy of being reviewed once in a while, above all when analyzing what is being done and how it is being done.

Now the program is something else. The program should not be a reference source, really. The program should be a study manual. I'm not going to mention study groups now; we're pretty grown up from a revolutionary standpoint, and we shouldn't be learning everything in study groups.

What we want the students to do, which is to take into

account their textbooks, to go over their lessons and study using their textbooks, is what we must do ourselves. We mustn't spend time on millions of study groups but instead individually study the program, read it, reread it, go over it, look for some chapter, look for some point on any subject of interest to us and be really informed as to the contents of the program, because the program is what is going to guide our work for the next fifteen or twenty years. I think this is a big task, a big goal, and we must follow that program. Although we wouldn't say it is the best program—I believe anything can be improved—it is unquestionably a good program.

Now, if we were able to do with this program what we did with the Moncada Program, that is, fulfill it, and not just fulfill it but overfulfill it, this would indeed be a worthy goal, a great overfulfillment, not of a soft norm—as has been the case in some places—but of a strong, difficult program; fulfill it and overfulfill it, and if we couldn't overfulfill it as to its content (it is possible to overfulfill as to content), we could still overfulfill it as to time, and no one can yet state how long it would take. Now, if we work well, we can fulfill it and overfulfill it as to time and I am also certain that we can overfulfill it as to content.

Some of the things in the program won't be too difficult, some are already being done. One little point we were discussing, the time it would take us to set up the exact sciences vocational schools, and already these schools have begun to function, the exact sciences vocational schools are already in existence. They opened this school year, although we can't say they are running perfectly for they also have their problems, as does education generally, what with the work load, contents, and that sort of difficulties, the test periods, etc., for those schools are very demanding.

The idea of introducing the teaching of computer science in all intermediate education schools—senior high schools, technological institutes, junior high schools—is something being put into practice; it hasn't been introduced in all the schools, but we have purchased an important portion of the equipment and means, I'd say about two-thirds of the necessary means are already in our possession. And we won't have to wait until 1990 for by 1989 the program will be applied in practically all intermediate schools.

THIS PARTY PROGRAM talks about the family doctor program. This family doctor has started to become a reality: in the city of Havana alone there are about 800 doctors—just in the city of Havana!—working in areas which we could say don't have the best living conditions, the best housing. They're working in old working-class neighborhoods, which aren't indigent neighborhoods because we don't have any indigent neighborhoods here, and they aren't slums because we don't have any slums. They're working in areas where the population needs them most and they're doing an excellent job.

This year, when more than 1,500 joined the program, we've built the doctors' housing as well as their offices. There are already mountain areas completely covered, such as in Granma Province, with the notable result that in the mountain areas where there are family doctors, the infant mortality rate is down to less than 10 per 1,000 live births. With this alone and in the mountains, with just a policy of education, the effects can already be seen in just two years. We are avoiding teenage pregnancies, avoiding accidents in the home, recommending methods of hygiene—with that alone, not counting the other elements the revolution is starting to put into effect, such as the recently opened children's cardiovascular surgery center, which will save the lives of many small children, and other programs that will be carried out, intensifying the work and raising the quality of maternity hospital services, especially for the first week of life, where we still have a relatively high index of infant mortality. Although the country's general index is now equal to those of some developed countries, we know that in regard to the first week of life we have to improve our work and health services, raise the technical training of the personnel, and improve the equipment.

This has occurred in the mountains, even without prenatal genetic counseling, which is being extended throughout the country. I think the prospects in this field are really very good, I think it's an area in which we can go beyond the requisites of the party program.

IF WE MAKE A GREAT EFFORT in education and do it well, if we utilize all the human and material resources at our command, if we overcome our difficulties, there's no doubt we can meet the requisites of the program and even go beyond them in education as well. I'm mentioning things that are already being done and that are in the program. We won't take long to complete them.

We can advance so much in the development of cooperatives, for instance, in the countryside; in the development of agricultural production; in the use of technology; in our scientific research centers; the fabulous things that can be done if we put ourselves to the task, the things that we can do in production and the services in general, if we overcome all these problems we have been discussing here.

All of you, the delegates who have been present here and the public in general, know the content of these debates. I'm not going to repeat or enumerate everything that was said, every one of the conclusions we have reached, because our people have been keeping up with the debates at the congress sessions. I have no idea what has been broadcast on television and radio; a little while ago I was watching television for a minute, the eight o'clock news, and I saw part of the report on the congress. Right now I don't know all of what's come out on television, I haven't had time to find out what's been broadcast but I do know, from what I've heard, that it's been covered in depth. There are probably very few things that have not been reported on television and radio, although there are always some things that must stay within the family, that shouldn't be widely publicized so as not to give information to the enemy. But the public has been given a maximum of information on the subjects discussed.

Something else and very significant: about 200 Cuban journalists took part in the debates along with almost 2,000 delegates who include the main cadres of the party, and also the Union of Young Communists, the mass organizations, the main cadres of the Revolutionary Armed Forces and the Ministry of the Interior, the main cadres of the socialist state, all of whom were elected as delegates to the third congress. And I'm sure that very few have ceased to function in these positions in the period from the first session of the congress until this session.

Matters were discussed with great clarity, as I said before, with great frankness, and for that reason it's not necessary to repeat all these issues.

I think we must get to the heart of things. There are two, three, four, or five clear fundamental things that can be taken out of this congress, much more than in the first session.

There is a fundamental issue, which is that we have a party. It is very clear that we have a party. It's so important to have a party!

TODAY IS THE THIRTIETH anniversary of the *Granma* landing. Some years before that, when we started the revolutionary armed struggle, we didn't have a party. We had a small contingent of men, there was a political organization and we had clear ideas, but we started the struggle with just the embryo of a party. At the time of the *Granma* landing there was a movement and we eventually had a large movement, but not what could properly be called a party, in the true sense of the word.

At the beginning of the revolution we had the Rebel Army, which, as Raúl [Castro] recalled today,[4] I had described as a "unifying factor for all the people."

We all know how the party, this new party, the Communist Party of Cuba was created, how it was built up, how unity among the various revolutionary forces emerged, how it evolved, overcoming difficult obstacles, errors, even, like those that surfaced initially and were analyzed, discussed, and overcome in due time; how it was built up slowly and carefully, selecting the best workers in the country, the best fighters. We were just a handful in the first years of the revolution.

The party devoted a great deal of time to its own creation, its own development, its own growth, its own internal affairs, its own ideological training. It was also being built, gaining experience in its active participation in these almost twenty-eight years of selfless and heroic revolutionary struggle.

Of course, right from the time the party was founded it was present in everything, but it still had a modest educational level. It had a great patriotic consciousness, a great revolutionary spirit, but not a great political education—although our members, from the very moment we started moving down the path of socialism, had what could be called a revolutionary consciousness. They knew what they wanted, despite the fact that they were not equipped with many ideas or knowledge. That was the task of ideological education, the work of the revolutionary schools, the work of our press, the work of our mass media, which simultaneously educated the party and the people.

It is really very gratifying and encouraging to see that today we have a party with a large number of members, with experience, a high educational level, a broad political awareness, and a high revolutionary consciousness, a party that knows what it wants and is really learning how to achieve what it wants. This emanates very clearly from what we have seen in these days.

The party now has more than a half a million members and candidate members. Half a million! Imagine, half a million! How can we compare that figure to what we had during the days of the attack on the Moncada Garrison? We were just a few hundred comrades, and we already thought we could carry out a program, make a revolution, bring the revolution to power, overturn the dictatorship, and carry out a revolutionary program. There are now 3,500 Communist Party members for every one of those who took part in the Moncada attack—3,500! Plus another 3,500 Young Communists and in addition millions of workers, Committees for the Defense of the Revolution members, women, peasants, students. It is really a colossal force.

At that time we didn't even have a modest radio station to spread our ideas. Maybe we would have had it after taking over the garrison; we surely would have had it because it was planned. There was no newspaper. Today we have modern mass media, scores of publications, several important national newspapers, provincial newspapers, magazines of all kinds, powerful television channels and radio stations, the whole educational system in the country, all the resources to spread ideas. It's so important to spread ideas! We saw very clearly that the struggle was impossible, victory was impossible if we could not spread ideas and if the masses did not adopt those ideas. We always saw that the masses were the basic factor in the revolutionary struggle, the great force that makes history, and that if the masses were exposed to those ideas nothing could stop our victory.

So what did we have at the time of that first program and what do we have today? Immense, tremendous, extraordinary resources and half a million Communists! At that time there was maybe one of us for every 50,000 citizens; now there is a Communist for every 20 citizens, including newborn babies. Today there is a member of the Union of Young Communists for every six or seven young people, depending on the ages as a point of reference, and the masses are members of our trade unions, our Committees for the Defense of the Revolution, all our mass organizations, under the party's leadership. Under the party's leadership! They are not under the leadership of the state; they are under the leadership of the party, because the Leninist idea of the role of the party in a revolutionary process is becoming clearer and clearer.

That's what having half a million party members means. And as I said during the sessions, it's a healthy party, a very healthy party, even though some members have made mistakes, a party with a high morality, a party of honest people. There may be a dishonest party member unworthy of membership in our ranks that we haven't yet discovered, but the party, its members, and its cadres are very moral and humane.

It was starting to go to pot, but we have reacted in plenty of time so that the party members will not be corrupted, the party will not be corrupted, the young people will not be corrupted, and above all our working class will not be corrupted. (*Applause*) I'm not falling into wishful thinking; I'm expressing what we have been seeing in this rectification process.

The peasants were also getting corrupted. We no longer knew if a cooperative was an agricultural production cooperative, an arts and crafts cooperative, an industrial cooperative, a commercial cooperative, or a middleman's cooperative. We were losing our sense of order; the trading between the cooperatives and the state enterprises, state enterprises exchanging products, materials, foodstuffs among themselves, like the case Raúl mentioned yesterday of a factory exchanging products with a farm, because while it sent the agricultural cooperative cement sweepings, the agricultural enterprise sent salted meat and who knows what else to the cement factory.

If everyone started doing that, if that proliferated, nothing would be left. There wouldn't be any meat for the schools, for the hospitals, for what has to be distributed to the population every day, every week, every month. If this kind of generalized trading developed among the state enterprises or between the agricultural production cooperatives and state enterprises, no one knows where this would all end, in what kind of chaos and anarchy. These are evident negative tendencies, extremely evident!

We offered examples of enterprises that sold their materials and charged the prices of finished jobs, be it paint, lumber, asbestos tiles, or anything else, to cite a few examples, for there are a ton of them. Enterprises that tried to become profitable by theft, swindles, swindling one another. What kind of socialism were we going to build along those lines? What kind of ideology was that? And I want to know whether those methods weren't leading us to a system worse than capitalism, instead of leading us toward socialism and communism. That almost universal chaos in which anyone grabbed anything he could, whether it be a crane or a truck. These things were becoming habitual and generalized.

If this is not combated energetically, the masses start to get skeptical, discouraged, and demoralized, and the ideas and objectives of our revolutionary process become discredited. This is serious, very serious.

We talked a lot about this subject and it's a subject on which a lot can be said, essential concepts about what socialism is and how it can be built.

In our meeting with journalists at their last congress,[5] I raised some of these problems, which are not only important for our country but for the whole of international revolutionary thought. Our party has explained with great frankness and courage the errors it has committed and how it happened; how at a given time we made errors along the lines of being extremist, so to speak, or being idealistic. And then we began to make worse mistakes, much worse, with more negative consequences, for the first kind were reversible, but the kind of errors I've been referring to could have reached the point of being irreversible. We had to rectify them in time, not only for the sake of our own process but also for the revolutionary process in general, since the construction of a new society, the construction of socialism, the road to communism is completely new to humanity; it's a new experience, a very recent one that must constantly be enriched by both theory and practice.

No one can imagine that it's all said and done, that all the problems were solved 150, 160, or more years ago, with the publication of the *Communist Manifesto* or the Gotha Program, or of Marx and Engels's or Lenin's books later on. It would be antidialectical to think that, it would be anti-Marxist to think that.

HUMANITY AND SOCIETY follow their course, and more and more new problems crop up. There are problems in this day and age that didn't exist then. At that time, for example, it seemed as though natural resources were unlimited, infinite, and that it was the social regime that was the only obstacle to the unlimited development of the productive forces and social wealth, especially material wealth.

Of course, there is a lot of truth in the great faith the founders of scientific socialism had in the possibilities of science and in the possibilities for development of the productive forces through the application of science. They realized that over 150 years ago, and now the socialist countries are beginning to see it very clearly. In the socialist countries there is a lot of activity surrounding the issue of scientific and technical development, for this is an indispensable prerequisite of the development of the productive forces.

Nowadays there are new problems, pollution for example, which is a reality and an enormous problem. There has also been an incredible amount of waste of nonrenewable natural resources, oil for example.

It is possible that in the brief span of 150 years man may exhaust all the hydrocarbons that accumulated over hundreds of millions of years.

A proven fact is that throughout its history humanity has engaged in all kinds of insane, abusive, unjust, cruel acts and wars, and this is especially true of man raised in the selfishness of class society. That is a fact proven over and over again. Man has unleashed world wars that have meant tens of millions of deaths; right now he is on the threshold of a war that may mean the end of all living creatures.

Man has also committed all sorts of outrages with natural resources—apart from the fact that they are unequally distributed, for nature gave some many riches in the soil, hydrocarbons and minerals, and others got practically nothing in the historical partition of the planet. Moreover, terrible situations of poverty and underdevelopment were created; we know about them from our ties with the Third World; we have thought about them, it's what we see in entire regions where thousands of millions of people live whose future is yet to be decided.

There are new problems, I repeat, enormous problems in this day and age, and it's up to the revolutionary, progressive parties and Marxist-Leninist theory to pinpoint, explain, and solve them. Some ideas have to be enriched by interpreting Marxism-Leninism correctly. All this is closely related to the construction of socialism.

We should point out that Lenin made a great contribution when he conceived of the possibility of building socialism in an economically backward country, in a country that wasn't an industrial power—the old empire of the czars. There was a time in revolutionary thinking when it was felt that revolution was only possible if it first occurred in the most industrialized countries and, what's more, in several industrialized countries at the same time. One of Lenin's great historical merits was to have thought of the possibility that socialism could be built even in an industrially backward country.

Of course, the construction of the first socialist state in such conditions took its toll in enormous, terrible sacrifice; in isolation and a blockade; in the need to develop and reinvent science and technology. It meant building a socialist regime with just its own resources, the lone resources of an industrially backward country which, moreover, was in ruins. This was a historical feat, one of humanity's greatest ever, although the consequences are still felt to some extent.

AFTER THAT, socialism continued to develop. Socialist processes were victorious in other industrially backward countries in Europe and later in the Third World. Of course, by then a Marxist-Leninist idea of tremendous scope was being practiced: internationalism. It was internationalism that made possible the phenomenon of a socialist revolution ninety miles away from the most industrialized and powerful imperialist country in the world.

In Marx's time imperialism didn't even exist. Imperialism is a new phenomenon which Lenin researched and analyzed to guide the revolutionary struggle under the new conditions. And this is what it's all about; we have many new problems to solve and many obstacles to overcome because this experience is very new and socialism is being built on a trial and error basis, so to speak. Yet some concepts are very important.

I believe that one of the worst things that happened to us here—I've said this before and perhaps I'll say it again more than once—is that we began to go off course; perhaps others have done it too, but I've seen the example of what was happening to us; the blind belief—or it began to be blind—that the construction of socialism is basically a question of mechanisms. As I pointed out at the journalists' meeting, I think that the construction of socialism and communism is essentially a political task and a revolutionary task, it must be fundamentally the fruit of the development of an awareness and educating people for socialism and communism. (*Applause*)

This does not deny the usefulness and value of certain mechanisms, even economic mechanisms, yes, economic mechanisms! But to me it's clear that economic mechanisms are an instrument of political work, of revolutionary work, an auxiliary instrument. I dare say that economic mechanisms are auxiliary means, auxiliary instruments of political and revolutionary work but not the fundamental way of building socialism and communism. I haven't the slightest doubt that the fundamental way is through political and revolutionary work.

We've lived through the experience—we've lived through two experiences, the one before and now this one, the two of them; we've seen the negative consequences of both of them and we could see even some positive things in both.

WE'VE HARBORED TWO TYPES of illusions. When the constitution was enacted; the country's political-administrative division was carried out; and the People's Power organs were set up,[6] which was a great advance, unquestionably, the naive belief came about that following these changes, these steps forward, the state was going to function perfectly, almost automatically. Later we started to realize that this called for a very important political work, an immense task for the party.

On the other hand, in the sphere of material production and the services, particularly in the sphere of material production, we started believing that everything would run perfectly with the Economic Planning and Management System, with the system of salary linked to the amount produced, a panacea that would almost build socialism by itself.[7]

This also partly explains the confusion in the party. Only such rather blind belief in mechanisms, such a lack of understanding of the idea that the construction of socialism and of communism is fundamentally a political and revolutionary task would explain (it wouldn't explain everything, but would explain it in a certain way or in part) that many party members and cadres did not detect the phenomena we are now tackling. Although I am also certain that many party members firmly believed that it had to be that way and that it was correct—it was part of the economic management system—given their trust and sense of discipline and because the basic decisions in the economic sphere were taken at a congress and because these decisions stemmed from the party leadership.

No leader, no cadre in this country had ever had any of these experiences in building socialism, and the knowledge that some of them had was, in any case, theoretical and, we might even say, too theoretical. No one here had real practical experience in the conditions of a country like ours, with our degree of development and our specific problems. No one knew or was in a position to know how those mechanisms were going to function, and this is why we have learned the lesson only now.

That is what was happening. How were we going to solve our problems of material production and the country's development? Apparently, we thought that by dressing up a person as a capitalist we were going to achieve efficient production in the factory and so after a fashion we started to play at being capitalists. Because it is only under socialism that you could dress up an administrator as a capitalist; if you wanted to make a capitalist out of him, you'd have to make him the owner of the factory and nothing else, return to the capitalist system, find a superefficient street vendor and make him the owner of the place.

Under the conditions of socialism, the only thing possible is to dress up an administrator as a capitalist, the only thing that can be done is dress him up and then believe that he's going to be efficient. And the characters dressed up as capitalists, many of our comrades dressed up as capitalists, began to act like capitalists, but without the capitalists' efficiency. Capitalists take better care of their factories and take better care of their money; they are always competing with other capitalists. If they turn out trash no one will buy it, and if they are not profitable they go bankrupt, they're sued and deprived of their property, they lose their jobs as administrators and stop being the owners.

So some thought that by dressing up a person as a capitalist he was going to make the factory run efficiently. What they actually succeeded in doing in many instances with such absurd beliefs was having these comrades start acting as capitalists, not by reducing production costs as capitalists do, not by turning out better quality products as capitalists do, for if they don't go bankrupt, if they can't sell, they're stuck with the merchandise. They didn't seek better work organization, full use of the workday with discipline, and a demanding attitude. Capitalists who manage to survive the competition are demanding, very demanding, or else they don't survive.

Our man dressed up as a capitalist produced anything and forgot about quality: if he had to produce 100 items, he did; he didn't solve the contradiction between quantity and quality, nor did he keep good checks on quality, nor did he care about it, he just cared about fulfilling his production plan. He began to sell at higher prices, he began to steal to have the factory be profitable, and in the end he didn't even care whether the enterprise or factory was profitable, for the state would come forward at the end of the year and shoulder the deficit. What were the problems facing our man dressed up as a capitalist? He could spend his entire life playing the role of a capitalist without achieving efficiency or else making shady deals and being paternalistic, solving individual people's problems here and there.

I'm not saying everyone behaved like that, since that would be unfair.

I'm pointing out the problem, which was becoming quite generalized and on the way to being much more so because we had gotten used to living with those problems and not seeing them.

NATURALLY, THE PROBLEM of unprofitability was rather generalized, so wholesale prices of many products were raised and even this failed to make many enterprises profitable. I repeat that even raising wholesale prices failed to make many enterprises profitable! Generally speaking, they became increasingly unprofitable. The larger the salaries paid in that chaos of norms and more norms, bonuses and more bonuses, these administrators dressed up as capitalists could even start to compete among themselves to see who got the best workers, paid the best salaries, was less demanding, and also played the role of populists, paternalists, what have you, making absolutely no demands, with all the consequences derived from this.

Our man dressed up as a capitalist could not solve these problems because it isn't capitalism or the capitalist methods that under the conditions of socialism can bring about efficiency in an enterprise. This doesn't mean we are giving up these mechanisms, no! We shouldn't give up the system of paying salaries according to the amount produced in the field of material production since it is impossible to do so in other fields—I've mentioned this before—it would be absurd. We can't give up paying salaries according to the amount produced, work norms, or the socialist formula of getting paid according to the quantity and quality of work, quantity and quality! (*Applause*) We shouldn't give up the idea of enterprise profitability or cost accounting. I'm not against any of those mechanisms or categories, provided we fully understand what political work, revolutionary work, is, the sense of responsibility instilled in cadres, the sense of responsibility of cadres, what can make efficiency possible, not dressing up as capitalists our administrative cadres in the material production sphere. (*Applause*)

YES, WE MUST LOOK for profitability but look for it seriously by discussing in-depth and exhaustively the reason the enterprises are not profitable; look for it not by some enterprises swindling or stealing from others, as we said, but by really cutting production costs, increasing productivity, making the most of the workday, using our know-how, organizing the work efficiently, deflating payrolls—none of which can be done in a day, of course. As we said here, in no case and under no circumstances can the remedy be worse than the illness, either when it comes to material production or education, where we're bent on solving the problem; but we were running the risk of using remedies worse than the illness; we must cure our illnesses with appropriate remedies.

Yes, we have inflated payrolls, that's one of the negative trends, and this is an old thing; it's not new, but it's possible that they became more inflated with all the confusion and mistaken concepts.

And we must cut costs, we must achieve quality. Actually, we are not going to have our socialist enterprises competing with each other, because that has nothing to do with the idea and conception of socialism; it has nothing to do with Marxism-Leninism. They can emulate each other but that's not competition in capitalist fashion, with its dramatic consequences.

When there's no competition, if the motivation prompting the owner in a capitalist society to defend his personal interests is out of the question, what is there to substitute for this? Only the sense of responsibility of the individual cadre, not just the collective's sense of responsibility; the role played by the cadres. The man who is in charge there must be a communist. It is unquestionable that whether or not he is a member of the party, the man who is in charge must be a responsible man, must truly be a communist, a communist, a revolutionary! (*Applause*) And not a communist playing at capitalism, a communist dressed up as a capitalist or, mark you, a capitalist dressed up as a communist. (*Applause*)

We have achieved success in other activities thanks to good political work, excellent things we have done, and so I ask myself, in the first place, the following: What economic mechanisms, what cost accounting will we use in such an important, decisive field as public health services? What cost accounting, what incentives, and what economic categories led us to develop a hospital like the Hermanos Ameijeiras hospital? What cost accounting led us to introduce science and technology there? What cost accounting enabled us to perform our successful heart transplants in that hospital and made possible all the major scientific advances it has achieved? Where is the hospital's profitability and the mechanism of profitability, and where is the hospital's system for linking salary to amount produced?

As we said during the congress—I don't know whether that was shown on television; at this time I don't know what the people know of what we have been discussing or the questions raised here—were we to remunerate a surgeon according to the number of operations he performed, if we continued along the road we chose in the material production sphere, we would be paving the way for a surgeon to perform twenty operations a day, any type of operation, even if the patient didn't need it, it wouldn't be important whether the person dies or not . . . unless we threw in a bonus for saving the guy, (*Laughter*) a bonus if the guy didn't die; twenty operations, a lot of operations; or in case the surgeon had to operate once or twice a day, to do it right and not try to do in one hour what should take three, lest he cut the patient's veins or nerves or kill him.

What system for linking salary to amount produced could we ever establish in this: what similar system could we establish in the case of the family doctor? For the family doctor must see his patients in the morning, visit them in the afternoon. He's got to sit down in his office, write up case histories, analyze, meditate. Were we to have doctors on this system, what would be the polyclinic's profitability?

There are extremely important spheres in social life and revolutionary work in which none of these mechanisms can possibly be used, so then, how are we to solve such essential services as public health, which have had such excellent results in our country like, for instance, the infant mortality rate. It's possible that this year it will be less than 14 per 1,000 live births, it's possible. And it will be less in the future. I already explained to you how things were going in the municipalities in the mountains which have their own family doctors.

WHAT ABOUT the family doctor? Well, that family doctor, in my opinion, gives us a glimpse of the communist man because he works well and works hard, and those in the mountains are young people trained by the revolution; they're not twisted nor are they under a deforming or corrupting system. The residents keep them highly motivated; they're influenced by the local population and are being trained in formulas of communist work.

What we have to do is work with these doctors, and that's just what we do from the time students are chosen to join the Medical Sciences Detachment; they have the approval of their classmates, they are interviewed by a commission to find out whether they have the vocation and they must make the grade. There are absolutely no exceptions to this procedure.

We must train them from their time as high school students and as university students, work with them and simply turn out communist doctors. I ask you, is there any other way? Is there any other way to turn out doctors with a communist consciousness? Now then, those who do heart surgery, for example, and other very complicated and difficult surgery, what about them? They earn a straight salary as specialists. That's why it was especially painful to see people selling garlic out there at any price, with a hectare of land and working a few hours a year and earning 50,000 or 60,000 pesos a year in the free peasant market, what those highly skilled surgeons earn in twelve years.

There were yearly individual incomes—I did the figuring—equal to what it would take surgeons, the best we have in the country, sixty years to earn. I know many good surgeons, many good doctors in this country, and I haven't seen any of them with that lust for money. They are dedicated to their work, they are true communists. (*Applause*)

The health sector leaves us no alternative but to train communists as of now, because there is no other way. Is there any other? Is there any other way?

Exactly the same thing is true in education. How could we possibly link a teacher's wages to the amount produced? We'll pay them according to the number of students passed, and then all the students will get 115 percent on their exams in every subject. (*Laughter*) Is there any way to link their wages to what they produce? What about the profitability of the schools, in all those categories, which I admit are necessary in the sphere of material production?

We have 600,000 or 650,000 workers in education and public health, and what are we doing? In the health sector the party here in the capital is waging a battle. Of course, the Ministry [of Public Health] and People's Power are working with the correct criteria, but the party and the communists in the hospitals are struggling tirelessly against deficiencies, poor service, all those things the people have been complaining about. And we can see some progress in the republic's capital as a result of political work, because there is no other way. Political work and a little bit of common sense, reason, sensibility, because in the hospitals, beds were being lost, rooms were being lost for lack of maintenance materials. That's a matter of bad planning, of erroneous concepts in the distribution of resources. We said to People's Power in Havana, "How are we going to maintain the hospital without materials? Why don't we allot them 2, 3, 4, or even 5 percent, if necessary, of the building materials destined for the general population." After all, it's for the population's benefit. Of course, hospitals should be allotted resources apart from this other channel.

So the hospital maintenance personnel began to regain hospital beds and do a heap of other things.

THE PARTY IS DOING a systematic job. The first secretary of the party in the city of Havana meets with all the secretaries of the party committees in the hospitals, and in the capital there are almost sixty hospitals. This party work is done every month, and it will have to be done for five years, or maybe ten years, depending on how we progress, creating a tradition, a real work tradition and a communist consciousness in those workers. Of course, society will recognize their efforts in terms of pay. There are pay differentials in the hospitals. Nurses' incomes have improved, and their abnormal working conditions have been taken into account. Also taken into account is the situation of health aides, who have to work with patients with certain illnesses and do a very hard job, because not all of them have the same working conditions. These things are taken into account. We should see to it that doctors are well paid and can have a decent life. But are we really going to make good doctors by paying them

2,000 pesos a month, making them through money? I'd like someone to honestly tell me if that is possible and where it would lead us. Tell me if we have any choice other than political and revolutionary work, from childhood on, from the time they are Pioneers.[8]

Communists must be formed from the time they are Pioneers, from the time they are in day-care centers, education, all levels of education, all the way through the university. Can this be done or not? Practical experience has shown we can, and I've seen many cases of correct political work. Political work isn't reciting a catechism about Marx and Lenin to people every day, but rather being able to awaken human motivation and morality. (*Applause*)

To put it graphically, comrades, we must look for the hidden seed that exists in every human being, to coin a phrase from the documentary called *The Hidden Seed*, because every human being has it. There can also be a hidden bad seed, and if we start cultivating bad seeds, we can create monsters.

I don't think anybody was born revolutionary or not. It depends on how you develop the positive traits in every human being. I have seen criminals who are ashamed to have people know that they are such. Pride is one of the hidden seeds in human beings, almost without exception. We must learn how to develop that pride of all human beings, their honor, their dignity, the finest traits people have. This is clear, in my view.

And in defense, comrades, what economic mechanisms do we use? What profitability can there be in a division, an army, a battalion, a company, a platoon, or a squad? What money could we use to pay the young men from the compulsory military service who volunteer for internationalist missions? What money could be used as an incentive? What money could we use to pay officers of our Revolutionary Armed Forces who have undertaken three, four, or even five internationalist missions? What material incentives could we give them?

With what money could we pay, what bonus could we give to the men who risk their lives and often do in fact risk or lose their lives? (*Applause*) If they work endless hours to assure the defense of the country, what bonus could we give them? If they spend years away from their families, what bonus or material incentive could we give them?

I HAVE SEEN many comrades in the military laden with awards and medals. What do we have? Communists. What were we obliged to develop in our armed forces, as a result of having a revolution and building socialism ninety miles from the United States? We were obliged to produce communists and have done so! (*Applause*) Is there any other formula or mechanism to solve the problem?

If there have been endless hours of preparation for the parade we witnessed this morning with discipline and organization, if we have organized the entire people, millions of men and women who spend one Sunday a month—a Sunday, a day off every month—on defense, what method have we used, how have we done so?[9] Simply by developing a communist consciousness.

Just imagine what would have happened if we had resorted to other methods in defense and law and order. We would have created alienation and corruption and taught people to think only of money. The officers of the armed forces and the Ministry of the Interior must have a salary in line with the work they do in order to have a decent life. They don't have an egalitarian salary, it is a socialist form of remuneration, depending on their capacity, experience, and work, but is that what has determined their conduct?

Here we have a comrade whom I saw over there, comrade Leopoldo Cintra, who was in Angola for the second time and had already been in Ethiopia. He spent several years in Angola as the head of the Cuban military mission, several years! I wonder, what bonus could we give him, what mechanisms could we utilize with him and the many thousands of men like him who have done their duty there? (*Applause*)

Then we can safely say that we have achieved our best results working with the pride and honor of people, with their consciousness, and instilling ideas. I have mentioned some of the fields in which these mechanisms could not be used, although on the other hand I do feel they are necessary in material production. There are research centers where people work fourteen or fifteen hours a day and think nothing of it. I'm not advocating that people work fourteen or fifteen hours a day, I'm simply explaining what the pride and honor of people can do.

WE MUST APPEAL TO people's consciousness, and the other mechanisms, the economic factors, are means, or auxiliary tools for political and revolutionary work required by a genuine revolution and, especially, required for the construction of socialism and the path to communism.

The same can be said for party members and cadres of the mass organizations. The best things we have, to tell the truth, have been obtained with political and revolutionary work, through the development of consciousness. These are not illusions, they are examples which are clear to all. And I say realistically, because we must all be realistic, that we must use these economic mechanisms in material production, but with this concept: as an auxiliary means or instrument of political and revolutionary work; because believing that these methods will give us the miracle of efficiency and economic and social development, the miracle of socialist construction is one of the most ridiculous illusions there could ever be. (*Applause*)

That's where the party's work comes in, that's what became clear, that's what's reflected in the summaries of the municipal and provincial plenums which have been held and the analyses that comrades have presented. In other words we have a strong party and the party has come to grips with the country's problems more than ever before, which is very important. Now it is dealing with many problems it never tackled for years. Now the party is in the center and vanguard of this battle to rectify errors and combat negative tendencies. All this became clear in the congress sessions.

At this congress session it became clear that the party knows what it wants and is learning how to accomplish it, and is also using a new work style.

We can't expect this rectification from our administrative cadres dressed up as capitalists. First we must remove the disguise, we must learn how to select and educate them. I don't mean to say we must change all administrative cadres; by no means, for there are many good ones. Many of them are not to blame for having been dressed up as capitalists and the fact that they worked and acted like vulgar capitalists and some have been deformed.

In this process we must have as many as possible mend their ways, all those susceptible to self-improvement and to adopting a really communist mode of behavior.

We admit the need for administrative cadres and the use of certain mechanisms. However, careful thought and study should be given to the use of those mechanisms. We have witnessed outright repudiation, more than rejection on the part of the workers when they understood certain types of bonuses that they were being paid. They were repelled and many rejected bonuses of this kind for which they had no justification, they were harebrained bonuses, (*Laughter*) unintelligible, incomprehensible, an effort to bribe people and play the role of the good guy.

CAPITALISTS DON'T do that. They don't give out a bonus that can't be measured in exact and precise terms and that doesn't yield a profit. But our cadres in capitalist garb were giving out bonuses all over the place for after all it wasn't their money. (*Laughter*) It was the bonus of the socialist state and the money of the people that they redistributed at will, creating chaos in wages.

It is clear and it was clear at this congress that the solution to the problems of efficiency, development, and the construction of socialism is the responsibility of the party. That was very clear! And as I said yesterday, not by managing, not trying to manage but simply by training, guiding, and leading men and women; coming to grips with all negative tendencies and errors of any kind; setting an example. That was an issue that was much talked about, the exemplary conduct that a Communist Party member must have. Yes, yes, there's no other way, or otherwise he or she can't be a Communist Party member, can't have that distinguished title. (*Applause*)

You know very well that being a communist means sacrifices; you know it better than anyone else. Sacrifices and efforts are always being demanded of you more than anybody else. This is logical under any circumstances and could not be otherwise; it must be that way.

There are citizens, workers with fine traits who have been honest enough to say, "No, I don't want to join the party," because they don't want to take on the obligations which party membership implies. This is the first thing we must make party members understand, that they must be ready for anything, be dedicated and self-sacrificing and assume a greater share of duties and responsibilities than other citizens. That is why exemplary conduct is required.

We say a communist worker can't work on his own. But that doesn't mean we will eliminate all categories of self-employment where there is a justification for them, where they play a useful role and don't contribute to theft, looting, shady deals, embezzlement; and where they really solve problems, they will be maintained. This issue was discussed at the Central Committee plenum, and I saw how some municipalities decided to make some exceptions on the idea that party members should not do work on their own. Party members renounced such practices and there were cases where the party said no because it was a retired person or somebody with a very low income, there was a special situation and the party made allowances for this. These were exceptions based on need and justice.

But on principle party members can't be working on their own or be involved in shady deals, private trading, or hold selfish positions such as those of which we have been critical, the people with that famous license, which was sort of a guarantee of immunity because they wouldn't go to work or would break something, doing whatever they could to be sent home on 70 percent pay so they could earn more money in addition to what they got from the state;[10] or they would leave an important project to earn more money on another, and they would leave a hospital being built with great urgency to go off and make more money on their own.

In this situation we will see who retains the famous licenses, who is really rendering a useful service to society. We must accept it, for it is a necessity under our circumstances and conditions; but with order, for this was also in complete disarray. Everything here fell prey to disorder, all measures led to some negative trend. It happened with those sent home on 70 percent pay, who have also been discussed here at the congress and the party has acted to solve the problems.

Clear principles and views repudiating these layoffs at 70 percent pay were expressed, but this doesn't mean we will ignore just concerns; but the limits and conditions must be determined in a country which needs workers in many fields. We will have to solve the problem which led to widespread vice. There is an incredible list of examples showing how this degenerated.

The work of the party can be seen in all of this; where the party gets involved, subjective and organizational problems are solved.

NOW WE ARE INVOLVED in this process of rectification and struggle against negative trends amidst a unique economic situation, as I explained. I won't say it is difficult because that would give the idea it is difficult in all aspects. That's why I said unique, because there are some branches of the economy with complicated and difficult situations, but not all. The country will have all the fuel it needs, for example; it will have many things which are assured by its economic relations with socialist countries.

But we will lack things that must be imported from the hard currency area. They will be in short supply, and we do have a complicated situation and there will be problems! This situation can lead to delays in the arrival of raw materials, difficulties with spare parts; there may be shortages of some, others may arrive late, due to our hard currency limitations, which are greater than ever!

At the congress I tried to explain to the comrades—I think some of this was reported in the press—that we would have half the traditional sum for hard currency expenditures. Imports valued at a minimum of $1.2 billion previously will be reduced to $600 million. And we will have to get by with that sum and be ready for those difficulties which will unfortunately turn up. There are times when you can't buy until you have the money; and you cannot spend unless some comes in. This also has to do with the foreign debt and related problems about which much has been said, and from which many countries are suffering. As I have explained previously, the situation is worse for us this year because of a series of objective factors such as last year's drought and the hurricane. But the work done enabled the damage to sugar production to be reduced to much less than what the drought has caused.

Re-exports of the oil we save, which had reached 3 million tons, underwent a price cut to less than half of the original price. Less than half!

Another financial and monetary problem associated with the economic blockade came when the dollar was devalued and all other currencies in markets where we buy our imports became more expensive. These three factors led to a drop of more than 40 percent in our foreign exchange earnings from one year to the next and created serious problems.

Such a small foreign exchange plan with such reduced imports of goods from the hard currency area is unprecedented and we are striving for the best possible use of those resources and seeking to limit the consequences as much as possible, but there will be inevitable consequences. We must see how we cope with the situation without sacrificing our development, maintaining our construction program, for example, of the nuclear power plant, which will mean a fuel savings of $500 million yearly. That can't be stopped, for it means the electricity we will need in the future. It may be that in the future we will be able to use electricity produced in this way in the kitchen, where we must now be using so many different types of fuel and often with difficulties.

This development must continue, construction and enlargement of oil refineries must continue, the development of nickel must go on. All industries which are important for the development of the country must continue under these circumstances and be given priority.

As I told the delegates, investments which reduce imports or generate exports will have absolute priority and we can't stop a single one. How will we get by? With the help of the goods and raw materials we get from the socialist countries and the indispensable minimum, very minimum, that we necessarily must buy from the capitalist world, we will draw up a rational plan that does not sacrifice development and attempts to meet the basic needs of health care, education, and food.

However, there will be inevitable consequences as a result of this external financial situation and even because of the quest for a balanced internal financial situation. We talked about this and some measures at the congress, although, of course, this issue will basically have to be dealt with at the coming meeting of the National Assembly, which will consider the yearly plan and where each of the measures we will have to take will be explained.

IN ADDITION TO THE PROBLEMS that so greatly affected us this year and gave rise to this situation, what factors threaten us or what factors play a role this year? Well, the drought this year was worse than last. I asked the Academy of Sciences to please gather data on rainfall in the 1981–86 period. It seems we are in a drought, without a doubt, for in all those years from 1981 to 1986 the rains have been less than average in those six years and including 1981 and 1986. There have usually been moderate droughts and intense droughts, although rainfall is always greater in some areas than others. In 1985 the drought was moderate to intense but in Havana Province, from which agriculture and our capital get their water, the rate was far less than average.

Now, about the rain we've had until late October—and we all know it didn't rain in November—despite the rain at a given time in Santiago de Cuba which helped fill some reservoirs, the average rainfall in the country this year was 68 percent of the average in the past, 68 percent, and in Havana Province it was 66 percent. In some places like in Holguín it was 52 percent.

The drought we've had this year is what meteorological experts call very intense drought, that's the name or category given to the drought we've had this year. It affects agricultural production and is forcing Havana Province to reduce its cultivated land for lack of irrigation water, in spite of the fact that we finished a canal leading from Mampostón dam to the town of Güira. We finally finished it, yet it doesn't compensate for the consequences of a drought which I believe came to 70 percent last year and 66 percent this year. Up to October this was the average rainfall in Havana Province, thereby affecting not just agriculture but also water supply for the capital. We have serious problems in that connection.

It has been decided to step up as much as possible the work on a new basin and complete it late next year. Yet canals, basins, dams are not much use if it doesn't rain.

I believe it is necessary for the population to be more or less informed about these facts and we must not live as if we ignored them.

ALL THIS will necessarily affect us. It has already affected our sugar production by over a million tons less, and since we are committed to honoring our obligations to the socialist countries and we no longer do what we did at times before—simply reducing our sugar deliveries to them so as not to affect our deliveries to the capitalist market—now we won't have much sugar available for the capitalist market in 1987. This is part of the group of factors I have explained and that makes it a tough year in terms of foreign exchange, with the added inconvenience that the drought also affects our production of other agricultural products like milk and root and garden vegetables.

That's why we are waging this battle that all these difficulties of an objective nature make more necessary to win, this being one more reason for us to work better in every sense, in every sense! We must wage a stronger battle against anything implying waste of resources of any kind: fuel, electricity, water, raw materials, what have you.

Above all, we must also be aware of our problems, we must be prepared to deal with them without sacrificing our future. We must do the best we can and be ready to cope with all the restrictions we may well have to face. (*Applause*)

We are now studying a series of measures, as I explained to you, and they will be taken. Coordinating these with the plan is already in its final stages, and the main goal here is doing the best we can with what we have now: a minimum of foreign exchange, making the best use of all resources, relying on the resources coming from the socialist camp, facing up to our difficulties and pushing ahead with development.

Development is the main thing and we are building very important projects.

Now, I confess to you that having witnessed, together with all the comrades from the party leadership and with all of you here, how the session unfolded, we have good reason to feel encouraged and rather optimistic, without pretending that the road will be easy. The road ahead involves difficulties and we must face up to them with a lot of political fortitude and a lot of political and revolutionary awareness. The party will have to play a decisive role in this.

We want the party to continue along the path it has taken and remain at the center of this battle; we want it to continue gaining experience, for we learn something every day.

As was explained here, in spite of what I just said, we're going to come up with more stone, more sand, more steel bars, more cement. We are going to launch in 1987 a bigger housing program than in 1986 and we are going to rectify our investment policy ideas and errors. We are going to keep close tabs on all priority projects, because in all these years we hadn't succeeded in having our priority projects—which are those having to do with our weakest point, the Achilles heel of foreign exchange—be built with priority, and we must give them all the attention they deserve.

We are going to go on doing things, we're going to go on building family doctor offices, another 1,500 of them. Next year we will fill the Santiago de Cuba mountains with family doctors. We will go on with our program to build new hospitals, the most important and urgent ones. We will not despair, nor will we sacrifice our future—neither the economic or social future—although, logically, the main emphasis will be economic investment; it couldn't be otherwise.

The party will have to follow everything closely; it must be in the center of all this, and we must enlarge our experience, the experience every one of us gains in facing up to the problems, the difficulties. Every day and everywhere we have the opportunity of learning something new, and judging by what we've seen this year, look at all the problems that are beginning to be solved now!

JUST LIKE WHEN I was critical at the first session of the congress, the enemy is listening to what we are saying. If I say we are not making the most of the workday or mention any of these problems, they immediately publicize it. They're interested in discrediting socialism, our interest is giving it prestige. Theirs is heaping trash on it, ours is freeing it of all trash. (*Applause*) We must free it of all trash and to do so we mustn't have the slightest fear of showing it for what it is! It's a good thing to wash our dirty linen out in the open. We're doing it and we can more and more count on our revolutionary press. To tell the truth, our press is contributing a lot to this battle, with a great sense of responsibility, great awareness, a great sense of its role and its mission.

And we're airing some of our trash. We still have more, but every day we are airing some of it.

Our enemies are fooling themselves, for they may be thinking that we are doing poorly or that socialism is not advancing. They may harbor illusions of that sort. But if they do, they are not thinking with the right logic, for what's excellent about this battle of ours is that we are clearing away the trash, paving the way for more rapid development of our revolutionary process. The fact is they don't realize that we are guaranteeing our future, that we are guaranteeing victory along the correct path, the correct path! (*Applause*) It's good if they're lulled by that, let's hope they're lulled to sleep for a long time, for then they will see how the revolution and the party will reemerge formidably from the dust of the trash. Once the dust settles, they will see the revolution marching on, the party marching on, and they will see that we have paved the way for overcoming objective and subjective obstacles in spite of the difficult conditions under which we have had to build socialism; that is, at the doorstep of imperialism and on the basis of the truly infamous economic relations such as the developed capitalist countries have with the underdeveloped countries, the Third World countries, in spite of all that. In spite of the miserable prices they pay us for our raw materials and our products, while charging us twice, three times, four times more for any object they export to us, even an ice cream machine! Even a little soft ice cream machine which sold for 2,000 pesos twelve or fourteen years ago. Back in 1970 we purchased a few hundred of them that went to factories and a few places run by People's Power. We used to have a little reserve around.

It occurred to me to ask what soft ice cream machines sell for nowadays, and the 2,000 peso ones we bought now sell for 8,000. So you see, and then they go on paying five cents, six cents for sugar in the so-called world market, and so it goes with any raw material, any resource from the Third World countries. A crane that used to sell for 25,000 pesos fourteen or fifteen years ago now costs 130,000, 140,000. Those are the conditions imposed on the Third World.

In spite of all that and thanks precisely to our status as a socialist country and our relations with the countries of the socialist camp, we will continue to advance. And just imagine the suffering, the poverty that is afflicting other countries that lack the privilege available to us!

Some day our enemy will understand and see all this, it will eventually realize what we are doing now in this historic moment in 1986. Some day they will realize!

OUR PROBLEMS are new, they are not the problems we had in 1959. Our problems in education are different. We don't have illiteracy, we don't have a lack of teachers, no. We have problems in education because we've built thousands of schools and we want these schools to function in the best possible manner. We have problems because we have 260,000 teachers and what we want is for these teachers to improve and do the best possible job. We have problems because we have built and expanded many hospitals.

We have problems because we have 25,000 and some doctors—not the 3,000 left here by the imperialists but 25,000 and all trained by the revolution—tens of thousands of nurses and health technicians and workers, and what we want is that they do the best possible job. We have problems because we have built thousands of industrial and agricultural facilities, because we have tens of thousands of tractors and pieces of construction equipment, and we want all these resources to be efficiently utilized. We have problems because we are building large projects and we want all this to go on at the right pace, with the necessary quality and efficiency. We have problems because we have huge resources compared with what we had in the past and we are waging a battle so they can be used correctly.

If we have a new factory turning out 60 million square meters of cloth, we want that factory to operate with maximum efficiency. And not with the idea of wearing all those clothes but instead exporting them to solve other problems, because we must first guarantee the supply of medicines and food. If we have another big factory of any type, many machine works which were nonexistent before and many construction materials plants that didn't exist before, we want them to work efficiently and in the best way possible. That's why we want to get rid of this trash and dust.

I spoke at the beginning about when the revolution broke out in the old tsarist empire, how they had to carry out the construction of socialism without help from anybody, depriving themselves of clothes, shoes, food, everything, to be able to rebuild the nation, and how later came the fascist aggressors who destroyed it all for the second time in less than thirty years. We have had, on the other hand, the privilege—as I explained—of having excellent relations, extraordinary foreign cooperation, satisfactory trade with the socialist countries. We have had many resources available to us and we are to blame for not having known how to use them efficiently, with all the necessary efficiency.

Unquestionably, if we run into problems with an adequate utilization of the workday in the countryside, if people decide to work without taking breaks so they can leave early, if people only work four or five hours in the fields, that's not the way to build socialism. If in industry, everywhere, we only utilize the workday to 80, 75, 70 percent capacity, that's not the way to build socialism in a country that still depends to such an extent on agriculture and that must develop its industries in order to free itself from that dependence on agriculture, and that in order to develop its industry has to work with great seriousness and efficiency and must turn out quality products. If we fail to make the most of the workday in sugarcane, in agriculture generally, in construction, in the factories, in lots of other places, that's not the way to build socialism!

We must understand this, it is the first thing we must understand, and it is what we are now learning quite clearly, because never before had we thought as much as we are doing now about this type of problem. Never before have we internalized, as they say now, these problems to such a great extent. The party is aware of that and is coming to grips with it, because all these negative tendencies must be eradicated, we have to make sure that work gets done.

It isn't written in any program and no one has said anywhere that a country can be developed and could progress and become prosperous without work. And we must learn how to have a dignified concept of work. All our honor and pride must be brought together to raise the value of our work, and to become conscious of the importance of our work. And we must dedicate ourselves to work. Work as established by law; make the most of the workday and do away with all those silly things of all kinds that have led to a lack of discipline. We must do away with all those silly things and absurdities we have analyzed and harshly criticized. And there's only one way of doing this: political and revolutionary work guided by the party, for the response of the workers everywhere is excellent, as you yourselves have pointed out in all the meetings that have been held and in which so much was said about understanding and support, which with very few exceptions were found everywhere.

There are people who don't understand, people who obviously don't even read the newspapers, or if they do they don't understand what they have read, or they don't listen to the radio, or they haven't had the problems explained to them, because the key lies in explaining the problems and explaining our realities. If the sun is shining out there you simply can't say: "The sun doesn't exist."

We must do this work of informing and educating our workers and our people. I am convinced that we will succeed in this and following these sessions, this meeting, I am even more convinced, more than ever before! (*Applause*) And I'm convinced that we will meet the requisites of this program of the Communists and of our people. (*Applause*) And not just meet the requisites but go on beyond them, as we did with our promises in the Moncada Program, (*Applause*) as we did with our promises at the time of the *Granma* expedition, (*Applause*) as we did with our promises in the Sierra Maestra. (*Applause*)

It is not a question today of tackling problems of illiteracy, a lack of schools, the problems of beggars, starvation. It is not a question of tackling the problems of men and women dying for lack of hospitals, doctors' assistance of any kind. It is not a question of tackling the problems of a bloody dictatorship that oppressed us and tied our hands and feet, that deprived us of freedom, deprived us of bread, sold us out to foreigners. It is not a question of struggling almost without arms, without everything, against a powerful and well-armed enemy, in the face of huge tasks. It is a question of solving and confronting new problems stemming from our progress, our development, and the great historical challenges of developing, building socialism, advancing along the road to communism, developing revolutionary theory and practice, demonstrating that socialism is not just overwhelmingly superior to capitalism in the fields of education, health care, or sports, or other things where they admit we have shown great progress, but also demonstrating to the capitalists what we socialists, we Communists are capable of doing—with pride, honor, principles, and consciousness—more capable than they are of being efficient in material production! (*Applause*) It is a question of demonstrating that a consciousness, a communist spirit, a revolutionary will and vocation were, are, and will always be a thousand times more powerful than money!

Patria o Muerte!

Venceremos!

(*Ovation*)

NOTES

1. Fidel Castro and other members of the July 26 Movement returned to Cuba from exile on December 2, 1956, aboard the *Granma* and resumed the armed struggle against the Batista dictatorship.

2. The Moncada Program is a reference to "History Will Absolve Me," Fidel Castro's reconstruction of his October 16, 1953, courtroom defense speech against charges arising from the attack he led on the Moncada garrison on July 26 of that

year. It became a basic programmatic statement of the July 26 Movement. It is printed in Marta Harnecker, *Fidel Castro's Political Strategy* (New York: Pathfinder Press, 1987).

3. One of the problems currently under discussion in Cuba is the fact that a disturbing number of young people, having finished their studies and military service, decide not to work unless they are offered the job they want in the area of the country they prefer. It is not difficult to get by on the income of other family members because food is subsidized, medical care is free, and rent and transportation costs are minimal.

4. Raúl Castro is minister of the Revolutionary Armed Forces and second secretary of the Central Committee of the Cuban Communist Party.

5. The Fifth Congress of the Union of Cuban Journalists (UPEC) was held October 24–26, 1986, in Havana.

6. After extensive debate and a pilot project in Matanzas Province, a new Cuban constitution was approved February 15, 1976. An administrative reform later that year divided the country's six provinces into fourteen, and national elections were held October 10, 1976, to select representatives for the new elective bodies, called People's Power. See Fidel Castro, *Fidel Castro Speeches, vol. II: Our Power is that of the Working People, Building Socialism in Cuba* (New York: Pathfinder Press, 1983), pp. 188–245.

7. The Economic Planning and Management System was introduced in 1976. Most of the economic mechanisms Castro refers to, including the current wage scales, production norms, and the bonus system, were initiated as part of this reorganization.

8. The José Martí Pioneers Organization of Cuba, the mass children's organization, organizes recreational, sports, educational, and cultural activities.

9. Following the revolutionary victories in Grenada and Nicaragua in 1979, the U.S. government stepped up military operations in the Caribbean and escalated its aggressive actions against Cuba. In response to these new threats, in the

spring of 1980 Cuba decided to organize the voluntary Territorial Troops Militias. Since then, well over 1.5 million Cubans, the majority of them women, have been armed and trained in what Castro has described as a "revolution" in Cuba's defense system.

10. Licenses are issued to individuals who want to be self-employed only if they are rendering services useful to society.

In recent years, one of the negative norms that has developed is temporarily laying off workers with a guarantee of 70 percent of their regular wages whenever a work place is faced with a shortage of raw materials, broken equipment, or a temporary power failure.

RENEWAL OR DEATH

by Fidel Castro

COMRADES, IN OUR nominations for election to the Political Bureau we applied the same line, the same principles, and the same criteria we explained this morning in relation to the list of candidates—both full and alternate—for the party Central Committee.

We talked about this at some length, but since these discussions weren't broadcast, and our guests weren't present, it would be useful to repeat—in broad strokes,

---

This speech was given by President Fidel Castro, first secretary of the Central Committee of the Communist Party of Cuba, at the party's third congress on February 7, 1986.

Delegates to the congress elected a new Central Committee which then reelected Fidel Castro first secretary of the Central Committee and Raúl Castro second secretary. The Central Committee also elected the new Political Bureau, Secretariat of the Central Committee, and president of the National Control and Review Committee.[1]

In the initial portion of his remarks, not printed here, Castro introduced the newly elected leadership to the delegates and guests.

The transcription, translation, and annotation are by New International.

ENDNOTES BEGIN ON PAGE 407

not in detail—some of the criteria. That is, it would be useful for the comrades of the Central Committee to explain the work carried out prior to the congress by the commission on candidates.

We followed some basic criteria, some very objective methods to draw up the list of candidates. But first we tried to reduce the size of the Central Committee, to reduce the number of full and alternate members. Then we decided not to reduce the size because an even more important idea had emerged—the idea of a thoroughgoing renewal of the party leadership bodies. In reality, this had never been done before; what renewals had been carried out were more symbolic than anything else. Because when the time came for a renewal we confronted the enormous merit, revolutionary history, prestige, and human qualities of the comrades who make up this list of Central Committee members, the provincial and municipal committees, the committees at all levels. And always the problem was resolved the easiest way—by increasing the size of the committee. So we had symbolic renewals, and these often required work to make sure the comrades understood correctly what was being done, for some saw it as a demotion, as a criticism, as a negative evaluation of their work. It wasn't that at all; we simply had to renew the committees. And to carry out a renewal you have to replace a number of comrades who have all the necessary qualities and merits. But it's a question of renewal or death.

If we had continued to follow the principle of increasing the size, we commented earlier, each congress would have added 80 to 100 full and alternate members to the Central Committee. Eventually we'd have to hold our meetings in the Karl Marx theater.

I've said it before in public and elsewhere, and I repeat

it here before the people and journalists who are listening: we all know the party has problems when it comes to carrying out a renewal, problems in regard to the size we set for the committees in the provinces and municipalities. It's a struggle, it takes persistence to assure we maintain the spirit of comradeship, of solidarity, friendship, and affection among comrades. We came to the conclusion this congress would have to set the example, including in the Central Committee it elects. That's how we arrived at the firm decision to maintain the Central Committee at its present size. To reduce the number of members would have been more traumatic, made it more difficult to apply the indispensable principle of renewal. We never had a real renewal before, merely symbolic ones. This time we set out to carry out a deep-going renewal of more than a third of the committee.

Once we had arrived at these conclusions and the initial lists of candidates had been drawn up, the Central Committee met, discussed the matter extensively, and assessed these questions. The most important thing we accomplished was to become more precise in explaining some of the concepts involved in renewal, such as why we have to do it, what the communist and revolutionary response should be among the comrades who are being replaced, why such a number have to be replaced, why this includes comrades who have served on the Central Committee for twenty years, comrades of indisputable merit.

IF WE WERE TO FOCUS solely on revolutionary background, on merit, the only solution would be one that was becoming wrong—to keep on increasing the size of committees. This was a difficult, traumatic decision, more traumatic for us than for the comrades who were going to be replaced, comrades with whom we had excellent relations of comradeship, friendship, and affection.

This was the first decision made. But we had to go further, including reaching agreement on reducing the size of a number of sectors represented in the Central Committee. I noted in my remarks earlier that the number of governmental ministers had been reduced. Also reduced was the number of members of the armed forces—a sector that includes a great number of comrades with enormous historical merits, veterans of internationalist missions. It was agreed to cut representation from the armed forces from fifty to thirty-four. The Ministry of the Interior was cut from fifteen to eight, and so on. The same thing was done with the workers' organizations, where we cut the number elected as leaders, not as workers but as leaders. Here we had an ample quantity, a relatively ample number, giving us room to carry out a policy we believed to be essential.

We spoke about this at some length earlier, but it's worth repeating for all our people, for all the members of the party who are listening. We decided to apply the policy, and to apply it consistently.

We had already applied it in a partial way at the second congress.[2] The second congress gave the candidate list for the Central Committee a strong injection of both women and workers—steps it was magnificent to take. Now we have to continue along the same lines, adding workers, and not just workers who have become leaders but workers from the factory floor. We had to continue along this course, we had to stress three questions, three categories requiring promotion, three injections—a strong injection of women, a strong injection of blacks and of mestizos.

I want to say something more about this because we aren't afraid to talk about blacks and mestizos. Hypocritical societies that practice discrimination may be afraid, but not revolutionary societies. (*Applause*) At issue here is simply the color of skin, and since for us everyone is equal and there's no problem using the term white or blond, why can't we also speak about blacks, mulattos, or mestizos? Above all in this country, where we are all the product of a mixture of races. And this is something we are very proud of because it's not a bad mixture, it's an excellent mixture. (*Applause*)

ASK THE IMPERIALISTS what they think about this. Ask them if this mixture has been easy to dissolve, divide, or crush. They haven't been able to do it. This little country continues to follow a radical, socialist evolution, inspired by the principles of Marxism, guided by the principles of Marxism-Leninism. They haven't been able to divide us, to toy with the revolution; they have failed because the mixture is excellent and above all because the mixture is free, because equality and solidarity predominate. This is what is important, these are the key questions.

So we said we had to administer an injection. And that it also had to be an injection of youth.

There were three principles we wanted to follow in the process of selecting a slate of candidates for the party Central Committee. Merit, to be sure, was not excluded. That's not what we were trying to do. We were trying to incorporate merit from the ranks, from the various sectors, from the state, the armed forces, the Ministry of the Interior, the mass organizations, the party. Still, we kept three basic ideas in mind.

As I explained yesterday, we have to act on the question of women, because women in our country were discriminated, horribly discriminated against. I explained in detail what tasks, what destiny this society assigned to women. It prepared young girls for marriage, if possible marriage to a bourgeois. Women were totally dependent on marriage. But the primary role capitalism reserved for women was in the brothel—open prostitution or concealed prostitution. Here there were many forms of concealed prostitution. I recalled how women were chosen for their beauty to work in the big stores, in the offices and businesses of the aristocrats, and of course in the bars, hotels, and other places. There were many forms of concealed prostitution, and preparing those young girls for matrimony, for being sold to the highest bidder, was one of them.

That was bourgeois society, capitalist society. The revolution changed all that and freed women. But prejudices about women continued to exist. Raúl recalled the first time we organized a women's platoon and set aside for them a quantity of good rifles.[3] We didn't have a lot of rifles but we set aside some twenty weapons, M-1 carbines, light semiautomatics. It set off a battle I personally had to take part in, because I wanted to demonstrate women could be excellent soldiers. The rebels were almost unanimous in protesting this, some asking "How can we give a woman a rifle when I don't have one," or "when all I have is this old one?" And I said to them, "Listen, and I'll tell you why. We're going to give the comrade a rifle as good as or better than yours. And do you know why? Because they are better soldiers than you are."

The extraordinary thing is the women proved to be unbeatable soldiers. This platoon, which we named after Mariana Grajales,[4] had its leader wounded on a bridge the first time it went into combat. In general rebels, irregular troops, retreat when their leader is killed or wounded. And these comrades—with their leader, who was a man, wounded—these women who were just beginning as soldiers, none of whom had yet emerged as a leader, continued to fight. They wiped out the enemy troops, rescued their wounded leader, brought him back behind our lines, and collected all the weapons. (*Applause*)

There are a number of indicators of the discrimination against women. We explained this with figures. Women constitute half the population. They have excellent revolutionary and human qualities of all types. However, only 21 percent, about 21 percent of party members are women. This is irrefutable proof of various social and historical factors that in some way limit, make more difficult, and obstruct the development of women in our society. This when in reality the revolution is more popular among women than among men, which is logical given that women were a sector discriminated against, an oppressed sector liberated by the revolution.

WOMEN MAKE UP 21 percent of the party. This has been a problem historically; the party was born in the factories and it is a fact the workers' sector was composed of men. But here also the problem stems in part from prejudices, because women had less access to jobs.

Although that factor may exert some influence, I am certain it is the legacy of the past—something we inherited from the old class society, from the ruthless society of exploiters—that explains why women still make up only 21 percent of the party even though they are the social sector that is the most revolutionary, the most enthusiastic, and the most determined. They are demonstrating this right now in the question of defense, in the organization of the territorial militias, for which 1.8 million women have volunteered. Hundreds of thousands of women joined the territorial militias and tens of thousands, 20,000 women cadres, local leadership cadres, have been trained. They are more disciplined, more dedicated, more objective than the male militia members. The first regular units with women officers have been established, units with regular army troops. Fifty-five percent of the country's technicians are women, but only 21 percent of party members. Even at the second congress, after the injection we administered there, only 12.89 percent of the Central Committee were women.

THE SITUATION in the youth organization is similar, which is even more serious because young people should be the bearers of more just, more equitable ideas. But there we have the same problem: although the proportion of women members is higher in the youth organization than in the party, women are still a low proportion of the leadership.[5] The same is true in the People's Power assemblies. When people go to cast a ballot and the candidate is a woman, they often say, well, she has children, she has this or that thing, and they vote for a man. So the people too, the popular masses are proof of this. The people select and vote for the candidates, and the outcome shows the people have prejudices; this is a fact.[6]

It is a reflection of historical prejudices that despite the injection of women on the Central Committee [in 1980], they still numbered only 12.89 percent.

And I tell you discrimination based on sex has proved more resistant than discrimination based on ethnic or racial motivation or whatever you want to call it; discrimination based on the color of skin. Because on that score we have made great progress, given the course of history, the legacy of history. The same thing happened as with women; the black sector was discriminated against. Slavery, which gave rise to some of the greatest atrocities of colonialism, endured for centuries. Tens of millions of men and women were taken from Africa and enslaved to perform work whites didn't dare do in this torrid, tropical climate.

And the same was true in the cold north. In the temperate areas slaves were used to pick cotton and to do other hard work. Slavery lasted in our country until 1886, one century ago. Once it was overturned, neocolonialism came in its place; the Yankees brought along all their racial prejudices and established them here. I mentioned earlier how there were schools, like the school I first attended and remained in until the fifth grade, that only admitted blacks who could pay. Other schools, like the Colegio de Dolores, Colegio de Belén, private, religious schools, didn't admit blacks at all. And I noted the arguments they gave. They seemed to be pious arguments, along the lines of "poor things, since there would be so few of them, they wouldn't feel comfortable." (*Laughter*) But even if they could pay they weren't admitted. And very few were in a position to pay.

Of course some children, especially those of the bourgeoisie, graduated, went on to the university, and had access to everything. And in the poorer middle sectors of the city there were a few workers who made great efforts, but if they were black, it was nearly impossible to gain access to these levels of training and education. Then there were the sectors that lived in the poorer areas, in the impoverished villages that existed here, descendants of the Haitians, of the Jamaicans.

It was with great pleasure I greeted today two newly elected members of the Central Committee, two comrades named Robinson, a young woman and a young man, brother and sister, originally from Guantánamo but one now living in Moa, the other in Havana—two young people who have distinguished themselves extraordinarily.[7] And I asked them where their parents were from, their grandparents. It turned out they were of Jamaican origin, descendants of Jamaicans who had emigrated to Guantánamo to cut sugarcane. They are brother and sister and today they are members, elected members of the new Central Committee chosen by this congress. (*Applause*) A brother and sister who have attained the highest levels of academic education, training, and honors, who have really distinguished themselves. Yes, today such a thing is possible, even though the legacy of the past is still with us.

AS I SAID EARLIER, discrimination is something unjust that gives human beings a sense of rejection, creates complexes, exerts influence. The victims of discrimination lived in the poorest neighborhoods, in vacant lots, in the poorest possible places, where there were no schools, no other possibilities, not even the slightest centers of culture, and I explained how this exerted an influence. On the other hand, in places where there is schooling, where there are centers of culture, where there is more culture, children tend to be better oriented in their studies; it helps them, it encourages them. I explained that in the regions we distributed the vocational schools by municipality. Some municipalities have more cultural centers, some fewer than others. Havana, perhaps, has centers with a higher educational level. The point I wanted to make was that when talent emerges, there is an opportunity for it to develop—independent of these conditioning factors, although they do exert an influence.

It is calculated—and as I explained earlier today, these are arbitrary calculations—that 34 percent of the population is black or mestizo. These are arbitrary figures because 100 percent of us have some mixture in our blood, no matter how "Spanish" we might be. Because Spain for centuries had at least a touch of the Middle East—the Moors—who are darker than the whites of Europe. In any event, mestizos and blacks are considered to make up 34 percent of the population. The revolution received broader support from blacks and mestizos because the bourgeoisie was white. No North American black owned a sugar mill; it was whites who owned them. I don't know of a single black who was a big landowner, or who owned a big store, a major industry, or a big corporation. There may have been a few blacks who were members of the liberal professions, a lawyer here, a doctor there, perhaps an owner of corner grocery store or some other small business.

Those who left for Miami were in their immense majority the rich white bourgeoisie. The black sectors on the other hand totally supported the revolution. Why? Because they had all suffered discrimination, discrimination because of the color of their skin. And this is a legacy of our history. Since then some have received education and training, some are doing one thing, some another. To be sure, an enormous mass has emerged—for the revolution is still young even though it's twenty-seven years old—tens of thousands, hundreds of thousands of young blacks and mestizos have entered our technical schools, pre-universities, and universities. And they are increasingly distinguishing themselves there.

But we can't leave it to chance to correct historical injustices. To really establish total equality takes more than simply declaring it in law. It has to be promoted in the mass organizations, in the youth organization, in the party. And that's why we said in the report that we should reflect the ethnic composition of our society, that we can't leave the promotion of women, blacks, and mestizos to chance. It has to be the work of the party; we have to straighten out what history has twisted. (*Applause*)

So we proposed an injection of youth. A list of candidates was drawn up; I explained earlier how this was done. No one said in a subjective way, I am going to make the selection. The party called on the provinces, the party in the provinces, to give us a list of those comrades who—no matter what their skin color or age—should be considered for selection as full or alternate members of the Central Committee. We also asked that the lists take into account the women, black, and mestizo comrades who met these conditions—in short, that they give us a list of everyone who met these qualifications.

A number of those included were young black women—they met all three requirements we were looking for. Some were young black men, others older. In all, 233 names of comrades were brought forward in this way. In addition, the mass organizations were consulted and they proposed a number of candidates. Comrades who hold important responsibilities, for example in the People's Power assemblies or, as I explained earlier, in the Central Committee itself, were considered. We took into consideration every comrade who is a member of a provincial executive committee. We looked in particular—but not only—at the comrades under thirty-five. In this way the list grew by another 160 names. In each case we studied the comrade's background, history, everything. That's how the final list, what we call the slate of candidates, was drawn up—with objective methods.

What I explained earlier is proof of this, because clearly

there are some who are well known and others who are not, who aren't known by many people. But I was thinking about young unknown people with merit, and I thought about two in particular who aren't well known. When I saw the lists, after they had been drawn up following these methods, those two comrades' names were there. I, as president of the commission on candidates, didn't propose anyone for the slate; the commission simply followed the method outlined. And naturally when the final list was drawn up, nearly all the women who had been proposed were on it. The immense majority of black comrades were on it. Young comrades with merit—whether black or white—were on it.

OTHER COMRADES of great merit who didn't fit any of these categories were on it. To give an example, this includes the director of the Ameijeiras hospital,[8] the best hospital in our country and one can probably say the best in Latin America. It is giving medicine a tremendous impetus, and its director symbolizes this. His effort symbolizes the effort of all the doctors, technicians, and scientists of great merit who work there.

We could have added at least five or ten people to the list of candidates because of the services they have performed for the country. Take for example the case of the comrade who was chosen to be a cosmonaut.[9] It wasn't by chance he was selected. He was a magnificent soldier, with great merits, selected to become a student pilot, an outstanding pilot, leader of his unit, a man of great human, moral, and revolutionary qualifications. He wouldn't have been elected a member of the Central Committee before he went into space. But he went into space and he was elected as a symbol.

I explained earlier at some length that it was impossible for anyone to assure these were the best. There are half a million members in the party and another half million in the youth organization. There are hundreds of thousands of persons with qualifications, who meet the requirements, and thousands, tens of thousands with great merit. The most we can do is come up with a list that more or less approximates, that ensures this great mass will be represented.

There are some of such great merit they can hardly be promoted. They have to be left at their work, where they are doing much more for the country. As we mentioned earlier, it is a fundamental principle that a communist never aspires to any post. You wouldn't be a communist if you aspired to posts or honors. (*Applause*) It is the party that promotes you. The party tries to select from among the best those who will represent it, knowing it's the great mass that's important, that is full of history and merit. The final selection of candidates was based on all these criteria: on merit, background, and outstanding qualifications.

We have to have confidence in the youth. I mentioned earlier today that the average age of those who began the armed struggle was twenty-two or twenty-three—and we thought we were capable of starting a revolution. I was a little older; I was twenty-six. When the revolution triumphed the great bulk of the combatants were around thirty years old. We were enormously inexperienced but we believed in our capabilities. Perhaps if we'd had a lot of experience we might have been inhibited, perhaps even converted into conservatives. But fortunately we weren't aware of our inexperience. (*Laughter*) We decided without the slightest vacillation to take the road of revolution, and in the end this proved to be the right decision. That is why we have to have confidence in the youth.

Now we have the privilege of combining something we didn't have in the past—the greater experience, the tenacity of some, and the energy of others. We have to push this process forward today and do it without any fear at all. (*Applause*) The addition of young people who have been through service in the armed forces, who have worked in production, is very important. And any young person we promote at a given moment will have been, as we said in our report to the Central Committee, through the experience of being a rank-and-file soldier, or of working in production or services. We must not be afraid of promoting young people. The years pass, the years accumulate history, and if we dedicated ourselves only to history, our average age would be high—it was already fifty-one; we have now dropped to forty-seven; in five years it will return to fifty-two. An injection of youth is necessary.

FOLLOWING THESE CRITERIA, we came up with a slate of candidates. The number of women elected is now equivalent to 18.22 percent of the full and alternate members of the Central Committee. If we were to look only at the full members, the percentage would possibly be somewhat lower, but adding the two categories together approaches the 21 percent proportion of women in the party.

Blacks and mestizos—I am referring to those who declare themselves as such (*Laughter*)—here we have to begin by counting because before nobody asked. The question was erased in our constitution and correctly so. But in the party we have to make a little notation, because we have to see how we're doing with our policy of promotion, how well all the sectors are represented. Before, we never asked anyone these questions and rightly so. Why go around asking such questions? In the past it was to discriminate, today it's for the opposite reason—so we ask.

Rizo, for example, had been down for white; he had no notation of any kind. But yesterday he was telling me he had his great-grandmother's certificate of freedom, that she had been an African slave. Risquet is a mixture of Black and Chinese, Asian, one could say Southeast Asian or Korean, I don't really know where Risquet's ancestors are from. And a mixture of white, too. From Canton? Well, you ought to know. (*Laughter*) In any event if we include them all, we'll have more, we all know we have more. We have now reached 28.44 percent, so we're approaching the same proportion as in the party membership.

THIS IS A POLICY of promotion, and we're really very satisfied with it. We saw it first today when we elected the Central Committee. The same policy of a broad renewal was also followed in the election of the Political Bureau, where more than 40 percent of the members are new.[10] It was very difficult. These were comrades we see constantly, comrades of great merit. If you'd like an idea of the firmness and fervor with which we applied this policy, I'll give you a few examples.

Among the comrades on the Central Committee who were replaced in the renewal process was Comrade Reynaldo Castro, a hero of labor, a man of great historical merits, a comrade who is a model of simplicity, of humility, an example in all senses. (*Applause*) This is an indication of the quality of the comrades who were replaced in order to apply this policy—it was a matter of renewal or death. Comrades like Braulio Maza; it's difficult to find another like him in the Central Committee. (*Applause*)

We left many areas of responsibility open, but we felt we could redistribute them better. Many of those who were in the National Assembly or the Central Committee will be given other responsibilities, some in one area, others in another; some will receive one recognition, others another recognition.

In the Political Bureau, the renewal included comrades with the history and merits of Ramiro Valdés.[11] (*Applause*) I remember, when we were preparing to attack the Moncada barracks and were selecting volunteers, Ramiro was one who volunteered to help take the installation. And it was Ramiro who disarmed the soldier, one of the soldiers in the post. I'll never forget that. Ramiro was in Mexico, he came on the *Granma,* he was in the Sierra Maestra; Ramiro came with Che in the invasion.[12]

It included comrades of such merit as Guillermo García, the first peasant who joined us.[13] (*Applause*) Comrades of such merit, noble spirit, simplicity, and modesty as Sergio del Valle, who took part in the invasion alongside Camilo.[14] (*Applause*) Comrades like Jesús Montané—(*Applause*) I recall that he too was one of the few comrades who volunteered to take the post at Moncada.[15] He was later taken prisoner, and then came over on the *Granma;* a comrade with a long history. There are more beloved comrades, too many more to mention them all. But they included Armando Acosta who was also with us in the war, in the Sierra.[16]

In other words, the Central Committee applied the principle of broad renewal. These comrades continue to enjoy all our consideration, our affection, and they continue fulfilling their responsibilities to the revolution. They spoke in a very encouraging way at the plenum. Comrade Ramiro spoke on behalf of them all. They are satisfied, they respect the decisions; the steps we have taken seem to them to be correct and fair. That means we have won a genuine victory. The comrades understand this fundamental, essential principle—that we have to renew to continue moving ahead; that it's not a demotion but a vital necessity for the revolution.

I have given you an idea of the consistent manner in which we have proceeded, the criteria by which the elections were conducted. Our Political Bureau also received an injection of blacks and women. (*Applause*) The policy was applied up and down the line. I think the Congress and the Central Committee have given an example of the policy of renewal we have to continue following. It's time to put a halt to simply increasing the number of members. Renewal is an intelligent policy because it means seeking merit, promoting it, looking for it, providing training wherever we come across it.

IT WOULD BE the most absurd thing in the world for a small group of us to believe we have all the necessary virtues and merits. It's the people who have the merits. Because as I said a few days ago to the comrades, wherever you have 100 men you have a great number of potential heroes. I remember that in our own war, when there were just a few left after our initial mistakes, many of them were great leaders, such as Che, Camilo, Raúl, and Ramiro. (*Applause*) No one could imagine what qualities men like Che and Camilo had. Che was the doctor for our troops; Camilo was playful, always joking. Who would have guessed what kind of heroes they would turn out to be? That's why I said when Camilo died that in our people there are many Camilos, and when Lázaro died that there are many more Lázaros.[17] (*Applause*)

We have to take into account the example of the men, of the leaders of the old party, of the first party, of the first Marxist-Leninist party—like the comrade who spoke here today, Comrade Blas Roca, who led the Popular Socialist Party for so long. (*Applause*) I remember very well, I'll never forget it, when Comrade Blas Roca, giving great proof of his generosity and greatness, despite the fact he had led the Marxist-Leninist party for so many years, and we had made a Marxist-Leninist revolution by uniting all forces and creating a new party, met with me and told me: "I am handing you the banner of the Marxist-Leninist party." (*Applause*) Now Comrade Blas Roca has set another example, very useful and very valuable for our people and for future generations. He knows the respect he has among all of us, the special consideration he receives because he has earned it. He sent us a letter dated January 31, 1986, before the congress opened, that said:

"Comrade Fidel Castro and other comrades of the plenum:

"The final touches are being given to preparations for the third party congress, which undoubtedly signifies important improvements in the methods and tasks of the party, whose strength lies in its close links with the masses. In considering these perspectives I am impelled to direct myself to you, dear comrades, to ask you, as I do now, to free me of my responsibilities and obligations on the Central Committee, responsibilities and obligations I have held proudly up until now. I believe even without such titles I can continue contributing in some areas, such as in the final stages of preparing the civil code, which is so necessary to the complete institutionalization of the revolution which, under the leadership of Fidel, and guided by the ideology of Marxism and Leninism, is building socialism. Communist greetings. Always faithful to the revolution and loyal to its principles, Blas Roca." (*Applause*)

Despite this letter from Comrade Blas Roca, we followed the criteria that there are three men who—because of their history, their prestige, the glory they have given our country, their personal merits regardless of their age—we want to have as symbols, as long as they live, on the Central Committee. They are Comrade Blas Roca, Comrade Fabio Grobart, and Comrade Nicolás Guillén.[18] They were elected. (*Applause*)

I am happy to be able to explain this policy fully before our distinguished guests; before our congress, where I was able to speak on this earlier; before all our people; before reporters from our own country and abroad. It is a correct, fair, and revolutionary policy, a proof of the unity and cohesion of our party, of our people, of the solidity of our principles. And as I told the plenum, the Central Committee, we are all one family—from the youngest rank-and-file member to one who holds the highest responsibilities in the party.

We are all absolutely equal, we are all governed by the same norms. We are all one family in the party. And we are all one family beyond the party—with the people. (*Applause*) No matter where we are, inside or outside the Central Committee, inside or outside the congress, in a municipal or provincial meeting, in a basic party unit or outside of it, our people, our party will always be one single fist, one single heart.

Patria o muerte!

Venceremos!

NOTES

1. The full members of the Political Bureau are *Juan Almeida Bosque*—commander of the revolution, president of the National Control and Review Committee, vice president of the Council of State; *Julio Camacho Aguilera*—first secretary of the Provincial Committee of the party in Santiago de Cuba; *Fidel Castro Ruz*—commander in chief, first secretary of the party Central Committee, president of the Councils of State and of Ministers; *Raúl Castro Ruz*—general of the army, second secretary of the party Central Committee, first vice president of the Councils of State and of Ministers, minister of the Revolutionary Armed Forces; *Osmany Cienfuegos Gorriarán*—member of the Council of State, vice president of the Council of Ministers; *Abelardo Colomé Ibarra*—general, member of the Council of State, first substitute for the minister of the Revolutionary Armed Forces; *Vilma Espín Guillois*—member of the Council of State, president of the National Leadership of the Federation of Cuban Women; *Armando Hart Dávalos*—member of the Council of State, minister of culture; *Esteban Lazo Hernández*—first secretary of the provincial committee of the party in Matanzas; *José R. Machado Ventura*—member of the Council of State, member of the Secretariat of the Central Committee; *Pedro Miret Prieto*—member of the Council of State, vice president of the Council of Ministers; *Jorge Risquet Valdés-Saldaña*—member of the Central Committee Secretariat; *Carlos Rafael Rodríguez*—vice president of the Councils of State and of Ministers; and *Roberto Veiga Menéndez*—member of the Council of State, secretary general of the Central Organization of Cuban Trade Unions.

The alternate members of the Political Bureau are *Luis E. Álvarez de la Nuez*—first secretary of the party provincial committee in Havana; *Senén Casas Regueiro*—general, member of the Council of State, first substitute to the minister of the Revolutionary Armed Forces; *José Ramón Fernández Álvarez*—member of the Council of State, vice president of the

Executive Committee of the Council of Ministers, Minister of Education; *Yolanda Ferrer Gómez*—member of the national Secretariat of the Federation of Cuban Women; *Raúl Michel Vargas*—first secretary of the party provincial committee in Guantánamo; *José Ramírez Cruz*—member of the Council of State, president of the National Association of Small Farmers; *Julián Rizo Álvarez*—member of the secretariat of the Central Committee; *Ulises Rosales del Toro*—general, first substitute to the minister of the Revolutionary Armed Forces, chief of staff of the Revolutionary Armed Forces; *Rosa Elena Simeón Negrín*—president of the Cuban Academy of Sciences; and *Lázaro Vázquez García*—first secretary of the party provincial committee in Camagüey.

The members of the Central Committee Secretariat (in addition to Fidel Castro, Raúl Castro, José R. Machado Ventura, Jorge Risquet Valdés-Saldaña, and Julián Rizo Álvarez) are *José Ramón Balaguer Cabrera*—head of the Central Committee Department of Education, Science, and Sports; *Sixto Batista Santana*—general, head of the Central Committee Military Department; *Jaime Crombet Hernández-Baquero*; and *Lionel Soto Prieto*—Cuban ambassador to the USSR. The president of the National Control and Review Committee is Juan Almeida Bosque. Unless otherwise noted, the responsibilities and ranks cited herein are those held at the time of the third congress.

2. The Second Congress of the Cuban Communist Party was held December 17–20, 1980.

3. This was during the revolutionary war against the Batista dictatorship.

4. Mariana Grajales was the mother of Antonio Maceo, a general in both of Cuba's wars of independence from Spain.

5. At the time of this report, women made up 41 percent of the membership of the Union of Young Communists (UJC) and 19.5 percent of its leadership cadre. One year later at the UJC's fifth congress held April 1–5, 1987, women were 40.3 percent of the membership and 28.4 percent of the leadership

cadre. Thirty-eight percent of the new UJC National Committee were women and 32.3 percent were blacks and mestizos.

6. At the time of this speech, 11 percent of the delegates to local bodies of People's Power were women, as were 22 percent of the National Assembly. In elections held later in 1986, these figures rose to 17 and 35 percent, respectively.

7. Gladys N. Robinson Agramonte was elected as full member of the Central Committee. She serves as the chief of technical control department of the Comandante Pedro Soto Albe Company in Moa, Holguín, and is a member of the party leadership committee in the plant.

Juan C. Robinson Agramonte was elected as alternate Central Committee member. He serves as first secretary of the provincial committee of the Union of Young Communists in Havana.

8. Raúl F. Gómez Cabrera is director of the Ameijeiras Brothers hospital.

9. Col. Arnaldo Tamayo Méndez, the first Cuban cosmonaut, participated in the Soviet Intercosmos program in a flight September 18–26, 1980.

10. Forty percent of the members of the Central Committee are new to it, as are, in fact, 50 percent of the newly elected Political Bureau.

11. Ramiro Valdés Menéndez is a commander of the revolution, vice president of the Councils of State and of Ministers, and a member of the Central Committee. He headed the Ministry of the Interior for a long period.

12. Ernesto "Che" Guevara (1928–1967), an Argentine revolutionary, joined Castro while in Mexican exile and participated in the *Granma* expedition and distinguished himself as a leader in the subsequent revolutionary war in Cuba. After the victory, he headed the Cuban national bank and served as minister of industry. He later left Cuba to participate in the guerrilla struggle in the Congo and Bolivia. He was captured in Bolivia and executed by the army with the assistance of the U.S. CIA.

13. Guillermo García Frías is a member of the Central Committee, commander of the revolution, and vice president of the Council of State.

14. Sergio del Valle Jiménez is a member of the Council of State and of the Central Committee. Camilo Cienfuegos was a guerrilla commander and one of the central leaders of the revolutionary war; he was killed in a plane crash in October 1959.

15. Jesús Montané Oropesa is head of the Central Committee General Department of Foreign Relations and a member of the Central Committee.

16. Armando Acosta Cordero is a member of the Central Committee and of the Council of State. He became national coordinator of the Committees for the Defense of the Revolution in 1980.

17. Lázaro Peña González was an early member of the Cuban communist party and central leader of the CTC from the 1940s until his death in the mid-1970s.

18. Blas Roca Calderio was general secretary of Cuban communist party from 1934 to 1961. It had several names during this period, adopting the name Popular Socialist Party (PSP) in 1944. He participated in the 1961 fusion of the PSP, Revolutionary Directorate, and July 26 Movement to form the Integrated Revolutionary Organizations and in the 1965 founding of the Cuban Communist Party (CCP). He served on the Political Bureau of the CCP from 1965–86. He died April 25, 1987.

Fabio Grobart is the only surviving founder of the first communist party of Cuba, called the Communist Groupings of Cuba, formed in 1925. He is a member of the Central Committee and president of the Institute for the History of the Communist Movement and Socialist Revolution of Cuba.

Nicolás Guillén is president of the National Union of Writers and Artists of Cuba and is Cuba's most famous poet.

Join the

PATHFINDER READERS CLUB

BUILD A MARXIST LIBRARY!

15% OFF ALL PATHFINDER BOOKS AND PAMPHLETS

25% DISCOUNT ON MONTHLY SPECIALS

Get your annual card for only *US$10*. Available at www.pathfinderpress.com or at Pathfinder book centers around the world.

The Cuban Revolution in World Politics

Our History is Still Being Written

THE STORY OF THREE CHINESE-CUBAN GENERALS
IN THE CUBAN REVOLUTION

Armando Choy, Gustavo Chui, and Moisés Sío Wong

Three generals of Cuba's Revolutionary Armed Forces talk about the historic place of Chinese immigration to Cuba, as well as over five decades of revolutionary action and internationalism, from Cuba to Angola and Venezuela today. Through their stories we see the social and political forces that gave birth to the Cuban nation and opened the door to socialist revolution in the Americas. $20. Also in Spanish and Chinese.

From the Escambray to the Congo

IN THE WHIRLWIND OF THE CUBAN REVOLUTION

Víctor Dreke

The author describes how easy it became after the Cuban Revolution to take down a rope segregating blacks from whites in the town square, yet how enormous was the battle to transform social relations underlying all the "ropes" inherited from capitalism and Yankee domination. Dreke, second in command of the internationalist column in the Congo led by Che Guevara in 1965, recounts the creative joy with which working people have defended their revolutionary course—from Cuba's Escambray mountains to Africa and beyond. $18. Also in Spanish.

Marianas in Combat

TETÉ PUEBLA AND THE MARIANA GRAJALES WOMEN'S PLATOON
IN CUBA'S REVOLUTIONARY WAR 1956–58

Teté Puebla

Brigadier General Teté Puebla joined the struggle to overthrow the US-backed Batista dictatorship in Cuba in 1956, at age fifteen. This is her story—from clandestine action in the cities, to officer in the Rebel Army's first all-women's platoon. The fight to transform the social and economic status of women is inseparable from Cuba's socialist revolution. $14. Also in Spanish.

www.pathfinderpress.com

NICARAGUA IS A CARIBBEAN COUNTRY

by Lumberto Campbell

COMRADE RAFAEL "Fafa" Taveras, President of the Anti-Imperialist Organizations of the Caribbean and Central America; Comrade Clement Rohee,[2] Executive Secretary of the Anti-Imperialist Organizations of the Caribbean and Central America; Comrades all:

The Sandinista National Liberation Front wishes to express its deep satisfaction for the selection of Nicaragua as the site for this meeting. We see this decision as a statement of solidarity by the organizations here against the war of aggression that the United States has launched against our country.

The parties and organizations that you represent in

On February 8–9, 1986, the Anti-Imperialist Organizations of the Caribbean and Central America met in Managua, Nicaragua.[1] *The delegates were welcomed to Nicaraqua in the name of the Sandinista National Liberation Front (FSLN) by Guerrilla Commander Lumberto Campbell, FSLN coordinator for Southern Zelaya province on the Atlantic Coast. Campbell is now also head of the regional government of Southern Zelaya.*

In this article we print the full text of Campbell's speech. The translation and notes are by New International.

ENDNOTES BEGIN ON PAGE 426

this meeting constitute our continent's highest expression of the principles of democracy, national liberation, social justice, anti-imperialism and self-determination. Your presence in Nicaragua in these times that are very difficult for us is one more demonstration that the Caribbean peoples are an indestructible unit, despite all the attempts by imperialism and colonialism to divide us.

Almost 60 percent of the territory of Nicaragua is what traditionally we call the Atlantic Coast. This is a deceptive label, since in reality what is called the "Atlantic Coast" of Nicaragua is the shore of the Caribbean Sea. Approximately 500 kilometers of Nicaragua's coastline lies along the West Indian sea and for half a century now, the West Indian sea has been the main socioeconomic and cultural link between Nicaragua and the rest of the world.

Through this coast area, Nicaragua shared the vicissitudes that marked the life of the other societies in the region: exploitation of their natural resources, brutal exploitation of the native peoples, introduction of slavery, installation of corrupt and venal governments, and isolation from one another as a way to tie each of our societies more tightly to the imperial yoke.

Because of its particular geographic location as a bridge between the Caribbean Sea and the Pacific Ocean, Nicaragua also became important as a possible canal zone site early on. This exacerbated the domination imposed by Yankee imperialism. The strategic position of the country added to the richness of its forests, rivers, and mineral deposits to stimulate imperialist plunder.

Foreign companies established economic enclaves in Nicaragua, just as in other Caribbean societies. These grew out of the generous concessions granted by bourgeois governments, or were imposed on the country through successive armed invasions.

Our natural resources were quickly exhausted or nearly exhausted; this was the case with mahogany, pine, and important mineral deposits.

Thus imperialist expansion used our Caribbean region, the Atlantic area, its geography, its economy, and its productive resources, to position Nicaragua within its sphere of domination.

But the Coast was also the region of our national territory where a large part of the liberation struggle led by General Augusto Sandino developed. It was there that Sandino recruited an important part of the Army for the Defense of National Sovereignty,[3] there where he besieged the U.S. Marines and the imperialist economic interests, and finally won the expulsion of the Yankee enemy.

THE PROMINENCE of the Caribbean profile of Nicaragua, and its position within the international capitalist economy, was lost after the capitalist crisis of 1929. The new wave of capitalist development after World War II was concentrated fundamentally in the Pacific Coast and the central region of the country. The Atlantic Coast was marginalized, forgotten, and isolated from the rest of the country. The close ties between the new forms of imperialist expansion in Latin America and the economic interests of the Somoza dictatorship condemned this immense part of Nicaragua to extreme misery.

Today, under extremely difficult conditions, Nicaragua must confront a brutal aggression by the U.S. government. The expansionism and militarism of Yankee imperialism cannot accept that in this small, impoverished country, located in what they have always arrogantly considered their "backyard," the people have stood up and resolutely moved forward for national liberation, popular democracy, for development with social justice, and for an end to isolation.

And since the national dignity of the Nicaraguan people is unacceptable to the government of the greatest military power in the world, this government has launched a war of aggression against our small country. The goal is to destroy the conquests of our revolution and restore the assassins of our people to governmental power.

Imperialist aggression has converted the Coast into one of the theaters of this war. Imperialism has taken advantage of the contradictions generated throughout the course of our history, contradictions between the two great regions of the country, arising from the way in which the colonial powers established their domination. Imperialism has tried to manipulate the particular demands of the Coast peoples to turn them against the revolution.

The Sandinista revolution has recognized that, in the initial measures we took on the Coast, we committed errors because of our ignorance. At first, we followed an economist and sectoral policy. We reduced the problems and historical demands of the Coast peoples to a problem of underdevelopment. We did not have an ethnic policy; we tended more to divide than unite the people.

But it is unquestionable that those errors, together with the political consciousness of many sectors of the Coast population, never would have led to such sharp contradictions had these factors not been skillfully manipulated by U.S. imperialism, using the many resources at its command.

The problems and contradictions have made the Sandinista People's Revolution recognize the just demands of the indigenous peoples and communities of the Atlantic Coast. Today we are carrying out a process of consultation on the autonomy project and developing autonomy statutes that for this first time in our history recognize the historic rights of our indigenous, Afro-Caribbean, and mestizo Coast population.[4]

The autonomy of the indigenous peoples and communities will serve to create a true national unity where all the social sectors that were previously exploited and oppressed will participate in the construction of a new, multiethnic and multilingual Nicaraguan society.

NICARAGUA not only shares a past of exploitation, misery, and colonial and neocolonial domination with the other countries of the Caribbean. It also shares their desire for liberation, justice, national dignity, friendship, and progress. Hence, Nicaragua shares many of their current problems and the challenges facing them in the immediate future.

In the first place, the struggle for national liberation: for the elimination of the most aberrant forms of colonialism, which still persist in our region, and of imperialist neocolonialism, which still holds sway over our people in many ways.

There exist situations of colonial domination in the Caribbean that deny the legitimate right of the people to constitute themselves as sovereign nations. The right of Puerto Rico to exist as an independent nation has been denied through almost a century of colonial domination. Puerto Rican patriots are persecuted in their homeland by the U.S. government.

At the present time, the Haitian people are struggling to eradicate the remains of Duvalierism, which with the help of the Reagan administration is trying to perpetuate itself without Baby Doc.[5] Somoza and Duvalier both had the firm support of the United States as a strategic backup for their rule. Both dictatorships used the bloodiest forms of repression, obscurantism, and state terrorism to remain in power. The Nicaraguan people view the current struggle of the Haitian people with great hope. This is a struggle that must unite the best traditions of emancipation, equality, and justice with which the Haitian people opened a new era in our hemisphere nearly two centuries ago.[6]

In recent years, various of our societies have been caught in the foreign debt, which has become one of the most serious problems for the entire continent. The unacceptable conditions imposed by international private banks have led some Caribbean countries to a condition of heavy indebtedness that has been the detonator of popular protests.

The economic weakness of our societies, their small area, their isolation from each other, their proximity to the United States, and above all the alienation of the ruling classes gave rise to conditions where economic domination was transformed into political domination. The classical image of the North American embassy as the real seat of power continues to be the reality in many of the countries of our region.

In the second place, the struggle for social justice. Foreign dependence and imperialist domination are the source of social inequalities, privileges, exploitation, and misery, and they constantly reappear on this basis.

One of the most visible aspects of imperialist domination throughout the Caribbean, as in all the Third

World, is the close alliance it establishes with elements of the local ruling classes. Thus, through their subordinate alliance with imperialism, and at the cost of increasing levels of social exploitation in their own relations, these ruling classes find the resources to continue their own domination.

Our peoples pay the price of this growing submission to imperialism: they are burdened with illiteracy, exhausting labor, the lack of land, housing, food. This price is paid by the suffering children who go about begging; by the young women who prostitute themselves in the cities; by the youth who fall prisoner to drugs; by the peasants who desperately scratch out a living on ever less fertile land; by those who sell their blood so it can be exported to the public hospitals of New York; by the tens of thousands whose only future lies in emigrating, to seek refuge in the slums of the Bronx, to forget everything, to flee to the most sordid strata of the imperial underworld.

In the third place, the struggle to develop our productive systems and more just forms of trade. Imperialism has seriously distorted the development of our productive forces. The relations of production imposed by the expansion of U.S. imperialism created enormous inequalities between different regions of the same country and between different sectors of its population. Once again, the Atlantic Coast is a tragic example of how deeply imperialism can distort the economy of a country, deforming its productive structure, expanding it in some regions while allowing others to deteriorate.

The development fostered by the multinational corporations comes from outside our countries, and the benefits leave our countries. The technology that they claim to share stays in the hands of the multinational companies. It is not made available throughout the countries where these corporations operate, nor is it transmitted to what few local technicians exist.

On top of this, the products that our economies export find themselves subject to a very harmful unequal exchange that, year after year, sucks more and more resources from our countries. The struggle for development, therefore, also leads to the necessity of establishing a new economic order where progress will not be a monopoly of a few and misery the daily lot of our peoples.

National emancipation, social justice, and development are issues and tasks that are closely linked in the challenges facing the peoples of the Caribbean. To put it another way: we can undertake the tasks of social transformation and the construction of a more just society, we can move forward on the road to real development only through the struggle for national emancipation and the establishment of effective national sovereignty for each and every one of our countries.

NATIONAL LIBERATION becomes, then, the central question for the Caribbean societies. Without it, development and justice are not possible, nor is peace.

Within this general framework, Nicaragua has a specific experience of suffering, of struggle, and of triumph. The Sandinista People's Revolution made possible the conditions for our people to confront foreign domination, backwardness, and social exploitation with courage and creativity.

Nicaragua respects other experiences. It is not trying, and has never tried, to impose its own view, its own manner of facing the problems of underdevelopment, of dependence, of injustice. There is no "Sandinista model" to export, because revolutions are the most authentic product of the historic experience of each people.

But it is undeniable that Nicaragua has a lesson to share: only the organized struggle of the people can confront the problems and the evils that afflict each of our societies.

Today, in revolutionary Nicaragua, the struggle for national liberation assumes the form of a people's patriotic war, of a national war of the entire people, of all patriotic and honest sectors, for national defense against the military, economic, and diplomatic aggression of the government of the United States.

The reason U.S. imperialism has such visceral hatred for our country is simple: Nicaragua, thanks to the Sandinista struggle, has shaken off its chains. Nicaragua is free, wants to remain free, and will remain free.

It is unacceptable to imperialism that little countries such as ours should be independent. The Reagan administration used trivial pretexts to invade Grenada. Now, it cannot tolerate the fact that the country that during the half century of the Somoza dictatorship was one of the most loyal servants of imperialism is today the example of what the revolutionary struggle of the people can accomplish.

Imperialism cannot accept the fact that the country from which it launched the invasion of Cuba in 1961 is today an active fighter in the cause of nonalignment, peace, and progress for all peoples.[7] The Reagan administration cannot accept the fact that the genocidal National Guard, which was complicit with the U.S. invasion of the Dominican Republic, has been smashed by a people's, anti-imperialist guerrilla army. Nor can it accept a Sandinista People's Army that keeps at bay the assassins financed with U.S. dollars.

Nicaragua does not want war. Throughout its history,

Nicaragua has learned the hard price the people must pay for war. It is the aggressive and militarist policies of U.S. imperialism and the administration of President Reagan that force Nicaragua to dedicate more than half of the government's budget to the defense of the nation's sovereignty.

Therefore, Nicaragua supports, always has supported, and always will support all possibilities and initiatives for a peaceful resolution of conflicts. Nicaragua strongly supports the Contadora process; our country has always been the most active in complying with recommendations of the Contadora Group and was the first to announce its decision to sign the original peace accord.[8]

Nicaragua applauds the spirit of the Caraballeda message of Peace, Security, and Democracy in Central America.[9] Nicaragua shares each and every one of the "Permanent Bases for Peace" defined in this message. Many of them are part of the principles of our own revolution, such as self-determination, nonintervention in the internal affairs of other states, democracy and pluralism, and respect for human rights. Others have been part of the foreign policy initiatives of the Nicaraguan government in attempts to contribute to peace in the region: the Latin American character of the solution to our problems, the elimination of foreign bases in the area, the departure of outside military advisors from the region, among others.

Nicaragua deplores the unilateral decision of the U.S. government to interrupt the bilateral conversations in Manzanillo.[10] Our government has indicated its willingness to resume that dialogue; we commend the fact that the Caraballeda message welcomes this dialogue.

Until now, the Reagan administration has responded to these peace initiatives and dialogue with war. At the present time, President Reagan is seeking $100 million dollars from the U.S. Congress in financing for the Somocista assassins whom he cynically calls "freedom fighters."[11]

During his campaign against the U.S. invasion, General Sandino had the support of courageous collaborators from several countries of the region. One of the most distinguished was the Dominican Gregorio Urbano Gilbert.

Gregorio Urbano Gilbert was a valiant patriot who had fought against the U.S. invasion that occurred in his country in 1916. This invasion aimed to carry out an imperialist plan similar to that which was being carried out at the same time in Cuba, Nicaragua, and Haiti. For this reason, Gilbert had to flee his invaded country, and upon learning of the Sandinista struggle, joined it and came to be part of the General Command of General Sandino. The example of Gregorio Urbano Gilbert testifies to the existence of a clear anti-imperialist and regional consciousness throughout the Caribbean Sea.

TODAY, the Nicaraguan people find themselves once again obliged to defend themselves with arms against the same enemy: U.S. imperialism. As in other occasions, the Nicaraguan people know they can count on the active solidarity of their brothers and sisters in the region. The enemy is the same, the fight is one.

The unity of our organizations and our countries is necessary so that our region will cease to be one of the most victimized by the outrages of imperialism and will be transformed into a region of peace, justice, and abundant development for our peoples and for humanity.

This unity is necessary so that the Caribbean will no

longer be an imperialist backyard and instead will become a scene of productive labor and social justice.

This unity is necessary so that the Caribbean will no longer be a sea of war, plowed by imperialist fleets that stifle popular rebellions, drown national revolutions in blood, overthrow patriotic governments, threaten and menace with giant military maneuvers, and impose puppet governments.

Through the valiant action of the people our organizations represent, the Caribbean must be converted into a *sea of peace.*

NOTES

1. For a discussion of the Anti-Imperialist Organizations of the Caribbean and Central America, see the "In this Issue" column.

2. Rafael "Fafa" Taveras is the general secretary of the Dominican Socialist Bloc and a leader of the Dominican Left Front. Clement Rohee is the international affairs secretary of the People's Progressive Party of Guyana.

3. Organized by Sandino in 1927, the Army for the Defense of National Sovereignty fought a guerrilla war in northern Nicaragua until the U.S. Marines were withdrawn in 1933.

4. The consultative process culminated April 22–24, 1987, in a Multiethnic Assembly composed of delegates elected by every village and community on the Atlantic Coast. The assembly, held in Puerto Cabezas, capital of Northern Zelaya province, adopted a draft autonomy law that guarantees the right of the Atlantic Coast peoples to use and develop their own languages and cultures, to elect and run their own regional governments, and to decide on a broad range of economic and social policies in the region. The draft statute will be discussed and voted on by Nicaragua's National Assembly.

5. On February 7, 1986, President-for-Life Jean-Claude "Baby Doc" Duvalier and his family fled Haiti aboard a U.S. Air Force transport plane. His ouster followed months of growing popular demonstrations against the hated dictator.

6. In 1791, Black slaves led by Toussaint L'Ouverture revolted against their colonial masters and seized control of the northern part of the French colony of Saint-Domingue; in 1804 they declared their independence and renamed the country Haiti.

7. The 1961 CIA mercenary invasion defeated by Cuba at the Bay of Pigs (Playa Girón) embarked from Puerto Cabezas, Nicaragua.

8. On September 7, 1984, the Contadora Group (foreign ministers of Mexico, Venezuela, Panama, and Colombia) proposed an Act of Peace and Cooperation in Central America. On September 21, Nicaragua announced its intention to sign the accord without any amendments or conditions. The U.S. subsequently rejected the accord.

9. Foreign ministers from the Contadora Group and the Contadora Support Group (Peru, Brazil, Uruguay, and Argentina) met in Caraballeda, Venezuela, in January 1986 and issued a document calling on the U.S. to reopen talks with Nicaragua, suspend its aid to the contras, and withdraw its military forces.

10. In June 1984, Nicaragua and the U.S. began bilateral talks in Manzanillo, Mexico. The U.S. broke off the talks in January 1985.

11. The U.S. House of Representatives voted June 25, 1986, to give the Nicaraguan counterrevolutionary forces $100 million for fiscal year 1987. The measure was subsequently approved by the U.S. Senate as well, and the money given to the *contras.*

REVOLUTION IS THE BIRTH OF LIGHT

by Tomás Borge

B*ernardo Marqués Ravelo:* Commander, I would like to begin by talking about Julio Cortázar.[1]

Tomás Borge: I think that since Julio's death, this is the first time that I will talk about that sweet fool who decided to die. There are those whose death hurts more than a thorn in the eye, and one has trouble talking about them. Before he died, I wrote the piece you are familiar with.[2] Other Latin American writers also wrote about his stature, his humanism, and his literary talent. Of course, the book *Queremos Tanto a Julio* certainly does not include all of the best Latin American writers,

---

This interview with Commander Tomás Borge first appeared in the April 1985 El Caimán Barbudo *(The Bearded Alligator), a journal of literary criticism published in Cuba. Borge is Nicaragua's minister of the interior and president of the National Autonomy Commission. He is a member of the National Directorate of the Sandinista National Liberation Front (FSLN). He was one of the founders of the FSLN in November 1961.*

The interview was conducted by Bernardo Marqués Ravelo in April 1985 in Cuba. The translation from Spanish and the footnotes are by New International.

ENDNOTES BEGIN ON PAGE 442

although some are there, nor are all of Cortázar's closest friends included. Those Julio loved the most are excluded: Roberto Fernández Retamar, for example; not to mention Ernesto Cardenal or Martínez Rivas.[3] But since his death, I have not wanted to read anything about him nor talk about him.

Cortázar left an open wound in Nicaragua that cannot be closed. His first visit coincided with the transferring of Carlos Fonseca's remains,[4] and I asked him to say a few words. He said a few simple words. Someone, a *compañera*—I don't remember who—said that Julio had no right to speak, that he lived in Paris, that he wasn't in Buenos Aires, that he didn't write revolutionary literature, and I don't know what else. In a similar situation, I am sure, Carlos Fonseca, who was near-sighted but who could see far into the distance to perceive horizons, would have asked Julio to say a few words at the tomb of a fallen brother.

Julio had a singular capacity for amazement. Everything surprised him: the air, a dark sky, a bright face, the tracks of ants, the inevitable rising of the sun, the sands of the sea. During the burial of the bones of Carlos Fonseca, the people riddled the sun with shots from their rifles, and Cortázar was witness to this solemn and unique Nicaraguan moment.

Later, Julio was here many more times. He came to learn, to drink from the well of our people, to spew forth volcanos. He visited the neighborhoods and the eyes of his new friends. He swam in the sea accompanied by Carol, his companion, that woman for whom it is impossible to find adjectives.

One day she told me that what she wanted most was to die after her husband. And when I asked her why, she brought a tear to my eye: "To spare him that suffering," she told me.

He was a big-boned man, full of love. A great writer of course, but—could you doubt it?—immensely greater as a man. When we said good-bye for the first time, because of the way he was, how he acted, and how he gave us his heart, I had completely forgotten that he was a world-renowned writer.

He loved Nicaragua as if she were a girl with crystal legs and the heart of a newborn bird.

Marqués: In Bluefields a few years ago, you said that with songs such as those of Carlos Mejía Godoy,[5] the Nicaraguans could not but have made a revolution. This statement attributes a revolutionary function to art as well. I would like you to elaborate on this.

Borge: I see a deep interrelation between art and revolution. The music of Carlos Mejía Godoy was a detachment of combat engineers in the consciousness of Nicaraguans, a detachment of agitation, without thereby losing its character as art, its roots, the color of our skin. I think that in our Latin American reality, music is destined to open the floodgates of the revolution. However, the aesthetic counterrevolutionaries—that is, the dull and tasteless, the bureaucrats—deny this possibility. They deny the right of artists to be creators of art.

Cuban and Nicaraguan music have the same common denominators: the people at the center of a great social upheaval create and express themselves through troubadours, poets, dramatists—that is, through prophets. It's the ancient struggle between the old and the new. Revolutions bring forth new creations because revolution is nothing more than a great change in man's consciousness; the possibility of a dialogue between man, the moon, the sun, and tractors.

Marqués: Theater—

Borge: I think that in Nicaragua theater is in a formative stage because, naturally, it is not an easy discipline. We have begun the march, but we are still at the beginning. We have our roots, hybrid roots, and we must take advantage of them to create our forest.

I know nothing of the level of development of Cuban theater, but in Colombia I witnessed the theater of that people. Plays that spoke to the common man, about the problems he faces, his vicissitudes, his daily quarrels, his sexual inhibitions, the class struggle, his worries, his violent, almost exasperating optimism.

We must pay closer attention to theater because we are beginning to see its first buds, expressions that recapture the traditions of the first years of the conquest and that were lost or numbed by centuries of indifference. We must set to work; there are many spectators and a huge stage.

Marqués: You have said that you will never publish your poetry. Why?

Borge: I have said that I am a clandestine poet. I think that this is something I should reflect upon, but at another time. Let me tell you, I have many clandestine loves.

Somewhere, in some magazine, they said that I have a clandestine love for surrealism, and this is true. And they said I had a clandestine love for Cuba. This is the falsest thing in the world. My love for Cuba is a public love for her people, for the beauty that her revolution has inaugurated. My love is a love that walks the streets and is not afraid to mention her name.

Marqués: On Ernesto Cardenal's sixtieth birthday you said that you preferred his *Epigrams*, that these were love poems that you would have liked to have written. You also cited his *Prayer for Marilyn Monroe.* From these examples, you seem to prefer Cardenal's love poems to his combative poetry. It is said that Maceo preferred Gustavo Adolfo Bécquer above all poets.[6] How do you explain that a man of epic stature has lyrical tastes?

Borge: Maceo, as a man of epic stature, had lyrical tastes. How could a man of epic stature not have lyrical tastes? Ernesto Cardenal's poetry, his *Epigrams*, is great poetry. I said so. I said so because perhaps I am a little jealous. It is sad to know that I'll never be a poet like Ernesto.

I think that today we are frustrating ourselves, we are making ourselves unsuccessful poets, because we have no time for creation. The major work of Ernesto Cardenal is still to be written. He has many years left to give us more beautiful pieces of verbal architecture, of magnificent seriousness, of intense ethical and aesthetic lessons. What is happening to Cardenal is what's happening to Sergio Ramírez,[7] who could be a successful novelist. Literature and his sensitivity turned him into a good revolutionary. Today we have a good vice president but probably, with every passing day, less of a great writer.

We are obsessed by the lack of minutes in each day, which has only twenty-four hours. For example, I don't give much freedom to Omar Cabezas.[8] I spend my life demanding things of him, and he, as a serious worker, always fulfills his obligations to the Ministry of the Interior and continues writing. I was told that he has finished or is about to finish another book. I don't know how he manages to arrange that when he barely has a chance to arrange the scattered lines of his mustache and maintain a neat appearance.

Marqués: Photography as an art, linked to cinema, photography that registers Nicaraguan reality, appeared since the final offensive and perhaps a little before.[9] How would you assess this medium at this time?

Borge: It's true. There has been a sort of rebirth of photography. We must not forget that the revolution is the birth of light. Unfortunately, cinema is an art in which talent and even genius are subsidized by millionaires, and we are a poor country. Some documentaries, some fiction films have been created. Brothers and sisters from other fraternal countries have come to film with us, in our land. Cinema must be among our priorities. If the Cubans have done something with few resources, we can attempt our works with hardly any resources. So it goes, and perhaps tomorrow we will discover an oil well—but it can be done. With imagination, talent, sensitivity, and love you can move the world, which is much more difficult than making a film. The Ministry of the Interior has made four or five films. And I have not wanted to encourage them for purely economic reasons. Television, however, is cheaper and is probably the road to be developed in our specific case.

Marqués: Commander, I have always been overwhelmed by the enormous number of poets, and good poets at that, that your country can claim. However, in narrative writing—

Borge: It is almost the same in another sense. A novel requires that you devote body and soul to it, while poetry can be written between one meeting and the next, between one battle and the next. Fundamentally, poetry is inspiration, whereas a novel—just ask José Coronel Urtecho—a novel is a sauna bath, freeing up hours and talent.[10] I am sure that if Sergio Ramírez dedicated all his time to literature, in no time at all he would become a great novelist.

Who can write novels in Nicaragua if all those able to do so have an overwhelming load of responsibilities? If Lizandro Chávez is busy,[11] if Sergio is vice president of the republic, if we don't give Omar Cabezas time to breathe—I have been told that the poet Julio Valle completed a novel, I think it is something about the Liberal revolution.[12] Fernando Silva,[13] between umbilical cords and whooping coughs, writes a poem and, once in a while, a short story. It's true, the potential novelists in my country are hospital administrators or members of the presidency.

Nicaraguan reality has captured all the writers. It is an extraordinary coincidence that all the intellectuals are revolutionaries, except Pablo Antonio Cuadra,[14] who wets his bed when he hears mention of imperialism. He wakes up every morning soaked with fear. Poor Pablo Antonio, who is a great poet. If from others we confiscated their landholdings, their palaces, their riches; from him we confiscated his poetry.

I think that behind Fernando Silva, who sometimes writes but always talks and talks, there should be someone with a tape recorder to record all that he says. It would be worth publishing. It is a monologue full of sparks and subtleties, but unfortunately, no one has thought of taping Fernando. He is a man who will tell you a story every ten minutes, but will take ten months to write down just one.

Marqués: Minister, the enemy speaks of your post in Dantesque terms: a repressive apparatus, gloomy prisons, police that torture. I would like you to discuss the cultural work of your ministry.

Borge: Well, we have laid out certain orientations to the fighters of the Ministry of the Interior.[15] Basically, it is a repressive body. We repress the counterrevolution and bad taste, which is exactly the same thing. The *compañeros* never mistreat counterrevolutionary prisoners and are even polite with them. Hence, in order not to break with Latin American tradition, we ask that they become torturers, that they torture lack of imagination without pity. We gave them these guidelines in an assembly, and we added another: that they should shoot down boredom without a trace of pity and that they treat the skin of the prisoners with more respect than their own skin.

I once spoke to Fidel Castro about this and explained my point of view, and he agreed with me. It would be an unforgivable error for the revolutionary police to become torturers. The only way to be competent and efficient in this profession is to reject any physical abuse. Respect for the integrity of every human being is sacred and inviolable. And we have been demanding in this regard, which is why all the counterrevolutionary conspiracies in Nicaragua have been neutralized by our security forces.

Within the ministry we have two great concerns: the development of the party and, connected to this and with the same importance, the cultural development of each and every one of the members of the ministry. I don't think that Nicaragua is alone in this, because I understand that poetry is also written in the police stations and army units in Cuba.

Marqués: It is said that realism is a paradigmatic form of revolutionary art. But so also is magic realism, the fantastic reality, above all in our countries. I would like to move on to this subject.

Borge: Marx appreciated Balzac's realism and realism in general,[16] just as he loved Greco-Latin sculpture. However, Marx did not say that realism was the only valid form of aesthetic expression. Without a doubt, if Marx had said that, he would no longer have been a Marxist. I sincerely believe that you cannot create something only in green or, to put it another way, you cannot create something only in red. This would be wanton aggression against art.

Under capitalism, profits lay siege to art. It is not right to surrender aesthetics because of hunger, nor to surrender it to the demands of the slogan of the day. It is reality itself that determines the form, the theme, and the artist's personality. Of course, the artist's social perspective is not separate from his traditions or culture. You cannot and should not separate artistic creation from the class struggle, but it is a crime to place it in the service of art dealers and bureaucrats.

Marx said that our duty as revolutionaries is to transform the world. And to transform the world, you must know it and love it as you do the woman with whom you make love. You must know its laws, its peculiarities, and its processes.

I think that socialist realism was necessary, just as, in other contexts, symbolism and surrealism were necessary. One must take into account that the Soviet revolution was the only proletarian revolution in the world, that it lived alone for many years, making incredible efforts to survive, surrounded by enemies, besieged by hunger and the most extreme poverty. It was forced to be heroic and distrustful. I sincerely believe that socialist realism was a necessity—although it is not now, and at the same time, it is. It was a contribution that seriously helped to show the profile of an enemy capable of mimicry and hiding in the shadows.

The peoples of Latin America have their great artists. It is these peoples who, with flaming torches, seek the art they need, require, and demand.

Marqués: In July, it will be six years since the triumph of the Sandinista revolution. Could you give a balance sheet of what has been achieved by the process during this time?

Borge: We have still not reached the projected economic goals. We have not built great buildings, though we have perhaps built a road or two, a hospital or two. We are still in the stage of social underdevelopment.

We have a severe economic crisis—that is even clearer than the face of the moon. However, we have had successes in international politics, but have not managed to solve, in practice, our pressing problems. The reasons for this are obvious: our poverty, the absence of a competitive industry, and a country that was plundered for decades and decades. It is also due to our inexperience, to our ignorance. However, revolutionaries learn quickly, though one pays a high price for initial ignorance. Add to this the exasperating imperialist aggression and the resources that we are forced to invest in defense. Almost all our resources, more than 50 percent of our wealth, goes to the war. But yes, we have accomplished a great deal. Indeed, we have planted some corn, a good deal of cotton, and a regular harvest of metaphors. We have planted and harvested hope.

The Nicaraguan people have faith in their revolution. That's the truth. How do you explain that in such a poor country, harassed by problems, with a high inflation rate, with shortages of basic goods, where the laws of the market economy, speculation, low wages, have not been conquered, with an acute housing problem, the people are still on this side of the fence? It is obvious that there is a will to find answers to the problems of health care and education of the people. There is a will to keep the remnants of corruption and disorganization from being generalized.

We have been successful with the Literacy Crusade.[17] We have been successful in lowering infant mortality and reducing illness. We have made progress in the development of culture in general. We have incorporated the youth into the universities and other educational centers. We have given away astronomical amounts of land.

But all the expectations of the people are on the Sandinista leaders. The people expected to get housing from the revolution. The revolution has given them hope, and the people have managed to feed their hopes. How else can you explain the support of the Nicaraguans for the revolution? The workers of the Dominican Republic have perhaps had fewer difficulties, yet in the Dominican Republic the people took to the streets and the police had to repress them. Not only there but in other countries of our America as well. How do you explain this except that the Nicaraguan people have confidence in the Sandinista Front?

I think that the first accomplishment—it is more than an accomplishment—is having planted this hope and having obtained a good harvest without previous fertilization or use of insecticides.

Marqués: Now, I would like you to speak about the foreign debt. A few weeks ago, Fidel Castro, in an interview published in Mexico, spoke about the agony we suffer: up to our necks in debt. I would like you to give me your opinion on this matter.

Borge: Fidel presented a clear picture of this acute, unavoidable, and irreversible problem of Latin America. And, in effect, the Latin American people have been united around legitimate passions in politics and solidarity. They have been united at certain moments by the development of solidarity with Cuba or Nicaragua or, as Fidel points out, with Argentina at the time of the invasion of the Malvinas.[18] The problem of the foreign debt, however, unites the peoples who are stabbed by this crisis, and on the other hand, it can unite governments that have no choice but to rebel or perish. The debt leaves only one alternative: to reject the hands that squeeze our necks, trying to choke us.

What Fidel presented was a detailed picture that demands an answer. Fidel prefers a political solution. But of course, we must recognize that other types of solutions may exist outside of man's control. It could be that this debt, this agony of the Latin American countries, is a bomb that is about to explode, that only needs to have its fuse removed. In the next few years, we will be eyewitnesses to the prophesies of Fidel Castro, who has thought deeply about this topic. A rebellion against the debt is possible.

I think that all the changes of a democratic character that are taking place have much to do with this explosive reality and, of course, with the Sandinista revolution and the Central American conflicts. I am sure that if the Nicaraguan revolution were to disappear, all traces of democracy on the continent, regardless of the class interests that these governments represent, would also disappear. These governments are no longer entrenched military regimes. Their existence provides the objective base for the struggle against the crushing debt.

The big corporations and the big banks also have an interest in eliminating the factors that are giving rise to these democratic changes in Latin America. One of them is, of course, the Sandinista revolution. Mister Reagan is not trying to destroy us just because he feels like it.

Marqués: Commander, do you see an immediate solution to the Central American conflicts?

Borge: No. I think that the Central American conflict does not have a short-term solution. I think that it is a problem that will be solved in the medium term. It will be solved because the Central American conflict will have a solution some day, no one should have any doubt of that.

Central America will recover its sovereignty, its right to listen with its own ears to the flow of its rivers and the chirp of the cicadas, and to see with its own eyes the upright dignity of its trees. It will recover its ability to decide, and the wounds inflicted by imperial domination will heal.

But it will not be easy. Imperialism still has reason to have faith in itself. It seeks, between light and darkness, with all its brute strength and resources, to block the triumph of the Central American peoples. What is happening is that the epicenter of the Latin American revolution that is now in Central America is shifting toward the southern cone. When a volcano erupts in the southern cone, along with the volcanos in Central America, I don't know how in the devil imperialism will be able to extinguish the rivers of lava. It will not have enough strength or ability.

Imperialism is able to intervene and block, but not in the end to prevent, the development of the Central American revolution. The revolution is such a natural thing that even with all their resources, with all their strength and intelligence, they have not been able to freeze the Salvadoran revolution. The revolution in El Salvador survives and develops even though it did not take maximum advantage of its possibilities.

I would say that the Salvadoran revolutionaries have

advanced notably in the field of unity, but they have not completely overcome their sad and useless differences. And as long as that unity is not total, so long as there is no joint effort, so long as they do not take refuge in the same foxhole and shoot with the same rifle, victory will be lost in the fog and the blood.

I am not pessimistic. I believe in the Salvadoran revolutionaries. I think that the unification process is difficult, it is a process and not an earthly paradise. If they really achieve unification, they will be strong like horses, intelligent like snakes, and sensible. They are making great and praiseworthy efforts in this sense. One must have the courage to tell them so. At the same time, they are an example of courage, audacity, and political clarity.

Marqués: Besides magical realism, I think one can speak of a historic realism in Latin America. This is the case with Galeano and other authors:[19] history and magic; poetry, history, and fiction; of a burning quality. I would like, lastly, to speak of this.

Borge: I think that when we really write the history of Latin America, we will be strong enough to rescue lost tigers and riches. I would suggest Eduardo Galeano as historian of Latin America, because our history has yet to be written and Galeano is its best chronicler. Recently, we began writing it, not in the traditional way but as a living being that breathes and sweats. Let me tell you, *One Hundred Years of Solitude* by Gabriel García Márquez is just one chapter of this history,[20] because the history of this part of the world is one of solitude since the arrival of the colonizers. It began to cease being a history of solitude on January 1, 1959, when the Cuban revolution triumphed.

NOTES

1. Julio Cortázar (1914–1984) was an Argentine novelist and author of short stories.

2. Borge's tribute to Cortázar, "Julio Cortázar: Compañero de Prisión y Libertad," [Julio Cortázar: comrade in prison and in freedom] was published in *Queremos Tanto a Julio* [We love Julio so much] (Managua: Editorial Nueva Nicaragua, 1984), a collection of essays about Cortázar and his work. In addition to the piece by Borge, it contains articles by twenty other authors, most of them Latin American.

3. Roberto Fernández Retamar (b. 1930) is a Cuban poet and literary critic. He is currently president of Casa de las Americas, the most prestigious institute of Latin American culture, based in Havana.

Ernesto Cardenal (b. 1925) is a Nicaraguan Catholic priest and a poet. He is currently Nicaragua's minister of culture.

Carlos Martínez Rivas (b. 1924) is a Nicaraguan poet.

4. Carlos Fonseca Amador (1936–1976) was the Nicaraguan revolutionary leader and founder of the Sandinista National Liberation Front. He died in combat fighting the Somoza dictatorship's National Guard and was buried in the northern village of Waslala. On November 7, 1979, his remains were reinterred in Managua.

5. Carlos Mejía Godoy (b. 1943) is a Nicaraguan composer and singer. Currently he is an FSLN delegate in Nicaragua's National Assembly.

6. Antonio Maceo (1845–1896) was a leader of Cuba's war of independence from Spain.

Gustavo Adolfo Bécquer (1836–1870) was a Spanish author and poet.

7. Sergio Ramírez Mercado (b. 1942) is a Nicaraguan author and currently is vice president of Nicaragua.

8. Omar Cabezas (b. 1950) is the author of *Fire from the Mountain: The Making of a Sandinista* (New York: Crown Publishers, 1985). At the time of the interview he was a vice min-

ister of the Ministry of the Interior. He is currently a member of the Managua regional committee of the FSLN.

9. A reference to the 1979 Sandinista-led insurrection that overthrew the Somoza dictatorship in Nicaragua.

10. José Coronel Urtecho (b. 1906) is a Nicaraguan novelist and poet.

11. Lizandro Chávez Alfaro (b. 1929) is a Nicaraguan author.

12. Julio Valle Castillo (b. 1952) is a Nicaraguan poet.

The Liberal revolution refers to the 1893 uprising led by Liberal Party leader José Santos Zelaya. It ended thirty years of rule by the landed oligarchy organized in the Conservative Party and opened a period of accelerated capitalist development.

13. Fernando Silva Espinosa (b. 1927) is a Nicaraguan poet, author, and pediatrician.

14. Pablo Antonio Cuadra (b. 1912) is a Nicaraguan poet, novelist, and dramatist.

15. The Ministry of the Interior includes police, prison guards, firefighters, immigration officers, internal security forces, and special military units.

16. Honoré de Balzac (1799–1850) was a French novelist and author of *The Human Comedy*.

17. In 1980, Nicaragua mobilized 180,000 young volunteers in a five-month campaign to teach reading and writing throughout the country. Illiteracy was reduced from 50 percent to 12 percent.

18. In 1982 Britain waged a war against Argentina to maintain control of the Malvinas (Falkland) Islands, Argentine territory occupied by Britain since 1833.

19. Eduardo Galeano (b. 1920) is a Uruguayan novelist and essayist.

20. Gabriel García Márquez (b. 1928) is a Colombian novelist and the winner of the Nobel Prize for literature in 1982.

CLASS STRUGGLE IN THE UNITED STATES

Is Socialist Revolution in the U.S. Possible?

A Necessary Debate

MARY-ALICE WATERS

In two talks, presented as part of a wide-ranging debate at the Venezuela International Book Fairs in 2007 and 2008, Waters explains why a socialist revolution in the United States is possible. Why revolutionary struggles by working people are inevitable, forced upon us by the crisis-driven assaults of the propertied classes. As solidarity grows among a fighting vanguard of working people, the outlines of coming class battles can already be seen. $7. Also in Spanish, French, and Swedish.

Cuba and the Coming American Revolution

JACK BARNES

The Cuban Revolution of 1959 had a worldwide political impact, including on working people and youth in the imperialist heartland. As the mass, proletarian-based struggle for Black rights was already advancing in the US, the social transformation fought for and won by the Cuban toilers set an example that socialist revolution is not only necessary—it can be made and defended. This second edition, with a new foreword by Mary-Alice Waters, should be read alongside *Is Socialist Revolution in the U.S. Possible?* $10. Also in Spanish and French.

Revolutionary Continuity

Marxist Leadership in the U.S.

FARRELL DOBBS

How successive generations of fighters joined in the struggles that shaped the US labor movement, seeking to build a class-conscious revolutionary leadership capable of advancing the interests of workers and small farmers and linking up with fellow toilers worldwide. 2 vols. *The Early Years: 1848–1917,* $20; *Birth of the Communist Movement: 1918–1922,* $19.

TRANSFORMING THE TRADE UNIONS
INTO INSTRUMENTS OF REVOLUTIONARY STRUGGLE

Trade Unions in the Epoch of Imperialist Decay

LEON TROTSKY, FARRELL DOBBS, KARL MARX

Food for thought—and action—from leaders of three generations of the modern revolutionary workers movement. Invaluable to the practical education of militant workers who are relearning today what a strike is and how it can be fought and won—militants who, in the course of such struggles, become interested in ideas of fellow unionists about how the entire system of capitalist exploitation can be ended. $16

Labor's Giant Step

The First Twenty Years of the CIO: 1936–55

ART PREIS

The story of the explosive labor struggles and political battles in the 1930s that built the industrial unions. And how those unions became the vanguard of a mass social movement that began transforming US society. $30

Selected Articles on the Labor Movement

FARRELL DOBBS

Articles from the *Militant*, written in the mid-1960s. Includes, "Unions Lose Ground," "Steel Union: Case History of Bureaucratism," "The Case for an Independent Labor Party," "Unions Need Class-Conscious Leaders," and more. $5

The working-class fight for power

The Workers and Farmers Government

JOSEPH HANSEN

How experiences in post–World War II revolutions in Yugoslavia, China, Algeria, and Cuba enriched communists' theoretical and practical understanding of revolutionary governments of the workers and farmers. "What is involved is governmental power," writes Hansen, "the possibility of smashing the old structure and overturning capitalism." $10

For a Workers and Farmers Government in the United States

JACK BARNES

Why a workers and farmers government is "the most powerful instrument the working class can wield" as it moves toward expropriating the capitalists and landlords. How this opens the road for working people to join in the worldwide struggle for socialism. $10

Dynamics of the Cuban Revolution

A Marxist Appreciation

JOSEPH HANSEN

How did the Cuban Revolution unfold? Why does it represent an "unbearable challenge" to US imperialism? What political obstacles has it overcome? Written as the revolution advanced from its earliest days. $25

The Rise and Fall of the Nicaraguan Revolution

JACK BARNES, LARRY SEIGLE, STEVE CLARK

Based on ten years of socialist journalism from inside Nicaragua, this issue of *New International* magazine recounts the achievements and worldwide impact of the 1979 Nicaraguan revolution. It traces the political retreat of the Sandinista National Liberation Front leadership that led to the downfall of the workers and farmers government in the closing years of the 1980s. Documents of the Socialist Workers Party. $16

INDEX

C

G

H

O

P

Q

Y

Z

FURTHER READING

MAURICE BISHOP SPEAKS

THE GRENADA REVOLUTION 1979–83

with an introduction by Steve Clark

Twenty-seven speeches and interviews by the murdered prime minister of Grenada on the gains of the revolution, defense against US imperialism's hostile actions, and Grenada's solidarity with freedom struggles throughout the Americas, Africa, and Asia.

Includes the official statements by the government of Cuba following the counterrevolution that ended with Bishop's murder, and the speech by Fidel Castro honoring the Cuban internationalists who died while defending themselves during the October 1983 US invasion. $25

SELECTED SPEECHES OF FIDEL CASTRO

Includes 1961 speech, "I Shall Be a Marxist-Leninist to the End of My Life," explaining why only a socialist revolution could bring about the profound changes Cuban working people had overthrown the Batista dictatorship to achieve. Also, two 1962 speeches analyzing the danger posed by the Stalinist secret faction of Aníbal Escalante, and the Cuban Revolution's stake in defeating it. $15

NOTHING CAN STOP THE COURSE OF HISTORY

Fidel Castro

In this book-length 1985 interview, Castro takes up US-Cuba relations, Cuba's role in the fight against apartheid rule in South Africa, the overthrow of the Grenada revolution, and the social consequences of the foreign debt in Latin America and the Caribbean. $19

New International

A MAGAZINE OF MARXIST POLITICS AND THEORY

NEW INTERNATIONAL NO. 12

Capitalism's Long Hot Winter Has Begun

Jack Barnes

and *"Their Transformation and Ours," Resolution of the Socialist Workers Party*

Today's accelerating global capitalist crisis—the opening stages of what will be decades of economic, financial, and social convulsions and class battles—accompanies a continuation of the most far-reaching shift in Washington's military policy and organization since the US buildup toward World War II. Class-struggle-minded working people must face this historic turning point for imperialism, and draw satisfaction from being "in their face" as we chart a revolutionary course to confront it. $16. Also in Spanish, French, Swedish, and Arabic.

NEW INTERNATIONAL NO. 13

Our Politics Start with the World

Jack Barnes

The huge economic and cultural inequalities between imperialist and semicolonial countries, and among classes within almost every country, are produced, reproduced, and accentuated by the workings of capitalism. For vanguard workers to build parties able to lead a successful revolutionary struggle for power in our own countries, says Jack Barnes in the lead article, our activity must be guided by a strategy to close this gap.

Also in No. 13: "Farming, Science, and the Working Classes" *by Steve Clark.* $14. Also in Spanish, French, and Swedish.

NEW INTERNATIONAL NO. 11

U.S. Imperialism Has Lost the Cold War

Jack Barnes

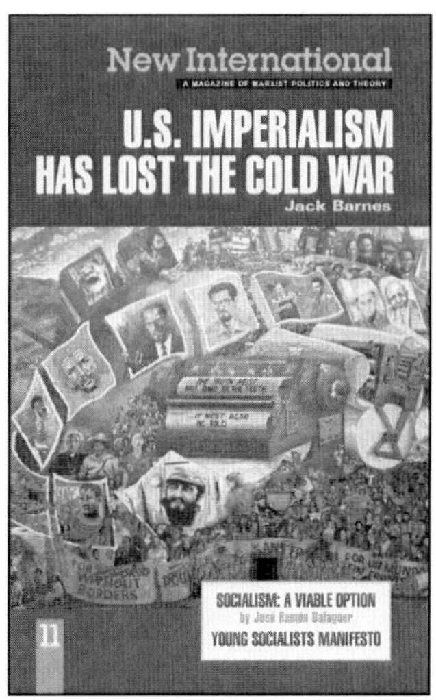

Contrary to imperialist expectations in the 1990s in the wake of the collapse of regimes across Eastern Europe and the USSR claiming to be communist, the workers and farmers there have not been crushed. The toilers remain an intractable obstacle to imperialism's advance, one the exploiters will have to confront in class battles and war. $16. Also in Spanish, French, Swedish, and Icelandic.

NEW INTERNATIONAL NO. 8

Che Guevara, Cuba, and the Road to Socialism

Articles by Ernesto Che Guevara, Carlos Rafael Rodríguez, Carlos Tablada, Mary-Alice Waters, and Steve Clark and Jack Barnes

Exchanges from the opening years of the Cuban Revolution and today on the political perspectives defended by Guevara as he helped lead working people to advance the transformation of economic and social relations in Cuba. $10. Also in Spanish.

IN NEW INTERNATIONAL NO. 10

Defending Cuba, Defending Cuba's Socialist Revolution

Mary-Alice Waters

In the 1990s, in face of the greatest economic difficulties in the history of the Cuban Revolution, workers and farmers defended their political power, independence and sovereignty, and the historic course they embarked on in 1959. Waters addresses discussions and debates in Cuba on voluntary work, income taxes on wages, farm cooperatives, and much more. In *New International no. 10*. $16. Also in Spanish, French, Swedish, and Icelandic.

THE RUSSIAN REVOLUTION

LENIN'S FINAL FIGHT

Speeches and Writings, 1922–23

V.I. LENIN

In 1922 and 1923, V.I. Lenin, central leader of the world's first socialist revolution, waged what was to be his last political battle. At stake was whether that revolution, and the international movement it led, would remain on the proletarian course that had brought workers and peasants to power in October 1917. Indispensable to understanding the world class struggle in the 20th and 21st centuries. $20. Also in Spanish.

THE HISTORY OF THE RUSSIAN REVOLUTION

LEON TROTSKY

A classic account of the social, economic, and political dynamics of the first socialist revolution as told by one of its central leaders. "The history of a revolution is for us first of all a history of the forcible entrance of the masses into the realm of rulership over their own destiny," Trotsky writes. Unabridged edition, 3 vols. in one. $38. Also in Russian.

THE REVOLUTION BETRAYED

What Is the Soviet Union and Where Is It Going?

LEON TROTSKY

In 1917 the working class and peasantry of Russia carried out one of the most profound revolutions in history. Yet within ten years a political counterrevolution by a privileged social layer whose chief spokesperson was Joseph Stalin was being consolidated. This classic study of the Soviet workers state and its degeneration illuminates the roots of the social and political crisis in Russia and other countries that formerly made up the Soviet Union. $20. Also in Spanish.

NEW INTERNATIONAL AROUND THE WORLD

New International is also published in Spanish as **Nueva Internacional** and French as **Nouvelle Internationale**. Selected issues are available in Swedish as **Ny International** and in Icelandic as **Nýtt Alþóðlegt**. All are distributed worldwide by Pathfinder Press.

AVAILABLE AT

WWW.PATHFINDERPRESS.COM

and at the following locations

United States

(and Caribbean, Latin America, and East Asia):
Pathfinder Books, 306 W. 37th St., 13th Floor
New York, NY 10018

Canada

Pathfinder Books, 7107 St. Denis, Suite 204
Montreal, QC H2S 2S5

United Kingdom

(and Europe, Africa, Middle East, and South Asia):
Pathfinder Books, First Floor, 120 Bethnal Green Road
(entrance in Brick Lane), London E2 6DG

Australia

(and Southeast Asia and the Pacific)
Pathfinder, Level 1, 3/281-287 Beamish St., Campsie, NSW 2194
Postal address: P.O. Box 164, Campsie, NSW 2194

New Zealand

Pathfinder, 188a Onehunga Mall, Onehunga, Auckland 1061
Postal address: P.O. Box 3025, Auckland 1140